Hugh Falkus

A Life on the Edge

Hugh Falkus
A Life on the Edge

Chris Newton

2007
THE MEDLAR PRESS
ELLESMERE

Published by The Medlar Press Limited,
The Grange, Ellesmere, Shropshire.
www.medlarpress.com

ISBN 978-1-899600-73-1

Produced in England by The Medlar Press Limited, Ellesmere.
Designed and typeset in 11 on $12^{1}/_{2}$pt Baskerville by
Jonathan Ward-Allen.

Contents

Acknowledgements

I would scarcely have been able to write a word of this book without the help and trust of Hugh Falkus' family and friends, and I have received both in abundance.

My thanks are due firstly to Mary Falkus and Malcolm Falkus for taking me into their confidence and talking to me at length and on record about difficult family matters; to Bill Arnold, whose devotion to Hugh and Kathleen, supported by his late wife Marie, sustained them through the last years of their lives, and who knew more about Hugh's affairs than anyone living; and to Fred Buller, the closest ally Hugh ever had, and the wisest critic.

Next, my thanks to a handful of people who belonged to the Falkus inner circle and whose contributions to the book have accordingly been indispensable. They are Peter Behan, his friend and medical advisor; David Burnett, his publisher; Michael Daunt, his professional successor; Anthony Desbruslais, friend to both Hugh and Kathleen and executor of the estate; Malcolm Greenhalgh, Hugh's friend and co-author; Jo Rippier, in whom he confided over many years; Fred J. Taylor, who gave Hugh as good as he got both on and off the river-bank, and earned his deep affection and respect; Tim Thomas, his confidant and supporter in his failing years; and Bar and Joe Woodall, part of his Eskdale bedrock.

Jane Charlesworth, Marjorie and Geoff Mallinson, Daphne Crutchley and Daphne Smyth were able to provide vital information from the family perspective. Bill Fowler's ex-wife Toni Richards cast considerable light on Hugh's postwar years, while Tessa Sharp was willing to share with me something of what her family went through in the aftermath of the events of 12th May, 1951.

David Profumo's insight into Hugh's character was of enormous help. Andrew Moir deserves particular thanks for responding to my queries about Hugh's service career by doing a sizeable chunk of my research for me and elucidating the workings of the Royal Air Force. Lesley Robinson at Culford School unearthed the story of Hugh's schooldays, and Brian Clarke ransacked his notes of an interview with Hugh to help the book.

I am grateful to Anne de Courcy, Lady Mairi Bury and Lord Londonderry for helping me to assemble the story of Hugh's marriage to Lady Margaret Vane-Tempest-Stewart, and to David Beazley for helping with my research into the history of the literature on sea-trout fishing.

Between them, Jeffery Boswall, Keith Hopkins, Mike and Val Kendall, Hans Kruuk, Hugh Maynard, Lary Shaffer and John Sparks enabled me to piece together an account of Hugh's film-making career.

Important detail in other areas was supplied by Keith Allan, Piers Brendon, Vanya Hackel, Dave Hatwell, Sandy Leventon, Crawford Little, Mark Monaghan, Grace Oglesby and Anne Voss Bark, while personal accounts were contributed by Mark Bowler, Chris Falshaw, Peter Mason, Gregor Murray, David Pilling, David Steel, Frederick Treves, Janet Waddington and Margaret Walden.

In and around Eskdale, thanks must go to Benny and Les Armstrong, Tony Barrow, Roland Carson, Tony Corkhill, Lee Cummings, Willie Heap, Paul Hopwood, Roger Putnam and Eileen Tonge, and in Ireland to Sheila McHugh, Michael and Anthony Gielty, Ned Minihan, John O'Malley and John O'Shea. Sir Edward Dashwood, Tony Davies, Cyril Fox, Graeme Harris, Lynn Hughes and Moc Morgan helped to illuminate the Welsh perspective.

In memory of my father,
Tony Newton
'A very kind man'

Foreword

Michael Daunt

Most boys in their early lives have a hero. Usually it is a sportsman of some sort, either a cricketer or a footballer. In my case it was always a fisherman. Firstly it was my godfather, the country writer John Moore, whose most acclaimed work was the Brensham Trilogy - *Brensham Village*, *Portrait of Elmbury* and *The Blue Field*. He it was who gave me a fishing rod while I was still in my mother's womb, so determined was he that I should be an angler. It was to him I turned for advice when I had found a young tawny owl and when I kept a pet leveret (he advised me to breed white mice for the one and to feed the other on Complan). Both survived and were released in to the wild. When John died in 1967, I moved directly on to a new hero - Hugh Falkus.

I had known of Hugh for most of my life, for he was a friend of my father's and they had flown fighter aircraft together before the war. Then I read *Sea Trout Fishing* and watched *Salmo the Leaper* on television and knew that I badly wanted to meet him. I invited him to dinner in my London flat. He politely refused, despite my offering of oysters, to which I knew he was addicted. It was not until later, when I was the fishing correspondent for *The Mail on Sunday*, that I finally got my wish. I persuaded the paper to allow me to do an in-depth interview and Hugh, who always courted publicity, readily agreed. I forget now what I wrote in that long-ago article but I do know that it was the beginning of a lasting and true friendship. We immediately found huge amounts in common. Fishing, of course, but also literature, poetry, the countryside, shooting, women and much laughter. I came to love him as a father, and I know he loved me as a son.

When I wrote his obituary for *The Daily Telegraph* and *Trout and Salmon* magazine I remember the tears running down my cheeks as I typed. I would have hated to even attempt to write his biography as Chris Newton has done.

Not having been one of Hugh's circle, Chris has been able, without personal involvement, to delve into the secret caves, forbidden lands and arcane rivers of his life and write about them dispassionately. He has done a wonderful job. I am sure that, if he had known Hugh personally, he would have come under his spell and been prejudiced in his favour. What Chris has written is a description of the true Falkus; the man behind the public mask.

Nothing was small or mediocre about Hugh. He had huge talents and vast attributes but his failings were glaring and gargantuan. People who met him either loved him or disliked him intensely. A large majority felt the latter. This was because he was so outspoken (and usually correct) in his views and assertions and conventional humanity does not like this combination.

Hugh never cared what anyone thought. He loved his close friends and was intensely loyal and kind to them, but most of the human race he either ignored or fought with.

There is no doubt that he has had more influence upon me than any other person. He taught me so many things. Salmon and sea trout fishing certainly; but also how to read poetry and the art of writing. We used to sit in his study at Cragg Cottage, drinking whisky and discussing everything under the sun until the early hours of the morning. It was nearly always I who crawled to bed first - Hugh had an amazing constitution.

In all the years that I knew him we only once fell out. This was when I had made a cassette tape for public release called *Eskimo Nell and Other Blue Verse*. 'How dare you waste your undoubted talent on pornography!' stormed Hugh. He didn't speak to me for six weeks.

I still miss him dreadfully, as there are so many occasions when I want to discuss something with him or ask his advice. I loved him most dearly, both despite and because of who he was. I count myself unbelievably blessed to have known him and shared part of his life with him.

Introduction

*What do men do with their stolen time? Everyone lives in the tight
little house of his mind, each with its own façade, and no one
really knows what goes on in the next house.*

HUGH FALKUS, *The Stolen Years*

In the summer of 1994, after several seasons of failing to impress the great
sea trout of the Towy, I struck lucky at last. In the watches of a misty July
night I managed to land three, the biggest a shade over eight pounds. As I
had taken one of them on a Hugh Falkus Sunk Lure, two on a rod he had
designed and all three as a direct result of his writings, it occurred to me
that I ought to write Hugh a thank-you letter.

To my astonishment, he replied by return of post. Just a postcard, but it
was covered on both sides with the exuberant handwriting I have since
come to know so well.

'I'm delighted at your success' wrote Hugh. 'Persist with the sunk lure -
it is far and away the best 'fly' for catching sea trout late at night - fished
deep on a sunk line. *But* if you are not giving the surface lure a try as well
you are depriving yourself of some dramatic moments. *Always* give it a try
- as described in my book.'

Thrilled by this response, I resolved to obey Hugh's instruction without
delay so that I could write back to report the results. I imagined a correspondence developing between master and pupil, leading perhaps, one
far-off day, to a meeting. Failing that, I could always short-circuit the
process by stumping up the price of a speycasting lesson. But it didn't
happen. By the time I managed to get a sizeable fish on the surface lure as
Hugh had specified, he had left us.

Perhaps it was as well that I never did seek an audience with Hugh Falkus.
Though he was kindness personified to people who won his trust and
favour, he did not hesitate to express his contempt for those he thought
shallow, pompous or pretentious, or to anyone who challenged his teachings
without first-class evidence. Not knowing his ways and being young and

cocky, I could so easily have taken a false step and earned a summary dismissal.

The obituaries - I raided the newsagents for them - gave glimpses of a life rich in glory and adventure, yet shaded by grief and depression. The care-free bliss of boyhood days afloat, the thrill and terror of flying a Spitfire in battle, the shock of personal tragedy, the triumph of those pioneering wildlife films; five years in prison camp, four marriages, four disregarded children. All set against one enduring image; the peace and beauty of Hugh's Cumbrian valley and those glorious summer nights, now so very long ago, when the Esk ran silver with sea trout and 'the sky caught fire behind Scafell' as Hugh and his Trusties laid out the night's catch.

What a tale his life would make! I waited eagerly for the book which would tell it, but the millennium passed and it failed to appear. By now I was dabbling in writing about fishing myself, and had come to know Jon and Rosie Ward-Allen at Medlar Press. Knowing Medlar had published *Some of it Was Fun*, an assemblage of what Hugh had managed to finish of his autobiography, I asked Jon about the matter.

"No one's doing one as far as I know," said Jon. "Come and talk to me about it."

I drove up to Shropshire to talk to Jon and Rosie and came away with an agreement to write Hugh's story, along with the phone numbers of some of the people who could help me. I couldn't believe my luck.

The journey through Hugh's life that followed has been quite the most fascinating I have ever made, or hope to make. It has taken me the length and breadth of Britain, from Eskdale to Pembrokeshire, from the Sussex coast to Scotland, from Essex to Devon and from the Somerset Levels to the west coast of Ireland. It has brought me into contact with some of the kindest and most interesting people I have ever met, many of them well-known personalities in their own right.

It has been the journey of a lifetime. If you find it half as interesting as I did, I will have succeeded.

Chris Newton
July 2007

Prologue

The south-western corner of Achill Island, County Mayo, Ireland; four o'clock on a dull May afternoon. A long rolling swell from the Atlantic was breaking with an impressive, echoing crash on the rocks below the 800-foot high Moyteoge Head. The day had been fine enough, if sunless, but now curtains of drizzle were closing in and an unfriendly offshore wind was beginning to stir.

In the lee of the headland, anchored in the sandy waters of Keem Bay, lay a flotilla of fishing boats. Most of them were curraghs, two or three-man rowing boats, designed for the hunting of basking sharks; one was much larger. She was the *New Choice*, a 65-footer out of Keel and the property of Joe Sweeney, the man who controlled the local shark-fishing business.

Most of the fishermen had finished their work for the day and were plodding up the cliff road in ones and twos back towards their homes. As they passed above the bay, one of them, Paddy Kelly, thought he heard a shout. He called to his mates to stop.

The shout came again, and this time several men heard it. They studied the cliff face above them; a shepherd, perhaps, calling his flock. But they could see nothing.

Another shout, and this time the men looked down into the bay. To their astonishment, they could see, clinging to the anchor chain of the *New Choice* in the clear water a couple of hundred yards offshore, the figure of a naked man.

The fishermen turned as one and ran back down the cliff road to the bay. Two of them, Hughie O'Malley and Thomas McNamara, seized a light two-man curragh, pushed it out into deep water, jumped aboard and rowed hell for leather for the *New Choice*.

They were alongside her within a couple of minutes, positioning the curragh under her bow ready to seize the man before he gave up his grip and slipped away into the depths - they could see that he was drifting into unconsciousness. In fact his fingers had locked on so tightly to the anchor chain that it was all they could do to prise them free.

Trying to drag the man on board the little curragh would have been an invitation to disaster. Instead they put a rope round his body, tied him to the stern and towed him, with furious strokes, back to the beach.

The men waiting and watching on the shore ran into the surf to help O'Malley and McNamara to haul their strange catch up on to the sand. They could see that he was a young man, big and powerfully built, but he was now unconscious, ice cold and as white as death. Strangely, he wore not a scrap of clothing, nor so much as a ring by way of identification.

Surely no casual fisherman or recreational sailor who knew what he was doing would have been at sea on that cold spring day. Perhaps the man was a French poacher - there had been a lot of trouble with that sort of thing lately. One of the men even made a little joke about chucking him back.

But then a young lad, Michael Gielty, stepped forward. "I know who that is," he said. "He's staying with us at the guest house. It's Hugh Falkus."

I

The Call of the Running Tide

It seems to me now that people were kinder when I was a boy; that despite,
perhaps because of, their material hardship, the years of depression formed a more
compassionate age than that of today, when charity is laid on with trumpeting publicity;
when integrity and morality are so often supplanted by selfishness
and greed, and violence predominates.

THE STOLEN YEARS

JAMES Everest Falkus was born in 1875 in Cheam, Surrey, the son of
Richard Uriah Falkus, a bank clerk, and his wife Margaret, from Lelant
in Cornwall. James followed his father into a city banking job and at
twenty-four married Alice Musgrove, from Westcliff-on-Sea in Essex, who
was a few months older.

The couple settled in Beddington, Surrey. Their first child, Elsie, was
born in the spring of 1901, and a boy, Arthur Everest, followed in 1904.

The Falkuses had been married for eighteen years by the time their third
and last child arrived. They had by now moved to Melton, a large new
semi-detached house at the established end of Cornwall Road in James'
home town of Cheam.

Their second son was born at home on the night of Tuesday 15th May,
1917; according to his own account in later life, a Zeppelin raid was in
progress at the time.[1]

Although he was known as Hugh throughout his life by family and friends
alike, his birth certificate reveals that Falkus was baptised Hubert Edward
Lance.

Falkus' antecedents can quickly be traced back to his paternal great

The house in Cheam where Hugh was born in 1917.

grandfather, Richard John Falkus, a carpenter, born in Marylebone around 1818. Contrary to suggestions he made in later life to some of his friends, there is no sign of a link with a Danish banking family. The name seems to be commonest in Germany, and occurs more frequently both there and in England than in any of the Scandinavian countries.

All three Falkus children were brought up as members of the Plymouth Brethren. This cannot have made for an easy childhood; the Brethren were, and are, an evangelical and fundamentalist Christian Protestant sect characterised by extreme simplicity of belief and lifestyle. They disapprove of all forms of entertainment, including sport, dancing, cinema, theatres and gambling, with public houses and alcohol particularly frowned upon. Children are treated with the utmost strictness and greatly limited in their opportunities to play, or in the friendships they are allowed to make. According to Terry Norman in his Internet history of the Brethren, from which the author has gleaned the above information:[2] 'The untold tensions that such severe restrictions can cause between parents and children may easily be imagined, especially when mass entertainment took off explosively from the 1920s onwards.'

The Falkus home was no holiday camp, even by pre-war standards. Work and worship dominated, seven days a week. Theatre and cinema were beyond the pale, and the radio was allowed only for the news. Even photography seems to have been frowned upon; to the end of her days, Alice would not allow anyone to take her picture. She drove the boys hard in their schoolwork and insisted that they practise daily on the piano, an instrument which (in later life, at least) they both, unsurprisingly, professed to hate.

A thirteen-year interval between the second child and the last arouses the suspicion that Hugh's conception may have been an accident, or at least an afterthought, particularly as Alice was forty-two by the time he arrived - an advanced age for motherhood in those days. Was he a wanted child? Apparently so, if *The Stolen Years*, his collection of reminiscences from his early life, can be relied upon. Though he scarcely mentioned his mother in the book, he wrote of returning to 'my own circle of light and love and affection' and went on: 'It is the fashion nowadays to write of an unhappy childhood and to denigrate one's parents. Happily, I can write otherwise. My own home life was secure, and there are many memories I cherish.'

Despite this, there is strong evidence that all was not well between Hugh and his mother. He told the angling writer Brian Clarke that he had had 'a very happy childhood, except for my mother' and to his friend Tim Thomas he said his antipathy towards her had chiefly been provoked by the way she treated his father. He described her to other friends as having been slightly unbalanced, and once told his friend Bill Fowler (according to Bill's ex-wife Toni) that in a fit of anger she had torn the cloth from the dinner table, sending food, crockery, condiments and cutlery flying around the room. To several friends he said that he had tried to have as little to do with her as possible; none can remember him saying anything positive about her.

He was nevertheless capable of writing to her in affectionate terms. A postcard from prison camp dated November 1942 addresses her as 'Mother darling' and concludes 'Do hope you're keeping well. Please don't worry about me. All my love, write soon.'

In truth, the fragmentary evidence we have is not enough to provide a useful understanding of the relationship between Hugh Falkus and his mother. Suffice it to say that it does not appear to have been a good one.

Arthur's daughter Daphne, born in 1929, remembers her grandmother as a 'little old lady in a wig' (she apparently had some form of alopecia) who ran a tight ship at home and rarely laughed. The chief diversion for the women of the house - Alice, Elsie and Aunt Betsy, James' sister - was reading to each other from popular books and magazines.

Outdoor recreation did not figure highly on Alice Falkus' agenda. For her husband, however, it was a very different matter. The phrase 'messing about in boats' was coined by another Edwardian banker, Kenneth Grahame, but it fitted this one like a bosun's whiskers. James Falkus, 'a great big broad fellow with a merry mouth and an astonishing constitution', as Hugh described him, does not sound much like a sober son of the Church. His happiest hours were spent pottering about on the muddy creeks and tidal inlets of the Essex marshes, ambushing ducks with the 12-bore or chucking out a line for eels and flounders. Particularly, he loved boats; and in the 1920s and 1930s he owned dozens of them, their size and quality depending, as his younger son later wrote, on available finances.

'There were motor launches and fishing boats, racing one-designs, sailing punts, a converted naval pinnace, broads boats, dinghies and sundry small sloops and cutters' Hugh wrote in *The Stolen Years*. 'None stayed with us for very long.'

So dedicated was James to life afloat that in the mid 1920s James, Alice, Elsie and Hugh decamped from their suburban existence and went to live on a houseboat full-time. The *Neptune* was moored in a backwater of the creek that runs along the north side of Canvey Island.

'She was a beautiful boat' recalls Daphne, who remembers playing on board *Neptune* as a small child. 'My grandfather did the conversion in style, with brass and mahogany everywhere - he must have spent a great deal on her, though where he got the money from I have no idea. The sleeping quarters were below decks and the living quarters above. They even had a piano on board.'

Both boys shared their father's love of boats, and Arthur was old enough to play an active role in these adventures from the early days. Hugh was not long in joining him, acquiring his first boat, a double-ended punt with lug-sail and centre-board, by the time he was in his teens and learning to sail in the shallow lagoon where *Neptune* was moored.

By the mid 1930s, James Falkus had decided that City desks and gospel hall pews could not compete with leeboards and bowsprits and had for-saken the tedium of city life for good. Still in his fifties, he retired from the bank to spend every available minute on his beloved Essex marshes, sailing, fishing and shooting.

This seems to have been accepted with equanimity at home. 'When Father went fishing there was an understanding that domestic life main-tained its even tenor' wrote Hugh. 'No meals were to be kept hot: there was to be no waiting up, no worrying and no looking out of the window. That was the way of it, and everyone was happy.'

By the time of James' retirement Arthur had begun a career in electrical engineering, and was not free to share the waterborne life with his father except at weekends and holidays, whether he wished to or not. Hugh, however, was still living at home and could go out on the marshes with James whenever it was not a school day, and sometimes when it was.

This evidently suited both of them down to the ground. Not only was Hugh available, he was mightily keen - in contrast to his elder brother, he shared their father's passion for fishing and shooting from his earliest years. From the moment he was big enough to pull on a pair of gumboots, he became James' constant companion. Later in life he talked happily of these early days among the 'wader-haunted flats and saltings' to friends and journalists, relating how he shot his first wigeon and caught his first fish, a whiting, at the age of four from an East Coast jetty.

'I can still sense the feeling of wonderment and predatory elation as that silvery little fish came flashing into the sunlight - a moment never quite to be recaptured' he wrote. 'It is true that my father had other interests besides fishing - boats and budgerigars, for instance, and occasionally the world of commerce. But fishing was the thread that bound his life together and he fished, as he lived, with infectious and inexhaustible enthusiasm.'

By the age of six Hugh had already learned the basics of shotgun handling, though at this early stage his chief role lay in acting as a human retriever during his father's many wildfowling outings - he claimed to have been able to swim fully-clothed from the age of five. He would even earn pocket-money by ferrying the old fowlers across the creek for a halfpenny a time.

By his own assessment Hugh was a 'moody, introspective little boy' who lived outside the herd. He had few friends in boyhood, but counted prominently among them a one-eyed former sailing-barge skipper called Puggy Dimmond who lived on an old houseboat on the Essex marshes and spent his days fishing and wildfowling. Hugh worshipped Puggy and spent long summer days - often when he should have been at school - listening to his colourful stories or fishing with him from a duck-punt. 'He seemed ever genuinely pleased to see me, which, for adult human behaviour, was itself unusual' Hugh wrote.

School clearly came a poor second to all of this. Certainly Hugh never professed an interest in education. He reflected in *The Stolen Years*: 'It is difficult to understand why schooldays should ever have been expected to provide any particular form of happiness. They include the most delicate and awkward stages of our development, and being imprisoned in the company of several hundred other insensitive young beasts makes one's own

The earliest known picture of Hugh Falkus (right), with a friend on the Essex marshes at the age of ten or eleven - he is wearing his East Anglian School cap.

Hugh in his school uniform, probably aged eleven or twelve.

emotional awakening no easier or happier.' His school life, he went on, was neither unhappy nor riotous but 'something to be endured with as much stoicism as one could muster'.

Despite this, Falkus did quite well at school. In 1927, at the age of ten, he became a boarder at the East Anglian School for Middle Class Boys in Northgate Avenue, Bury St Edmunds (motto: *viriliter agite estote fortes* - 'strive manfully, be courageous'). The East Anglian School was founded in 1881 to provide a Christian education for secondary school pupils, and it soon gained and retained a reputation for being one of the most progressive schools in the county. It was much favoured by the older country families of Suffolk, and many a gentleman farmer or landowner would send his sons there. In the 1930s the school moved to more spacious accommodation in the rural setting of Culford Park, since which time it has been known as Culford School.

H. E. L. Falkus was one of the last pupils of the school when it was still the EAS, attending as a boarder until 1932. When his name first appears on the new boys' roll for the summer term of 1927, the school is recorded as having one hundred and nineteen boarders and forty-four day boys.

A wander through the school's annual report for 1928 reveals Culford as a place of achievement, culture and wit. There is great pride in the successes of pupils in the examination halls and on the sports field. A costly new gymnasium and laboratories for science and physics are planned, along with a new dormitory with a separate cubicle for each boy. Twenty-six pupils - a record - had won the Cambridge School Certificate. Culford, its headmaster, Dr Skinner, reminds us, had 'always striven to send out into the world the highest product possible - the Christian gentleman'.

Falkus may not have embraced Christianity with much enthusiasm, but Culford's records show that he was a good all-round pupil who pulled his weight on the sports field and particularly in the swimming pool. The academic lists generally show him in the upper half of his form and improving - never attaining brilliance, but very far from duncehood. He reached fifth place twice, in form IVb and again in Vb.

His achievements in individual subjects are not recorded, though he later told friends that his best subjects had been English and classics and that he had been poor at maths, a subject he was to struggle with throughout life. His one subsequent trial by examination, when he had to get through RAF Flying School, was dealt with through lateral thinking rather than deductive logic. He offered to complete the written papers for a group of less verbally-skilled friends while they looked after his maths and navigation papers. All the group scored high marks.

On the sports field at Culford, Falkus played for the 1st XI hockey team and the 2nd XI football team. He did not apparently win a place on any of the school cricket teams, though he told his friend and protégé Mike Daunt that at school, cricket had been his favourite boyhood game.

Falkus acquitted himself well on Sports Day 1931, when he was fourteen. He came second in the 100 yards and long jump and third in the 220 yards and high jump. These achievements helped his house, Floyd, to carry off the Sports Cup that term.

At swimming, he excelled. On 20th June, 1930, at the town's Corporation Baths, he won the junior length and came second in the two-length event. The following April he was awarded the Royal Life Saving Society's Bronze Medallion.

In December 1931 Falkus inhaled an early whiff of greasepaint. In the school production of *As You Like It* he is credited with playing Charles, a wrestler. He is also listed among the stage crew.

Despite these successes, his own account of his schooldays paints a disaffected picture. 'Boys are for the most part unkind, dirty little animals, many of whom grow up into unkind, dirty little men who continue to snuffle and grunt in the big adult jungle' he wrote. 'Content within my shell, I was lucky to escape much of the miserable bullying that made school life so wretchedly unhappy for many of my contemporaries. Ever a peaceable soul, I would fight with ferocity if pushed too far. And as a boy I could fight very well. Those early days spent plodding around marshes and rowing boats up and down windy creeks had developed strong limbs.'

In adulthood Hugh was free with stories about his youthful fishing, shooting and sailing adventures, and indeed built *The Stolen Years* upon them. But rarely did he divulge hard facts about life at home or in school. According to the angling writer and historian Fred Buller, his great friend for thirty years: 'The only time he would refer to his childhood was at three in the morning after a good deal of Scotch. Even then he would not dwell on it long, and refused to be drawn on the details.'

James Falkus appears centre stage in almost every chapter of *The Stolen Years;* Hugh's mother is referred to in passing just four times. This is handsome coverage, however, compared to his brother and sister, whose existence is not acknowledged at all. It seems a strange omission, particularly in Arthur's case. Daphne puts it down to his reluctance to defer to anyone else (a trait for which Falkus became famous), and to the fact that Arthur and Elsie were so much older.

It is clear from their later successes in competitive sailing that Hugh and Arthur could work as a team when afloat. Perhaps on dry land they had less in common. Where Hugh went his own way from his earliest years, Arthur was a conformist who liked to get on in the world conventionally, through study and a career. At eighteen, after a diligent passage through school which brought him distinctions in English, maths and chemistry, he won a place at the University of London, going on to take a first-class degree in electrical engineering. He went into the radio manufacturing business and later rose through the ranks at Cable and Wireless. There was very little contact between Hugh and Arthur in later life. Arthur died in Cambridge in 1993, at the age of eighty-nine.

Of Elsie, as the daughter of a highly traditional English family, less academic achievement was expected and more in the way of domestic duty. Just as well, it seems; Elsie was neither beautiful nor gifted, and she lagged behind her brothers in the IQ department too. Daphne remembers her aunt as a 'lump', kept always in the background by her parents, though she was kind enough to her niece, reliably saving back numbers of *Woman's Weekly* for her.

Hugh's son Malcolm's description is more graphic. 'Her looks were unfortunate - fat and heavy and chinless' he says. 'My mother said Hugh used to

Arthur Falkus with his daughter Daphne in the early 1930s.

A post-war studio shot of Daphne Falkus, taken when she was working for Lucie Clayton, the modelling agency.

stroke his chin to avoid getting the same affliction. She spoke with a strong provincial twang and had some preposterous ideas - until she was twenty-one, she thought a woman could get pregnant if a man touched her knee.'

As a latecomer to sex Elsie was besotted with men, and pursued anyone who seemed vaguely eligible. She became a Catholic, Malcolm's mother told him once, in order to make a play for the church organist, and developed such a crush on the Paignton librarian that he had to leave town.

'For all that, I remember Auntie Elsie as a kind and cheerful soul' says Malcolm. 'She certainly felt, and was, ignored by Hugh - Mum said he was ashamed of her - and I think Elsie and Mum found some common ground in their rejection by him.'

Elsie did acquire a suitor at one point, but the relationship was vetoed by her parents. She lived at home in the role of housekeeper and domestic dogsbody until she was thirty-eight, when she was briefly liberated by the outbreak of the Second World War. Taking advantage of the call to both sexes to serve their country, she enlisted - against her parents' wishes - with the WRNS. But happiness eluded her. In the 1950s, as a result of joining a marriage bureau, she met and married a man called Ted Morley, who eventually committed suicide by jumping from an upstairs window of their house. She died, childless, in 1980.

Elsie on the sea front at Goodrington in 1955.

Elsie Falkus in later life.

Arthur and his wife Nora on board Neptune.

Hugh striding along the seafront.

Falkus got his *valete* from Culford in the spring term of 1932, when he was fifteen. By then the family had acquired a foothold - along with an anchorage - in Devon, where they bought an old 60-ton straight-stemmed cutter which they named *Nora*, after Arthur's wife.

As a young man Hugh earned pocket money from at least one source which is not mentioned in his writings. Arthur, who had by then settled with Nora in Westcliff-on-Sea, owned a radio repair shop in nearby Old Leigh with a distributorship for Echo radios. In the early 1930s Hugh and a friend, Tony Chapman, would run the shop when Arthur was away. Falkus' civilian occupation for 1936-1938 is listed on his RAF record as 'assistant engineer'; a tongue-in-cheek reference to his job in the shop, perhaps.

At this time Hugh seems to have divided his time between the family home in Goodrington and Arthur's cottage in Old Leigh, where he would arrive without notice, staying for weeks at a time before disappearing again. During his stays in Essex it was not Arthur who accompanied him on his wildfowling expeditions but Nora, who, unlike her husband, shared Hugh's love of shooting. Daphne remembers him 'bullying' Nora into going out with him on to the marshes.

By the time the family moved its centre of gravity to Devon, Hugh and Arthur were highly competent sailors. They raced against some of the best-known yachtsmen of their day - Uffa Fox, Morgan Giles and Peter Scott. Two silver trophies survive from the period for the achievements of the brothers on board their dinghy 'Penguin'. Both are dated June 1934 and inscribed with the name A. E. Falkus, though Daphne says the brothers crewed the boat together.

It was soon after this that Falkus acquired a boat which for the first time would teach him to fear the sea. According to *The Stolen Years*, he bought an old 18-foot three-quarter decked yacht for £5 from a Devon boatman. Enchanted by her beauty and deaf to the vendor's warnings about her rotten timbers, he christened his acquisition *Night Wind*, and spent a winter doing her up from tiller to bow.

One evening at summer's end he was sailing home after a cruise up the Channel when, with little warning, a storm blew up:

A curtain of rain came hissing across the sea. With it came the real wind: no zephyr now, touched with soft caress, but a gusty brawling wind that whined in the rigging and stretched the sheets bar tight, heeling the boat over so that a lather of foam ran along her deck. The long slow swell had changed to a heaving switchback of yeasty water and the yacht's forefoot, plunging into waves now curling and white-capped, sent a mist of spray

Nora Falkus in her ATS uniform.

James Falkus fishing from the shore at Goodrington.

An elderly James Falkus.

A youthful Hugh Falkus digging lugworms.

flinging up over the weather bow . . . For mile after mile the little yacht plunged on into the blackness. Suddenly, without warning, the mainsail ripped from luff to leach. Loud above the tumult of wind and sea, the pieces of torn canvas thundered like gunfire.

As the storm drove the sinking boat headlong towards the rocks, her teenage helmsman managed to steer her through a gap into a sandy cove and run her aground. Exhausted by the battle to keep her afloat, he slept on what was left of *Night Wind's* shattered boards till daybreak before climbing the cliffs for home.

The final chapter of *The Stolen Years* recounts another, even narrower, escape from the sea. Falkus returned home one December night (it would have been 1938, from the age he gave for his father at the time) from an evening with friends to find his mother distraught because James had not returned from a fishing trip out in the Dart estuary. Hugh had been with him earlier in the day, so he knew where to look. After finding the dinghy half-sunk and awash, he calculated that his father's only chance of survival on that freezing night would have been to have swum, somehow, to the *Susannah*, a fishing smack which was kept in the channel through the winter months, and to have climbed up the anchor chain on to the deck.

Falkus described how he had found an unsecured rowing boat - complete with oars and rowlocks - dragged it down into the water and rowed out into the darkness. When he reached the *Susannah*, there, just as he had prayed, was his father, crouching half-naked in the icy cockpit and close to death from exposure. Hugh wrapped his coat around him and rowed him home.

The 'stolen years' - nineteen of them, from sixty-three to his eventual death at eighty-two (not, as Hugh wrote, eighty-five) - were the years James Falkus would have lost had it not been for this nigh-supernatural feat by his son. 'It is hardly credible . . . it did not make sense - it does not now', Falkus wrote, and the sceptical reader would agree.

Daphne, the closest we have to a surviving contemporary witness, does not dismiss the story. 'Something like Hugh's account did happen' she says. 'James, Arthur and Hugh took risks regularly and were always getting into scrapes with boats. Some of them were pretty serious. Hugh was a great storyteller and he certainly used poetic licence. But *The Stolen Years* rings true, even if he exaggerated the details. It captures the atmosphere of those years.'

In May 1935, on the day after his eighteenth birthday, Hugh joined the 2nd Battalion of the Devonshire Regiment. This does not seem to have worked out too well; his RAF record indicates that he bought himself out the following April (or much more likely, persuaded his father to do it).

Unsurprisingly, Falkus had been fascinated since boyhood by *The Riddle of the Sands*, Erskine Childers' pre-First-World-War spy thriller about a lone yachtsman's discovery of a German plan to invade Britain via the Dutch canal system. In the mid 1930s, probably in 1936, his interest in the book led to his spending a summer helping to crew a large sailing boat plying along the German coast west of Hamburg. He told friends later that he had got on extremely well with the Germans he met, particularly the young women.

There were occasions when Falkus saw a less attractive side of Germany. One night in Hamburg, he got into a dispute with a band of Hitler Youth. Words were exchanged, fisticuffs ensued and Falkus was lucky to escape without serious injury.

While in the city he befriended a young German who proceeded to open up to him about his opposition to the Nazi regime. Falkus told friends later that he had realised they were being spied on, but had no way of warning the young man; he was arrested and marched away by Nazi officials, apparently to be shot the following morning, and Falkus felt guilty ever afterwards for having been unable to prevent it.

His sailing exploits continued until, at the onset of war in 1939, all boats were ordered out of the water to remove any danger that they might be used in an invasion. But it was not the Senior Service that managed to recruit the services of Hugh Falkus for the battle against Germany. He had discovered the thrill of flying.

At the launch of a new boat at one of the Essex sailing clubs, July 1936. Hugh is third from the right, back row, with Arthur to his right.

II

Prisoner

Life is damnably monstrous. There's not very much I can write about. I'd give a lot for a few pounds of chocolates and some cigarettes.

LETTER TO DORIS

HUGH FALKUS was not a man to shirk active service for his country. At nineteen he joined the Air Corps, and by the time the Second World War began he had had his pilot's licence for well over a year.

After basic training in the summer of 1938 at a civilian flying school at White Waltham near Maidenhead, Falkus undertook his military training at 11 Flying Training School at Wittering, near Stamford, Lincolnshire. The unit operated two-seater Harts and Audaxes and single-seater Hawker Furies, all adaptations of the basic Hart airframe and used respectively in the light bomber, army co-operation and fighter roles.

Pilot's licence no 15152 was issued on 29th July, 1938, to Flying Officer H. E. L. Falkus of no. 11 FTS, RAF Shawbury, Shropshire. In August that year he was given a four-year short-service commission as an Acting Pilot Officer in the General Branch of the RAF. He got his 'wings' (his Flying Badge) that December, and became a substantive Pilot Officer in June 1939.

Falkus' first flying job was with the Met Flight in Northern Ireland, part of 2 ATS (Armament Training School), which was based at Aldergrove in County Antrim. At that time, according to his account, the BBC weather forecast largely depended on 'readings taken down in pencil on a knee-pad from instruments tied to the wing struts of an open-cockpit, single-seater, Gloster Gauntlet biplane fighter'. The Gauntlet was already outclassed by

Newly-commissioned: Flying Officer Hugh Falkus, 1938.

A young Doris Walter.

the beginning of the war and was relegated to support duties, but the attachment proved an enjoyable one, with plenty of time for leisure.

In a passage which was eventually published posthumously in a collection of his autobiographical material, *Some of it Was Fun*, Falkus remembered the posting as a time of great happiness. 'Flying one of the most manoeuvrable aerobatic fighters ever made, playing plenty of cricket, whisked off on frequent fly-fishing trips by by a commanding officer who was angling crazy, riotous parties in the mess most weekends with the chaps from City of Belfast Auxiliary Squadron - life was idyllic and, in later years, never quite to be equalled' he wrote.

The angling-crazy CO was a man called Atlantic Sam, who had earned his nickname through an attempt to fly the Atlantic after a champagne party. Their relationship did not get off to a good start. On one occasion he put Falkus in charge of the camp - not a welcome duty, as Falkus had just discovered a particularly productive fishing spot that contained some large trout and had planned to tackle them that night. When Sam returned for his notes and found Falkus absent, he put him on a charge. Unaware of all this, Falkus sneaked back into camp under cover of darkness and climbed into his room, leaving the lights off to avoid attracting attention.

Unfortunately he had found the wrong bedroom. The light went on to reveal the CO sitting bolt upright in bed. Thinking on his feet, Falkus behaved as if nothing was amiss. "I've brought you a few fish, sir," he said. The size of the trout, and the promise to reveal where they had been caught, ensured the charge was dropped.

It was Sam who first introduced Falkus to sea-trout fishing. The job made few demands on their time, and the pair were free to drive from their Belfast base to the banks of Ulster rivers such as the Foyle, the Bush and the Bann - all of which were then rich both in fish and free fishing - or sometimes over to the wilder waters of County Donegal.

When the Gauntlet was superseded by the Gladiator, Falkus had the job of taking delivery of the new aircraft from the Bristol factory where they were made. He would check them out at the Gloster airfield before flying them back to base.

Falkus hit it off immediately with Gloster's chief test pilot, Michael Daunt. More than forty years later, in *Salmon Fishing*, he recalled his first encounter with Daunt. 'A gleaming new silver Gladiator came zooming down, skimmed the line of trees fringing the tiny airfield and hurtled over the grass at head height. As he passed, the pilot gave us a cheery wave. Michael Daunt, upside down.'

On subsequent missions to Bristol the pair would party into the small hours with Daunt's friends and some 'friendly birds'. In later life Daunt's son, Michael Daunt junior, would become Hugh's friend, protégé and professional successor.

Falkus told his friend Tim Thomas that at the outbreak of war he had been in charge of a flight of Blenheim fighters which were being used to protect convoys along the east coast. He was due to lead a flight out to protect British troops in Norway, but two hours before the flight was due to leave he was replaced by another pilot, who had earned his CO's disapproval by dallying with a young divorcee in the village. None of the men returned.

By 1939, Falkus had a new responsibility to think about; a wife.

Doris Marjorie Walter was born on 23rd October, 1913, in Derby, the first child of a London-born jeweller and freemason, Harold Walter, and his wife Eileen. Eileen was glamorous, headstrong and extravagant, and the marriage was a stormy one. Harold, whose business was successful enough to allow him to run a shop in Buenos Aires as well as his base in Ipswich, acquired a large house which he named Gyppeswick (the old name for Ipswich) in Westcliff-on-Sea, Essex. When the couple finally split up, Eileen

The marriage of Sheila Walter to Peter Hayward-Surry. Hugh's mother-in-law Eileen is bottom right, his father-in-law Harold is top left in glasses. Daphne Walter is immediately behind the couple, Hugh at her left shoulder.

made a half-hearted attempt to turn Gyppeswick into a guest house, keeping the best rooms for herself.

Doris, the eldest of three daughters, was clever and artistically gifted. She was also sensible and well-grounded - sufficiently so to embark on a nursing career, at the famous John Radcliffe Hospital in Oxford. She enjoyed the theoretical side of nursing but soon found that the business of giving bed baths and changing dressings was less to her taste, so she left the Radcliffe to join her mother at Gyppeswick. She spent part of her leisure time looking after a group of Cub Scouts on Canvey Island.

Hugh was working in his brother's shop at Old Leigh when he met Doris, on a visit to Gyppeswick in late 1937 or 1938. Initially it was the middle Walter girl, Sheila, who attracted his interest. Sheila was as pretty as Doris and eighteen months younger than Hugh (Doris was nearly four years older than him). But Sheila was already spoken for - she was engaged to a young officer called Peter Hayward-Surry - so Hugh turned his attention to her older sister.

In 1938, the guest house went out of business and Eileen moved to Torquay to look for employment in the burgeoning hotel industry there. Doris secured a job as a receptionist at a hotel in Brockenhurst, in the New Forest, and it was at Chichester Register Office that Hugh and Doris were married, on 11th July, 1939. Her sister Daphne, who was allowed an afternoon's leave from the ATS to attend the wedding, remembers that there were few guests and no reception, though Doris looked very pretty in a pink suit.

The honeymoon was in Buxton, Derbyshire, the town of Doris' birth. Presumably it was brief. Hitler had marched into Czechoslovakia, and Poland was to follow. Servicemen's leave was in short supply, and the couple saw little of each other during what remained of 1939.

No. 222 Squadron of the RAF, disbanded since 1919, re-formed at Duxford, Cambridgeshire, on 5th October, 1939. Falkus was posted there four days later, making him a founder member of the re-formed squadron. Among his colleagues on 222 was Douglas Bader, the great air ace who carried on an outstanding flying career despite the loss of both legs. The squadron flew Blenheim fighters in a shipping protection role until March 1940, when it re-equipped with Spitfires to function as a day fighter unit.

At the end of April 1939 Falkus took a conversion course to Heyford bombers, probably to give him twin-engined experience before the transfer to 222's short-nosed Blenheims. The Handley Page Heyford was unusual among bombers in that it was possible (just) to loop it. Falkus was not happy until he had proved this to his own satisfaction, taking the four-ton behemoth up to 17,500 feet and finally pulling out of the loop five hundred feet from the ground. When he told this story at a smart luncheon in London after the war, he finished it off with some four-letter words about the aircraft's designer, at which point the man at the far end of the table smilingly introduced himself as Sir Frederick Handley Page.

Falkus would often say that while he could live with the thought that enemy fire might kill or injure him at any moment, he was terrified by the idea of a bullet coming from underneath. He even procured a piece of sheet steel for the defence of his most sensitive areas, and would take it with him on every mission.

The next posting was closer to home. The job was to fly Blenheims between the Wash and the Thames Estuary, protecting East Coast food convoys from Heinkel bomber attacks. Falkus did not think much of the Blenheim, which was heavy and cumbersome, poorly protected against enemy fire and not designed to take the stress of combat flying.

He wrote that a dawn wildfowling foray on the Essex marshes during the first winter of the war gave him a moment of terror greater than anything he had endured in the pilot's seat. Having been assured that there would be no target practice that day, he was crouched on one of the struts that supported the target, nursing the 12-bore given to him by Puggy Dimmond, when he heard the drone of Spitfires and realised with horror that the Range Controller had decided that the weather was fine enough for practice after all. Falkus ran from cover and waved furiously at his fellow pilots, just in time to stop their bullets from cutting him to ribbons.

Falkus wrote very little poetry, often claiming that it was beyond him. Yet he made some creditable attempts. The first on record is a seventy-eight-line poem entitled *Cloud Set*, found among his papers. There is no date, but it was clearly inspired by these early pre-war years in the air and so was probably written fairly early on. An extract:

> *Crosswind check, then a moment's wait*
> *Calling the tower for take-off clearance;*
> *Okay to go - (then take off straight,*
> *It gives the Squadron a nice appearance).*
> *Open the throttle and hold her steady,*
> *Tailplane's up and she's nearly ready*
> *Then ease her off as you feel her lift.*

The final lines show Falkus reaching into a romantic vein:

> *You're a little boy in a land of dreams*
> *Where the raths outgrabe and the Jubjub flies;*
> *You're in Xanadu with its mystic streams;*
> *At the rainbow's end where the treasure lies*
> *You're a Quixote tilting at twisted sails;*
> *You're with everyone in the fairy tales.*
> *You're sailing a sieve in a milk white sea,*
> *Past the land of Nod and the Isles of Care,*
> *Where Toad of Toad Hall and the Wise Men three*
> *Disport with the snark and the mad March Hare.*

Chamberlain declared war on Germany on 3rd September, 1939. Hugh wrote that his war began the following day, with an air-raid warning. He was sent up in a two-gun Gauntlet to deal with a reported high-level

Luftwaffe attack, but the German onslaught never materialised, so the mission came to nothing.

On the return leg Falkus decided to test his guns on a floating oil-drum. To his horror, both guns jammed almost immediately; yet again, the greatest threat to a British airman's safety seemed to come from his own side.

Back home that winter, Doris was dealing with the happy (one hopes) burden of a double pregnancy. Christopher and Malcolm Falkus were born at Eileen's rented home at 121 Station Road, Leigh-on-Sea, on 13th January, 1940. Her sisters Sheila and Daphne, as well as Sheila's husband Peter, were living with them (Sheila gave birth to a daughter, Sally, a month later). The twins' birth was difficult and the boys had to be taken to hospital after delivery.

If Hugh was able to see his firstborn, it must have been for a short time only. The war was gathering pace, and in May 1940, 222 Squadron moved to Hornchurch, Essex, to cover the Dunkirk evacuation.

Christopher and Malcolm Falkus, 1940.

It was at dawn on Saturday, 1st June, two days before the evacuation ended, that Falkus embarked on the adventure that would put an early finish to his part in the war. It had been a week of hectic action on both sides of the English Channel. On the news that morning, the BBC reported that the Allies had reconquered the area around Abbéville and crossed the Somme. Meanwhile the disembarkation of British and French troops from the shore was almost complete, though they were being relentlessly attacked from the air and four of our destroyers had been sunk offshore.

Falkus' squadron was scrambled at dawn to fly to Dunkirk. He wrote that there had been no time to put on his uniform, so he had simply pulled on his flying suit over his pyjamas.

According to the account Falkus gave so vividly in *The Stolen Years* (which has a long pedigree, incidentally - it made its first published appearance in an interview with the *South Devon Journal* in 1951), he shot down two German bombers over the Channel before making the mistake of getting greedy and chasing a third, when he found a Messerschmitt on his tail. The Spitfire crash-landed in a French wood and he was pulled out, dazed and bleeding, by German troops, who took him to a nearby farmhouse for questioning. His captors refused to believe he was an RAF officer because he was not wearing his uniform. Accused of being a spy, he was handed over to the SS and taken to another farmhouse, where he was interrogated and beaten before being made to stand in a corner of the courtyard throughout that night and the long, hot summer's day that followed.

Falkus wrote that as the sun began to set that evening, the SS men lined up on the other side of the courtyard and levelled their rifles. As they drew back their bolts, he turned to look for one last time at a trout he had seen rising in a stream on the other side of the wall. That split-second's delay, he wrote, saved his life; even as his captors' fingers tightened on their triggers, a senior German officer swept in, called off the firing squad and bundled him off to safety. From that moment he was treated as a prisoner of war. He went on to tell the same story to countless friends and interviewers over the years.

It is all very *Boy's Own Paper*. The thrill of airborne battle; the courageous young British officer, beaten and forced to stand against a wall without food or water; the little trout, a sweet reminder of home, rising bang on cue; the split-second escape from death at the hands of his evil SS captors. As with other Falkus stories, one feels a suspicion that historical accuracy may have been sacrificed for dramatic impact.

It was. The bare facts of Hugh's war are recorded in black and white on a single sheet of paper which has lain buried in an MoD file for the past sixty years. It is an RAF PoW 'interrogation report' on Falkus, the statement he made upon liberation to officers of MI9, the top-secret Government agency set up to help Allied personnel caught behind enemy lines. The statement, located and identified through the good offices of the RAF Air Historical Branch, reads:

I took off from Hornchurch in a Spitfire aircraft at 0430 hours on 1st June, 1940, on a fighter sweep over Dunkirk. The aircraft was hit by flak and then shot down by six ME 109s. I crash-landed in a field south-west of Calais and started to walk in the direction of the river Somme.

I continued walking for about 48 hours, being captured twice by German soldiers, but managed to get away each time. Finally I was captured again and taken to an army head-quarters in a château, where I was interrogated briefly.

I was then taken to a place near Fréville, where I was told I would be shot, and was kept in a courtyard for about 24 hours, after which I was taken to Fréville and then to Doullens, where I was put into an old gaol for several days.

I was taken on foot, by train and lorry, to the transit camp at Trier, where I spent about two days, and was then taken to the camp at Limburg, where I spent a further two days. I was then taken by train to Dulag Luft, where I was interrogated and kept in cells for about 3 days, and was then put into the camp.

The statement lists the eight camps where Falkus spent his war. From Dulag Luft (*Durchgangslager der Luftwaffe*, the RAF transit camp at Oberursel on the outskirts of Frankfurt) he was quickly moved to Oflag XIA at Prenzlau, then to Stalag Luft I on the north coast at Barth, where he stayed for fourteen months[3]. From October 1941 to September 1942 he was at Oflag VIB at Warburg, then there was a spell of eight months at Oflag XXIB at Schübin before he was transferred to Stalag Luft III at Sagan, where he spent most of the rest of the war.

So must we dismiss that wonderful story about the firing squad as pure fiction, as Falkus' friends have long suspected? Perhaps not entirely. Late one night many years later, over whisky and chat at the home of his BBC Natural History Unit friend Mike Kendall, Falkus told another, more believable, version of the account which appears in *The Stolen Years*. It makes a marginally less dramatic story, though a more harrowing one, and is not contradicted by his official statement - although one would have expected the salient points to have been mentioned in it.

Falkus told Kendall that he had been kept captive in a room in a farmhouse, and that from his window he could see a river. This led to his talking to his captors about his interest in fishing. Word of this reached a senior officer who also happened to be an angler. This man paid a visit to Falkus, during which they talked about their shared hobby.

After some days in captivity, Falkus and several other prisoners were told they were to be executed, and were marched out into a courtyard to be shot. Their guards were tying them to posts ready for the firing squad when the officer who had visited Falkus happened to drive up to the gate. He called on the SS men to stop, and took it upon himself to rescue his fellow angler by pretending that he needed to take him away for interrogation. For the other men, there was no reprieve.

Mike Kendall appears to be the only surviving friend who heard this story, although Falkus did provide an additional detail to Tim Thomas - that the death sentence had been imposed because he had struck a guard during one of his attempts to escape.

Whatever the truth about that long-ago summer's day in the Pas de Calais, there is no disputing the tedium and hardship that Falkus had to face as a prisoner of Germany for the next four years and eleven months. Nor should we underestimate the sense of failure and uselessness he must have felt at having been taken prisoner so early in the war - six weeks before the Battle of Britain got under way - without having managed, so far as we know, to fire a single shot for his country. For a courageous, talented and experienced pilot who had grown up with a gun in his hands, and whose brilliance at what Americans like to call 'shooting flying' was to impress his friends throughout life, being called out for a duck in the first over must have seemed an appalling ignominy.

Prison camp brought Falkus down to earth in both senses. Imprisonment was an ordeal for any officer, but for Falkus, a man with an immense lust for life who had enjoyed freedom and his own way since childhood, it must have been particularly hard to bear. For the first, and last, time in his life he found himself confined, far from friends and family and far from the tang of the ocean and the sound of running water. His letters reveal that his mood frequently oscillated between episodes of anger and rebellion - often leading to a stay in the 'cooler' - and periods of black depression when he would avoid human contact. Always there was the fear, the uncertainty, the discomfort, the sickness, the smell of maggot-infested latrines and the appalling food; black bread, rotten potatoes, boiled swedes, reconstituted meat, tinned jam, *ersatz* coffee and condensed milk.

The conditions in Oflag VIB were particularly grim. This camp was appallingly overcrowded, with as many as a hundred and thirty men in a barrack fifty feet long by twenty-six feet wide, and a toilet consisting of an open cesspit crossed by crude planks for the men to sit on. But Falkus was a brave and resourceful man, and (black moods notwithstanding) he appears to have made a brave and resourceful prisoner. According to Rollings' book, while at Barth he assisted in the making of clothing, compasses and maps; he also discovered the noble sport of building escape tunnels. By the time he was transferred to Oflag VIB, he had evidently become an accomplished tunneller.

In the early days tunnelling was largely a freelance business, with individual prisoners allowed to mount schemes of their own. Later it was to become much more organised. As Charles Rollings tells it in his book *Stalag Luft III, the Full Story*:

Hugh Falkus' first tunnelling effort was a 'blitz' scheme similar to one he had tried at Barth. Not far from the tripwire was a potato clamp and he decided to start there, thus reducing the length to be dug. Burrowing into the clamp, he excavated a cave. It was dark inside and he worked by touch.

Crawling out of the camp one evening, he bumped into a sentry who demanded to know what he was doing. Rather than face another sentence in the cells, Falkus thumped the sentry and took to his heels, the sentry shouting after him.

The tunnel was discovered a few days later, and Falkus, in collaboration with a group of his comrades, turned his attention to a longer-term project. This one was much more ambitious. It eventually produced the longest tunnel ever built in any of the camps, at 140 yards.

Work began in the summer of 1941. Clad only in long-johns - or sometimes combination undergarments, which protected the stomach, elbows and arms from the abrasions caused by tunnelling in cramped conditions - Falkus and his comrades began by sinking a shaft using a trowel made from the tip of a zinc jug with a wooden handle attached. Then they began to drive a tunnel towards freedom, twenty feet underground - an unheard-of depth at the time. Eventually they hoped to get a hundred men through it and out beyond the perimeter wire before the guards realised what was going on.

Filthy, sore and often barely able to breathe, the men laboured underground twenty-four hours a day, as many as sixty on a shift. It was an extraordinary project, and success would have been even more extraordinary. All went according to plan (apart from a series of terrifying collapses) until, in May 1942, the tunnel was finished and the way was clear for the big break. But that was the end of the adventure. The first escapers were immediately spotted by the guards, and found themselves back in camp within minutes. The furious Germans flooded the tunnel to make sure it could not be used again.

Such setbacks were never more than temporary. To these captured airmen, escaping had become a way of life, and giving up was unthinkable. Not only did it give them something to live for from day to day; by making life difficult for their captors, they could believe they were making some sort of contribution to the war effort.

The escape movement's eventual headquarters was Falkus' penultimate prison, Stalag Luft III, Goering's new purpose-built camp for British and American Air Force officers on the outskirts of the town of Sagan (now Zagan) in Poland, close to the German border about a hundred and thirty kilometres south-east of Berlin.

Stalag Luft III was supposed to be big enough to solve the overcrowding problems that had preceded it, but as more and more aircrew were shot down and captured it too became seriously cramped. Barracks designed for eighty or a hundred NCOs were packed with twice that number, and rooms built to hold six officers ended up with ten or twelve.

The terrain around Sagan was particularly dull, flat and featureless. According to Aidan Crawley's book *Escape from Germany 1939-45*, there was every incentive to get away from the place, even aside from the overcrowding, the boredom and the meagre rations. 'If any spur had been needed to induce prisoners to escape from the compounds at Sagan, the bleakness of the surroundings would have provided it' writes Crawley. 'The area inside the barbed wire was covered in tree stumps and without a blade of grass . . . outside the wire, a monotonous and unbroken vista of fir trees was all that prisoners could see.'

With nothing more constructive for the inmates to do than talk about home or play improvised games, escaping developed into a well-organised industry. Under the noses of the 'goons', as the guards were universally known to prisoners, tunnels into the sandy soil were repeatedly plotted, dug, disguised, aborted, abandoned and, nearly always, discovered.

Falkus did not officially claim to have tried to escape from any of the camps where he was incarcerated - there is a 'nil' opposite 'number of escape attempts' on that post-war debriefing statement. Presumably that was because he himself was never among those listed to make the break. He wrote, however, that he had helped with the construction of thirteen tunnels (entirely possible - in all, there were hundreds). He said that he had almost been buried alive in sand on one occasion, and on another was found naked underground in the dark, a fiasco which led to three months' solitary confinement. He told Tim Thomas that the greatest terror he had known in his life was the moment when a tunnel collapsed behind him as he and some friends were trying to dig their way under the wire, effectively entombing him in earth until he was able to dig his way out. Presumably that was the big tunnel at Oflag VIB.

The most ambitious, and the most notorious, of all the World War II ventures was the Great Escape of 24th March, 1944. Falkus said he had tried to dissuade his friends from going because he felt that the Nazis' increasing impatience with escapers and anger with RAF prisoners in particular would backfire on anyone who was caught. For this stance he was apparently scorned by his fellow officers, but he was proved right. Nearly all those who got out were recaptured. On the orders of a furious Hitler, fifty of them were summarily shot, one of the Reich's most shocking and despised acts. Ever afterwards Falkus referred to the Great Escape as the 'Great Blunder'.

Among Falkus' acquaintances in camp was Squadron Leader Roger Bushell, a charismatic former barrister, a natural leader and a fearless challenger of German authority. Effectively the leader of the Great Escape team, he was the original of the Richard Attenborough character, Roger Bartlett, in the 1963 feature film *The Great Escape*. Bushell was among the fifty who were machine-gunned by the Nazis.

One of those Falkus came to know well at Sagan was William Hardy, who became the last member of the Hardy family to head the world-famous tackle-making firm. Hardy said that he was one of those whose privileges had been taken away as a result of an escape attempt by Falkus which had involved an assault on a guard. He fished several times with Falkus in later life.

Another was Pilot Officer Bill Fowler, a bomber pilot who had been taken prisoner in July 1941 after he and his crew were shot down on a night-time raid over the Ruhr. Crag-jawed, moustached, six foot two and imperviously self-assured, William Menzies Weekes Fowler was the epitome of the swashbuckling flyer.

A shared love of fishing and shooting drew Falkus and Fowler together. Fowler's friendship proved a lifeline. At times, according to Fowler's account after the war, Falkus found prison camp almost unendurable. He would hide away alone in a corner, overwhelmed by depression and despair. Bill Fowler knew better than to challenge these moods, but he found that by

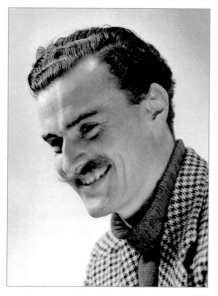

A civilian photo of Pilot Officer William Fowler.

encouraging Falkus to talk about his boyhood adventures, or drawing him into making plans for the good times that must surely come once the war had been safely won and the Germans sent packing, he could ease the despair a little and help his comrade to return to some kind of normality.

An incident involving Fowler has entered Falkus folklore. This is the story of the Kommandant's cat. According to an account quoted in *Stalag Luft III, the Full Story*: 'The cat, well-fed and plump, lurked outside the wire and had preyed on Falkus' mind for days . . . he and Wallace Cunningham lured the cat into the compound, stalked it, finally cornered it and put it to death. The stewed meat was divided among nine or ten men . . . Falkus used the cat's skin to make himself a pair of mittens.' Rollings goes on to point out that this is only one version of the story and that another officer, Peter Tomlinson, had disputed it, testifying that the cat had wandered into his room and was killed by another prisoner, 'Basher' Beauclair.

Brutal as prison camp life could be, there were lighter moments. Hugh's competitive instinct came to the fore when his fellow prisoner Pat Ward-Thomas, later to become an internationally-known golf writer, organised a golf club for the inmates of Sagan. According to Ward-Thomas in his 1981 autobiography, *Not Only Golf*:

When the membership had grown to twelve we had our first competition, a knockout, and Hugh and I reached the final. Falkus, no golfer but gifted with strong hands and a deadly aim, was expert at hitting the 'holes', such as they were. The fir tree would cause some discussion if its little trunk had to be hit, whereas Falkus would claim to have holed out if his shot whistled yards past the tree but grazed a leaf in passing. Fortunately Falkus was not as deadly as usual in our match and I became the first Open Champion of Sagan.

Falkus, six feet tall in his prime, with broad shoulders and large fists, also excelled at boxing. For years, his RAF Heavyweight Boxing Champion trophy decorated the mantelpiece of the family home in Devon.

Nothing did more for the prisoners' spirits than their own home-grown entertainment, and here too Falkus was much in evidence. 'Theatricals helped cheer us up' wrote fellow prisoner Jimmy James in his book *Moonless Nights* (2001). 'They were held in the dining room with tables placed together to form a stage and were organised mainly by Hugh Falkus, D. A. (Douglas) Ffrench-Mullen and P. E. J. (Pat) Greenhous, who wrote, produced and acted in comic skits, sometimes with a small "Greek Chorus" as supporting cast for the rowdier acts.'

James' book reveals that despite the censorship of letters, some news did creep through to give the prisoners clues as to what was going on in the world beyond the camp. They were all greatly cheered by a crumpled sheet of newspaper which arrived one day wrapped innocently around a parcel of clothing. It was the front page of the *Daily Express* for 15th September, 1940, and it announced that one hundred and eighty-four German aircraft had been shot down in a single day, the largest number to date. This was the first indication to the prisoners that their comrades back home had won the Battle of Britain (the date is now commemorated as Battle of Britain Day).

On the bitterly-cold night of 27th January, 1945, alarmed at news that the Russian army was advancing from the east, the Germans evacuated Stalag Luft III and neighbouring Belaria and marched more than nine thousand British and American 'Kriegies' out into the snow to relocate them to other prison camps to the north and west. It was a time of great confusion; Germany was losing control of the war, and it was becoming common knowledge that the Allied liberation could not be many months away.

With the guards low in morale and more concerned with their own interests than with trying to manage the security of the endless column of prisoners, there were now many opportunities for escape. Conditions were so grim - the men were driven along like cattle through the snow and frost, with inadequate clothing and very little food to sustain them - that some tried to break away through sheer desperation, feeling that almost anything was preferable to continuing the enforced march. Against this, the chances of survival on your own in such conditions were slim, and German discipline was collapsing; the danger of being shot in anger if you crossed the wrong man or got caught was now very real. Most prisoners, believing that freedom was imminent, felt that escape attempts were no longer worth the risk.

In fact only about thirty of the ten thousand RAF World War II prisoners ever did manage to escape from the German camps and reach home or neutral territory under their own steam. The rest were collected in dribs and drabs by the Allied forces as they advanced across mainland Europe during the spring of 1945, to be repatriated as soon as transport allowed.

The prisoners marched west, stopping by night to appeal to villagers to let them use whatever accommodation was available. Sheds and barns were eagerly invaded, while a heated building was a luxury to be shared by every man who could squeeze inside. Yet many, too sick, tired or cold to go any further, collapsed and died by the roadside. Some of the 'goons', scarcely better equipped than their charges, were among them.

When the column reached the town of Spremberg, about seventy kilometres west of Sagan, they were escorted into the station and put on trains to their new camps. Some were bound for Lückenwalde, south of Berlin, while others were being taken to Marlag-Milag Nord at Westertimke, north of the city of Bremen in north-west Germany. Marlag-Milag Nord had been built as a naval officers' camp (Marlag was the contraction for *Marinelager* and Milag stood for *Marineinterniertenlager*). The details Falkus gave on his MI9 statement indicate that he must have been among the latter party.

After a slow and tortuous train journey, the prisoners finally reached Marlag-Milag Nord on 4th February. According to *Not All Glory*[4], Victor F. Gambon's detailed synthesis of the testimonies of the RAF prisoners of war: 'Searches and delays kept some outside for up to eight hours. They were wet, freezing, cold, thirsty and near starvation, many at the point of complete exhaustion by the time they entered the bare rooms.'

Though for these men the war was now almost over, its hardships were not. Conditions were greatly inferior to those at Stalag Luft III and many of the prisoners were sick, exhausted and frostbitten from the long march. Their ordeal, and the uncertainty, were to continue for several more long weeks.

By early April the 'Kriegies' could hear from the south a sound that helped to raise their spirits a little; the roar of British guns pounding Bremen. The guards told them they were to be moved again, for their own safety. The prisoners were not reassured by this, fearing it more likely that their captors intended to use them as hostages, or even to kill them.

It was now that Falkus at last managed an escape, of sorts. On the morning of 10th April the prisoners were marched off towards the camp at Lübeck; two of the prisoners died in a 'friendly fire' incident when the column was strafed by RAF aircraft. Falkus did not leave with them. According to post-war accounts to journalists, he had managed to get hold of a pair of wire-cutters, which he used to cut through the ten-foot barbed wire fence surrounding the camp, and slip off into the night, living on nothing but 'short rations and berries' (*vide* the *Paignton Observer*), until he heard the rumble of approaching British tanks.

The concluding paragraph of his debriefing statement simply reads: 'I was liberated by the British Army at Westertimke, having hidden outside the wire from the time everyone else was marched away to Lübeck.'

On 27th April, Falkus was taken by truck to the aerodrome at Diepholz and put on a flight to Brussels. From there he was flown home. He arrived back in England on Sunday, 6th May, nine days before his twenty-eighth birthday. Two days later, he was joining in the VE Day celebrations.

Like many of his fellow prisoners, Falkus carried home with him a lasting hatred of Germany and Germans and an abhorrence of officialdom. 'No one is ever going to give me another order' he told friends on his return. In his case, having been knocked out of the war so early with so little to show for it, his feelings were compounded by a deep sense of failure, something that would dog him throughout his life.

The years of misery, humiliation and deprivation left Falkus with an urgent need to exorcise the horrors and hardships he had endured. He returned to England determined to squeeze every drop from the life ahead of him, and to do it on his own terms.

III

To Doris with Love

I think you'll find me absolutely intolerable. I can tell you now that my greatest desire
will be for decent cooking, then for a complete absence of noise and any kind of dirt.
So if you are ever going to organise yourself, start doing it now. If you still don't know
how to cook (you were useless before) then you've just got to learn.

LETTER TO DORIS, OCTOBER 1943

T HE prisoner-of-war's homecoming can prove a dreadful anticlimax. Conditioned to hardship, confinement and the company of men, he has been sustained through his ordeal by dreams of leisure, freedom and prosperity. The reality of domestic life is likely to bring him down to earth with an uncomfortable thud.

When Hugh arrived back in England in May 1945, Doris, Christopher and Malcolm were living at Paignton in Devon (Doris had felt it safer to move away from the embattled South East, and Hugh's parents lived in nearby Goodrington). The house, in Conway Road, was large, detached and rambling, with a sizeable garden, an apple orchard, a stable, a green-house and a cellar.

What happened on that homecoming Falkus never discussed in detail, but he gave his friends to understand that his wife had not been expecting him.

'He told us she thought he had been killed in service and had "made other arrangements"' says his friend, fishing companion and collaborator Fred Buller. 'By this we assumed he meant she had a new man in her life. He said he had stayed with her for a while to try to patch things up. But Hugh was a man of action. He hadn't a clue how to adjust to family life.'

Just how long Hugh stayed with Doris on his return is not recorded; it seems unlikely to have been more than a few weeks. But he did not abandon her entirely, at least not straight away. That she still counted for something with him is demonstrated by an event in late 1945 or 1946. Sir John Gielgud was playing Hamlet at the Haymarket that season, and Hugh claimed not only to have got to know the great actor but to have earned a great compliment from him; a box for one of the performances, which Hugh invited Doris to share with him. It was an evening she would remember with pride for the rest of her life.

The story that Doris had neither expected nor welcomed Hugh home was accepted by the Falkus inner circle throughout Hugh's life. It is very far from the truth. The real nature of the relationship between Hugh and Doris, and the circumstances in which their second set of twins, Mary and Anthony, were born, have not emerged until now.

The claim that Doris thought he had been killed in action has been demolished by the discovery of letters home from Falkus - more than four years' worth of them. They begin in June 1940, immediately after he was taken prisoner (Doris knew almost immediately that he had been captured; according to their son Malcolm, she heard his name read out on the radio by the traitor Lord Haw Haw), and continue until October 1944, not long before the prison camps were broken up. He ordered his wife to destroy them. She did not; they were found by their daughter Mary when she was going through her mother's papers after Falkus' death.

There are thirty of them, written in faded longhand on the narrow, flimsy, single sheets provided for prisoner-of-war correspondence, rather like a modern airmail letter. The sender would complete one half, then the recipient would reply on the other, already pre-addressed. PoW letters were closely censored - if Falkus wrote any which mentioned military or disciplinary matters, they would have been intercepted before they left Germany.

The first in Doris' bundle is dated 26th June, 1940, three and a half weeks after Hugh's capture, and identified as *Kriegsgefangenenpost* from Pilot Officer Hugh Falkus, prisoner number 2256, Oflag IIA, to Mrs Doris Falkus, c/o Cliff Park House, Paignton.

'My darling, just a line letting you know that I am well and missing you. Please tear this contraption down the centre and send your reply on the other sheet. I do hope you are keeping fit and well. Do look after yourself sweetheart and keep those eyes clear . . . I'll be back one day and then I'll be with you always.' He adds that he is 'endeavouring to learn German' and urges her to keep positive.

Some of Hugh's wartime letters to Doris.

A post-war picture of Hugh.

On 2nd July he tells her to 'concentrate on keeping yourself beautiful and the twins fit . . . ask my pater to look into my bank account and fix things up for you, there should be plenty of money.' He complains that he and his fellow prisoners are receiving only £3 a month of the £6 RAF pay to which they were entitled.

A few days later there was an isolated letter to his mother Alice: 'Dearest mother. Just a line to you all letting you know that I am fit and well. Have arrived at the final prison camp, which is for flying personnel only' [this must have been Stalag Luft I at Barth]. 'I shall be very grateful if you will send me some socks, handkerchiefs and underclothes and the blue sweater which was with my things. The Red Cross will tell you what I am allowed to be sent, quite a number of things are forbidden.'

He reveals that he is sharing a room with a naval lieutenant and that they have the use of a small garden outside, planted with lettuces and other vegetables.

'The authorities here are very decent to us and yesterday we went for a swim in the river. Look after Doris and tell her not to worry about things, I'll be back before long . . . your affectionate son.'

In a September 1940 letter the request for clothes is repeated to Doris, who is urged to send 'the warmest underclothes you can find'. 'I'm thinking of you every minute of the day and I long, how I long, to be with you . . . I'll be back one day when a little sanity returns to the world and then by God we'll find some happiness to make up for all this misery.'

Soon Falkus is thinking about the future in more practical terms. He suggests she hire a nanny - 'someone likely to be permanent'. But the early optimism that he would soon be on his way home appears to have faded. 'Lord only knows when I'll see you again. Be an angel and send some photographs of yourself, also a ukulele.'

In October the War Organisation wrote to Doris to tell her that Hugh was now at Barth and that they had received a message that he was 'anxious for news' of her.

'Life is damnably monstrous' he writes from Barth on 10th October. 'There's not very much I can write about. I'd give a lot for a few pounds of chocolates and some cigarettes.' Later that month he complains at her news that *Sport in Wildest Britain* (by H. Hesketh Prichard, 1921) is out of print and asks her to find a copy for his return. 'Very glad to hear the little brutes are keeping fit' he goes on. 'My spies inform me that sufficient discipline is not being enforced! Seriously though please don't spoil them, if you do they won't thank you for it later on . . . Don't forget that somehow you've got to save enough to buy a motor car, a new set of clothes (for me) and a gun (also for me) and a damn good holiday . . . I've given up worrying about how, where or with whom you are living, all I think about is when I'm going to get home, perhaps with any luck there'll be a second innings in the Far East. All of which is of course very selfish.'

A confined, deprived and desperately impatient young man of action, pushing as hard as he could on the only door open to him - his dream of the future. But what are we to make of that reference to the Far East? His thinking becomes clearer in a much later letter, dated February 1943, when he asked Doris: 'Would you like to sail round the world one day, after the war? You see I haven't much of a record and they'll probably chuck me out after the war's all over and unless there's the chance of a second innings in the Far East there won't be no job for little Hughie.'

There is no indication that Falkus ever officially blotted his RAF copybook; his only crime was to get himself shot down so early on. His RAF friend of later life, Andrew Moir, believes Falkus must have realised that any officer who had failed to distinguish himself in action or to gain much combat experience would struggle to find a job in the contracted post-war RAF. Falkus believed his only chance of a glorious finish was a second opportunity to fight, and understood enough of events beyond the prison camp to know that this was most likely in the Far East.

As the months go by, the tone of many of the letters becomes imperious to the point of bullying. He repeatedly chides Doris for not writing often enough, for not sending photographs of herself and the children and for failing to satisfy his demands for food, clothes and reading matter.

'I suppose by now you will have moved into a decent flat or house and acquired the services of a nanny . . . I suggest you get someone who will be permanent and stay until the boys are grown' he writes towards the end of 1940. 'I'm still fit but oh, how so sick at heart. Everything seems to have crashed.' A failed escape attempt perhaps, or just another bout of depression? Quite possibly both.

The following January he complains that she has still failed to send him any photographs, clothing or books. 'My present clothes are literally in rags and I was wearing only old flying clothes when I was shot down. Have you got a nanny yet? If not, why not?'

Falkus clearly had no idea how hard life had become for Doris. Their daughter Mary points out that she was frequently ill, short of money and exhausted from coping with the children. She must have been dismayed by his demands. Perhaps she did not want to bruise his fragile spirits by telling him how impossible they would be to meet.

No letters received by Hugh from Doris have survived from these years. Whether he kept any is not known, though it seems unlikely, given his determination to re-invent this period of his life. Many of his papers were lost in a fire much later. We are, however, given a glimpse of what life for Doris was like in the early stages of the war by a single unposted letter, probably dating from 1940. It is a request to him to send the twins' birth certificates, which she apparently needed in order to get them gas masks.

We've had lots of heavy gunfire lately and planes dashing about, supposed to be trying to lay mines. I am going out now to pick stinging nettles and dandelions, the Food Office say they are just like spinach, especially if you cook them with cream and butter. A poached egg on top makes 'a perfect meal'. So next time (if ever) you sample my cooking, you may be presented with a nice dish of 'weed purée' . . . hoping you are in good health husband dear, your loving wife, Doris.

'My mother was often ill in the war years, as she was later - I believe she nearly died after giving birth to my brothers' says Mary. 'Knowing how important it was to Hugh that she stay young and beautiful, she feared that if she told him the truth - how ill and tired she was - he wouldn't want to come back to her. All he could think of was that she was free and he wasn't. He had no idea what it meant to bring up young children in wartime, when food and clothing were so closely rationed.'

Falkus' references to his children, though indulgent enough on occasion, usually concerned the importance of their growing up fit, strong and untainted by any suspicion of mollycoddling. On the one occasion he mentions Malcolm's name, this paragon of good English spells it 'Malcom', a slight he repeated in a ninth birthday card, the only written communication his son ever received from him. His inability to communicate with his children is admitted in a later letter, in which he says: 'If we're still here over the New Year I'll try and think of something to write to the twins. It's awfully difficult though - I've been thinking about it for ten months now!'

On 25th February, 1941, he thanks Doris for the first books he has received, *Weekend Wodehouse* and *A Century of Horror*. He is feeling much happier. 'We're in great spirits here and I haven't the slightest doubt regarding the outcome of this year' he says. More photos are demanded - she must send one with every letter, to make sure some would get through. 'A copy of *The Field* will be met with tremendous enthusiasm' he advises her. And a little later he wants an 'ABRIDGED NAUTICAL ALMANAC - am getting pretty crack at celestial nav. but handicapped by lack of almanac.'

Still the complaints come about the quality of poor Doris' letters: 'Make them longer dear, they're so few and far between and so soon read.' And the Falkus family do not get a good press: 'Don't have anything to do with my various uncles and aunts and odd relations you may come across, they're a bloody weak lot - just tell them where they get off - from me.'

In November 1941 he thanks her for two letters with August dates, only just received. Clearly mollified by them, he tells her: 'I'm so terribly sorry to hear about the frightful time you've been having - I take back all I said in a previous letter, I think you've been coping splendidly. I didn't like your reference to 'feeling dubious', I promise there's nothing to feel dubious about, one of these days we're going to have one hell of a good time together, I feel frightfully optimistic about the future . . . so glad to know the offspring are so full of fun, I'm longing to see them - they must be getting awfully interesting. Please send lots of photographs of them, and you. Have you bought a motor yet? Save up and buy one and get out a lot.'

He goes on to announce his decision that they should all move to Norfolk 'in a cottage up on the coast with lots of wildfowling and sailing. You'll love it and it will be the best possible life for the twins . . . please send me some snapshots of the little brats crawling about. Can they swim yet? Make 'em practise in the bath! . . . there are so many people I know and I can sail a dinghy and shoot duck. The twins will have some decent country to play about in and if they drag coal into the lounge you can go and chuck them in the creek!'

On Boxing Day 1941 he promises that he is 'quite certain' that he will be back in time for next Christmas. Then on 15th January, 1942: 'Didn't think much of your last letter, can't understand why you haven't fixed some food parcels. Look here, write to anyone of note in America and ask them to send me some food and give them my word that I'll repay them after the war, but please do it at once and damn 'circumstances beyond my control'! Oh yes and write more often, two or three times a week in fact. You'll probably find it boring but you can call it your war effort! . . . brace up and get a grip on things, I feel you're slipping.'

The following week he is more sympathetic. 'I'm so pleased to hear the little brutes are fit and full of fun - they must be an awful handful, I do hope it's not too much for you. Don't forget honeypot, live up to your own resolution and write bigger, better and more frequent letters!'

By 14th February his attitude has hardened again. 'This time it's a demand. To say you can't send any is nonsense - you can arrange for parcels known as Medical Comfort Parcels. I don't care how you arrange it - you can say I'm dying if you like . . . If you are donating anything to the Red Cross, cease forthwith (please acknowledge) . . . there's been enough balderdash from them to float an airship.'

Then on 11th March: 'I'm not sure when my gratuity ($£300$) will find its way into the bank balance. You touch this of course at the risk of awful peril!! I do hope you're happy in your present residence . . . but it terminates immediately upon my return.'

There is a gap until January 1943, when he adopts a more considerate tone, and for once reveals something of what must have been happening back in Paignton. 'I had no idea you were ill . . . for the twins' sake if not for mine take it easy. I've had pneumonia and I know how absolutely bloody it is. Get a really good nanny for the boys - I hope you've got one already. If you're short of money let me know at once, I've just bought some loan bonds with my gratuity and you can have those.'

On 19th February he has some rare praise for his wife. 'I've just had an amazing letter from you, easily your finest effort. Please don't take it to heart, I feel absolutely bloody sometimes and things get horribly distorted.'

Then a new plan: 'When I'm demobbed we can buy a 20-ton ketch and push off round the world for a couple of years. It would be a marvellous holiday for both of us and provide the perfect antidote for three years of hell. Of course the question you want to ask is, what then? Well I'm certain I can make the trip pay for itself by writing and afterwards we'll be fairly well known and I can start a yacht agency or something like that. Please don't condemn it out of hand, it's been a dream of mine for years . . . I've really only mentioned it now because you've been ill and I want you to know that I'm always thinking about what we can do *together* one day.'

On 28th July, 1943 he asks her: 'Have you got hold of a responsible general servant yet? I don't think we're going to have to wait too much longer now, in fact I think you can start to make some tentative arrangements.' And on 12th August: 'Your recent literary efforts are lousy, though to be fair I suppose there is a faint improvement - you see you don't write often enough to get sufficient practice! And what about those photographs I'm always asking for? It makes me hopping mad to sit here and read your evasive replies. Incidentally we'll have no more of your rather particularly soulful look - this time we'll have a picture with some oomph about it - if you can't conjure one up send me one of Sheila's or Daphne's! What I want is a series of photographs of you and the twins so that I can keep abreast of their changes of appearance, increase in size, whether they've worn my ties out yet and so forth.'

29th September: 'You might get hold of *The Psychology of Sex* and read it, will you. You can cut the religious angle - which is nonsense - but the rest might interest you, in fact inform you!'

8th October: 'The snaps are simply awful - the twins look like a pair of guttersnipes . . . next time, get a photographer who understands something about light.' He goes on to speculate about their reunion. 'I think you'll find me absolutely intolerable. I can tell you now that my greatest desire will be for decent cooking, then for a complete absence of noise and any kind of dirt. So if you are ever going to organise yourself, start doing it now. If you *still* don't know how to cook (you were useless before) then you've just got to learn.

'Oh by the way, on no account are you to meet me on my return. God alone knows exactly when that's going to be, but when it does come - don't forget, *I don't want to be met.*' He never explained why.

On 29th November, perhaps conscious that the shooting season is under way back in England, he asks her to 'get and keep a copy of *Instructions to Young Sportsmen* by Colonel Peter Hawker. Don't be content to tell me it has gone out of print, get one. Will you also get a driving licence in my name and keep that for me too . . . one thing I do know is that if I can't get a permanent commission we'll take a chance on something big, live near the sea and the country, at any rate out of the towns, and as unconventionally as possible. I've spent hours and hours here thinking of what to do in the future. What I shall finish up by doing God only knows, but I do know that I shan't ever work for anyone else and that if the Service refuses me I'll start a yacht station or sail round the world or write. Well, who knows? I'm honestly not worrying very much though, because you see I've found that I can do almost anything well (if) I take an interest in it . . .' The last part of this letter is missing.

The final letter, dated 7th October, 1944, is one of the most positive. 'Your news of the twins is tremendously cheerful - they sound absolutely splendid, I'm longing to see them' he says.

Sixteen weeks later Stalag Luft III was disbanded and the march to freedom began. There were no more opportunities for letters, or any other organised form of communication.

Hugh's homecoming must have proved a crash-landing of a different kind. Doris continued to suffer poor health - she endured several bouts of pleurisy and pneumonia - and was struggling to raise two lively young boys. There was very little money. Falkus' dreams of post-war family life must suddenly have seemed as absurd to him as they already did to his wife. Doris, who had spoken of her husband as a hero during his years away, found him impossibly high-handed and demanding.

'I remember the telegram that came in 1945 announcing Hugh's return after the war, and the tremulous excitement among the three of us' says his son Malcolm. 'Hugh did eventually arrive - two or three days later than expected, I think - and Christopher and I rushed to make him a cup of tea. I'll never forget his contemptuous "What's this?" and then ordering us to go off to "bee-byes" - an expression I had never heard before and have never heard since.'

Malcolm recalls that despite the illness and hardship, his mother had somehow saved enough to buy the car Hugh craved, a small red sports convertible, and had parked it in the stable to wait for him. 'Hugh was not at all satisfied with it, and never thanked Mum' he says.

*Above: Christopher and Malcolm Falkus
around 1944.*

*Right: Malcolm Falkus with his
mother Doris.*

Doris never did get that cottage on the Norfolk coast, the round-the-world cruise or indeed the round-Britain one; nor did she find another man to replace Hugh. They divorced in 1947, Doris having little choice (given the dispensations on marital matters at the time) but to divorce her husband on grounds of adultery, with all the co-respondent paraphernalia that went with it.

For a time, Hugh paid her, unreliably, maintenance of £2 a week. She took odd jobs to get by, at one time selling boat trips around Paignton harbour.

Shortly before the end of the war, Doris had persuaded the Marist Convent in Fisher Street, Paignton, to accept Christopher and Malcolm as pupils. The convent was primarily a girls' school, but it would take boys of junior-school age. 'The nuns were marvellous to us and gave us opportunities to develop, such as tennis and piano lessons' says Malcolm. 'We also, perhaps inevitably, became influenced by the religious environment of the school. We came home one day and told Mum that we wanted to be Catholics.'

Soon after the boys were baptised to their new faith, Doris followed. When the divorce came, her faith empowered her to disregard it, and she wore Hugh's wedding ring until the day she died. 'I think she felt Catholicism was a way of perpetuating her marriage to Hugh, albeit in a spiritual way' says Malcolm.

When Doris struggled to find the £20-per-term fees for the boys' schooling the convent began to reduce them for her, eventually waiving them altogether. The boys were also given free school meals. On one occasion Malcolm remembers that a 'very special' nun took money from the poor box to treat the brothers to a visit to the circus in Torquay.

In 1951 Christopher and Malcolm started at St Boniface's College, a Catholic school some distance away in Plymouth, which Doris felt would be preferable to one of the local grammar schools. A charitable fund connected to the college paid the boarding fees, and the RAF Benevolent Fund, appropriately, footed the bill for the boys' uniforms.

For Doris and her sons the thought of living apart was unbearable, so they became weekly boarders, coming home at weekends. But it was an unhappy arrangement. 'Since there was Saturday morning school and we had a two-hour bus journey home, it was a most unsatisfactory compromise' says Malcolm. 'We could never settle properly. No sooner were we home than it was time to leave again.'

By this time their father had to all intents and purposes disappeared from the scene - though if Doris thought she had seen the last of him, she was mistaken.

Christopher and Malcolm were not alone in feeling unsettled. Their father, no doubt in a reaction to his years of captivity, spent the rest of the 1940s ricocheting around England, arriving at friends' homes with little or no notice and leaving for greener pastures as suddenly as he had arrived. He sought company and shelter with friends in London and Essex and with his family in the West Country. But increasingly he became drawn towards the North; and in particular, to Eskdale.

IV

London and Long Yocking

Eskdale, one of the loveliest of Lakeland's valleys, descends from the highest and
wildest of mountains to the sands of Ravenglass in a swift transition from
grandeur to beauty . . . it is a place of many delights, unspoilt by
commercial or industrial activity . . . a perfect arcadia in the hills.

WAINWRIGHT

THERE can be few places in England greener, grander, wilder and less spoiled by the hand of man than the valley of the Cumbrian Esk. It remains far less frequented by tourists than the eastern side of the Lake District, cut off as it is from the great lakes of Windermere, Coniston and Grasmere by unfriendly hills served by tiny, twisting, endless passes which become impassable at the drop of a snowflake. Lacking a major lake and largely free of souvenir shops and tourist facilities, Ruskin's 'gateway to Paradise' is left to the farmers, fellwalkers and fishermen.

The Esk begins life as a torrent high on the slopes of Scafell before running quickly down past the rocky fastnesses of Gait Crags and Hard Knott to bury itself in lusher terrain at Dalegarth, three thousand feet below. From here on its passage is intermittently disguised by low woodlands of oak, birch and alder. Over its last few miles, from Eskdale Green down to the tidal limit, the Esk becomes a gentler stream, with marshy slacks and meanders interspersed with stony pools and riffles.

At Ravenglass, the only coastal town in the Lake District National Park, the Esk joins two other bright little streams, the Mite and the Irt, before swinging out into the Irish Sea. Eighteen centuries ago the town was an important Roman naval base. Now, lacking so much as a convenience store, it is little more than a pleasant backwater of the A595. It must surely be the only town in England with more rivers than shops.

Hugh Falkus' first view of Eskdale was from the air, during his attachment to the Met Flight in Northern Ireland immediately before the war. He told friends many years later that its beauty had planted a determination to take a closer look once the war was over.

It is unlikely that this was much more than a notion. There is no mention of the Lakes in Falkus' letters from prison camp, in which his several visions of post-war life mainly involve the Norfolk coast.

Falkus owed his introduction to Eskdale to Bill Fowler, his fellow RAF officer and prison camp chum. Fowler came from a well-to-do Lakeland family. The Fowler seat at Long Yocking How in the heart of Eskdale had been built in the 1880s by his grandfather William, at one time Canon of Lincoln Cathedral. William Fowler was an expert on beetles; his six-volume magnum opus *The Coleoptera of the British Islands,* written between 1886 and 1913, still stands as the most comprehensive work on the subject ever written.

William's son Frank became the art master at Bolton School, spending term-time at the school and the holidays back home at Long Yocking Cottage (the big house was occupied by his older brother Philip). Art, angling and natural history were his passions. Frank's fishing diary chronicles his captures minutely, week by week; for those days of plenty, they seem to have been modest.

Frank and Beryl Fowler, also an artist (curiously nicknamed 'Jumbo' by her husband) doted on Bill, an only child, and spoiled him shamelessly; indeed the bond between Bill and Frank seems to have been as close as that between Falkus and his father. Bill's only domestic chore was the skinning, plucking, gutting and drawing of the fish and game he and his father brought home.

As Bill grew up, he came to share his father's passion for fishing. It is but a short walk from Long Yocking down to the Esk and the pair had the run of several miles of delightful water, at a time when most of the pools were available for the asking if you were known and trusted locally. They fished large sections of the river from Beckfoot down to the tidal limit above Muncaster, and generally had the water to themselves.

In February 1941 Bill married Mesnil Fowler (the shared surname was a coincidence), whom he had met during a brief tour with the Army in Norfolk. Mesnil moved in with the Fowlers at Long Yocking Cottage, but Bill had by now joined the RAF and there was no time for a honeymoon, let alone a decent start to married life. Within a few months, he had been shot down and taken prisoner. The happy chronicle of fishing exploits in Frank's diary abruptly dried up, replaced by bitter references to the absence of his son.

'Season spoilt by the blasted war, Bill still a prisoner of war in Oflag XXI B' Frank wrote in 1942, and the following year: 'This season about the worst in every way. Bill a prisoner still in the RAF camp at Stalag Luft III. The fish wouldn't take because of many blasted little thunderstorms, and any good fishing evening was sure to be a Home Guard parade.'

Frank also kept a nature diary, delicately illustrated with little impressionistic watercolours of details of the Eskdale landscape. Its pages for the war years are a catalogue of delight at the beauty of the wild plants and creatures of Long Yocking, soured on every page by pain and grief at the absence of his beloved son. Beryl was often away at her work as a portrait painter, so much of the time Frank was alone with his paintbrush, his fishing rod and his thoughts.

His son's name, or Bill's nickname, Jiff, appears in almost every paragraph. 'I do miss Bill, it's all wrong without him' writes Frank, and 'The Sweet Williams are very lovely now, how I wish Jiff was here to see them'.

There was a day of agony for Frank on 19th June, 1944, when the news came through of Hitler's callous slaughter of fifty of the officers who had taken part in the Great Escape. 'Felt in an awful sweat until I saw the list of names and Bill's not among them' he wrote.

On 30th June, the eve of the third anniversary of his son's capture, Frank once again had Long Yocking and its sunshine and birdsong to himself. He wrote: 'Very hot day, bluebells out in the wood. Went down the way Bill and I always go for a swim in the old bathing pool and took some soap with me. It was so hot that footmarks dried on the stones almost at once. The Lady's Slipper was out in the fields and the blue Speedwell and pink Ragged Robin were out among the new green grass. The willow wren was singing all day. I did wish Jiff was with me.' And a few nights later: 'A very beautiful sunset this evening. It began with a pink glow and turned to fiery orange, the whole western sky quilted and shining like a fiery furnace with great streamers of flame-coloured cloud reaching high up into the blue. The river coming down Bill's fishing pools looked like a stream of fire with steel grey ripples.'

By the last years of the war Frank was often feeling unwell, and his angling efforts had become spasmodic. Although his diary relates a near miss in the Road Pool on 7th July, 1944 - 'hooked a sea trout at the end of the shallows . . . it must have been a good fish, for it ran out my line although my finger was on it, but it didn't stay with me' - he did not, according to a later note by his son, manage to take a fish all season.

The following spring there was good news at last from Germany. Hitler was on the run, and the Allies had begun to reclaim France. On 4th May Frank heard that Stalag Luft IIIA had been liberated. 'I've been waiting for this news for nearly four years and it seems almost too good to be true' he wrote. When victory in Europe was declared a few days later, an exuberant Frank recorded his unqualified admiration for Eisenhower, Churchill and Field Marshall Montgomery.

Bill finally arrived back at Long Yocking on Wednesday, 30th May, 1945, and Frank's world was made whole again.

But for Frank Fowler, there were no stolen years. The bouts of sickness and pain he had been suffering were the early signs of heart disease. Returning from the river on the night of 2nd June, two days after his son's return, Frank collapsed on his bed in the act of dragging off his boots. He was dead within minutes, the victim, at sixty-six, of a heart attack. Frank lies alongside Beryl in the little churchyard of St Catherine's at Boot, a couple of miles up the valley.

A few weeks after the funeral, Bill invited Hugh Falkus to Long Yocking for the first time. Bill, taking over his father's fishing diary, recorded the occasion of Hugh's first attempt to catch a sea trout from the Esk; it was the evening of Saturday, 15th July, the weather warm, the river low. Bill took two 'smelts' (whitling), but Falkus was unsuccessful. They were not fly fishing but casting Norwegian spoons.

'Hugh came up to stay with us' wrote Bill. 'We went down in the evening - river fairly low. Caught this' (one of the 'smelts') 'on a long line - my first sea trout in five years.'

The following weekend they tried again, and the diary records Falkus' first Esk sea trout. He was fishing the Borrowdale (Bor'dale) Pool, just above Forge Bridge, near Eskdale Green; the date was Friday, 21st July.

Bill wrote: 'After four casts Hugh hooked first a 2½lb sea trout which he played out and was just going to net when it came off, then a salmon between 12 and 18lb which he had on for twenty minutes and then it cut the line on a rock. The first salmon to be hooked in the Esk this year!

'Hugh took the big rod' (a 17-footer) 'after the salmon had carried away the spinning tackle, and got this fish' (listed as 2lb 9oz) 'his first sea trout.' Again all the fish took the Norwegian spoon.

Falkus became a regular visitor to Long Yocking, and he and Fowler would explore the valley with rods in the summer and guns in the autumn

The Borrowdale Pool, looking downstream towards the bridge at Eskdale Green. Inset: Falkus with a sea trout, picture taken by Bill Fowler.

and winter. The Esk estuary and Drigg Marsh to the north were productive grounds for the wildfowler, and the men would bring back a rich harvest of birds, from mallard, teal, wigeon and geese to snipe and plovers. Falkus' dedication to wildfowling soon earned him his own nickname, 'Quack'.

'In the winter, shooting was and always has been my life, and to me no shooting quite equals the pursuit of wildfowl on salt marshes. It has a strong, weird mystique that demands an affinity with loneliness, a love of solitude' he wrote in *The Stolen Years*. The writer Maurice Wiggin, who became a friend of Hugh's, had this to say some years later:

My friend Hugh Falkus shoots wild duck. I think he would almost rather go duck shooting than anything . . . It is strange how wildfowling attracts men of marked individuality and poetic sensibility. You have to be out of the rut of commonplaces to fancy this rare, weird game of wildfowling, lying out on marshes and saltings, struggling through mud and across treacherous pills and creeks, crouching for hours in hides or lying motionless in a punt in the bitter weather of a wintry dawn. It is the wildest, most romantical of sports surviving to us.[5]

Bill Fowler in Gainsborough pose.

Falkus shot in those days mainly with a BSA magnum 12-bore which had belonged to his father, but he was particularly proud of a 4-bore fowling gun which he had apparently acquired soon after the war. This cumbersome weapon (the heaviest calibre it is considered possible to use from the shoulder) fired a quarter of a pound of shot, four times the payload of a 12-bore, and could take out a goose cleanly at eighty yards - if you could handle it, as Falkus obviously could. He told stories of using it as a light punt gun in the Essex marshes.

In 1946 Falkus returned Fowler's hospitality by inviting his friend down to Devon for a spot of West Country fishing. A note in the diary for May of that year refers to an unsuccessful sea-trouting expedition on the Dart, which was soon compensated for by the capture in the estuary of Bill's first bass. For 1947 Fowler reported that he failed to catch anything from the Esk at all, but the following year was more productive, with the fish running as early as mid-June and good bags recorded. Between 17th and 19th August Bill lists the capture of nine 'smelts' and two 'morts' (the old North Country term for mature sea trout). Some of these were taken on forays much further down the river, on waters controlled by the Muncaster Castle Estate.

Falkus with his beloved 4-bore.

Hugh Falkus displays a freshly-caught salmon. The date and location of this picture are unknown, but it would appear to date from the early post-war years.

There are intermittent references to Falkus until the diary finishes in 1952. On a September high-water outing in 1948 Bill and Hugh took a small fish each, although Falkus lost another good salmon. Their catch for the season was thirty-seven sea trout. Bill made a longer trip south in 1950, when the pair spent a month together and fished for bass at Dittisham on the Dart estuary.

Sea fishing was on the agenda back in Cumberland, too. Catches of crabs, lobsters and prawns are reported on expeditions with crab hooks and nets along Drigg Shore.

There is fragmentary evidence that Falkus' post-war fishing exploits took in visits to other parts of Britain, with or without Bill Fowler. He told the angling writer Brian Clarke that around 1950 he had regularly fished Blagdon Lake on the northern flanks of the Somerset Mendips, the birthplace of reservoir fly fishing, with Dr Howard Bell, the local GP and king of the lake. Dr Bell brought the naturalist's eye to lowland lake fishing; his contribution to this branch of the sport is considered by many anglers to have been comparable with those of Skues and Halford to theirs. He is still remembered for such patterns as the Amber Nymph and the Grenadier.

A studio portrait of Toni Briar.

Fowler and goat.

There were some returns to Essex too in these years, when Falkus would pursue his beloved wildfowl among the creeks and salt marshes of his boyhood.

Falkus and Fowler's 'local' when they were at home was the King George IV, down the road in Eskdale Green, or they would call at the Bower House on the Holmrook road. Sometimes social opportunities would take them further afield. In February 1946 Bill attended a Valentine's Day dance at Washington Hall, near Chorley, Lancashire, which had been laid on for the inmates of Woodlands, one of a series of camps run by the Young Men's and Young Women's Christian Association for newly-arrived prisoners of war. Among the junior staff of the camp was twenty-four-year-old Ursula Briar, known to her friends and family as Toni.

Toni was personable, educated, blonde and beautiful. Bill was the epitome of the dashing airman; tall, dark, square-jawed, witty and self-assured. The attraction was mutual and instant. An overt relationship was, however, out of the question. As if to underline the point, Mesnil Fowler gave birth to a son, Timothy, a few weeks later.

Bill and Toni nevertheless began an affair, taking advantage of the occasions when Bill was away from Eskdale. No one in the Fowler circle could

The Bower House, a favourite haunt of Falkus' from the post-war years on.

be allowed to escape without a nickname, and she quickly became known as Slosh. Some months after the Valentine's Day dance, she travelled down to Devon to see Bill, and it was there that he introduced her to Hugh Falkus.

'We met in a pub in Brixham' she recalls. 'They were such a well-matched pair. Like Bill, Hugh was charming and handsome, full of life and wonderful company. But he ignored me completely. I was Bill's property, so I wasn't available.'

Willie Fowler was as enthusiastic and skilful in the preparation and cooking of the game he harvested as he was with rod and gun, and it was Toni who suggested that he ought to write a book about it. With her help he eventually produced *Countryman's Cooking*, a comprehensive and colourful guide to the preparation, care and cooking (and, where necessary, killing) of everything from curlews and crabs to rooks, eels and pigs' trotters. There was much off-the-cuff humour, and a good deal of refreshing commentary on prevailing social and cultural prejudices and trends in food production. Fowler's targets ranged from food snobs and culinary ignoramuses to the modern trends towards 'incarceration and artificial feeding' in animal husbandry and the 'primrose-yoked, watery-whited rubbish' you got if you made the mistake of buying eggs laid by battery hens. Farmers, he claimed, were 'just about as callous and selfish a body of men as you could well find'. Among many lighter notes, a preposterously laborious recipe for cormorant ended: 'Finally, roast in a very hot oven for three hours. The result is unbelievable. Throw it away. Not even a starving vulture would eat it.'

The introduction contains a reference to the notorious incident in prison camp Falkus used to talk about, involving the stewing of the Kommandant's cat with 'a single black-market onion'.

Falkus appears, unnamed but unmistakable, in Fowler's chapter on fish cookery:

A few years after the war I was staying in South Devon with an old Air Force friend, a very experienced sailor and fisherman. At this time he owned a large Newlyn lugger, the Veracity, *and had her fitted out as a trawler. It was a hot summer's afternoon; the trawl had been shot, and we were sitting on deck, talking of this and that. I said, "Do you ever get any lobsters in the trawl?" He looked at me pityingly. "My dear fellow, you find lobsters among rocks, and we're halfway across Tor Bay in the middle of a square mile of sand." "Oh," said I, with deep humility. After another half hour or so, the trawl was hauled . . . there was nothing in it except one enormous lobster. My old chum's face was, as they say, a study.*

Countryman's Cooking was published in 1965 by Arlington Books, with a dedication 'to Slosh, whose idea it was'. It went on sale for ten shillings, sold a handful of copies and was quickly forgotten. Bill Fowler's only written legacy might have been lost for ever had it not been for the rediscovery of the book forty years later by David Burnett, for many years Falkus' publisher. Burnett recognised how readily Fowler's wit, wisdom and glorious lack of political correctness would appeal to a modern readership and in November 2006 he published a new edition under his Excellent Press imprint. He had a thousand copies run off, expecting it to take years to sell out, but the book and its author attracted such attention from the quality newspapers that sales were soon running into five figures. There has even been talk of a TV film about the life and times of William Fowler.

Falkus' responsibilities to his country had not ended with the war. He had been promoted during his imprisonment (on the basis of time served) from Pilot Officer to Flying Officer in 1940 and to Flight Lieutenant in 1941. After the war he remained on the Reserve of Air Force Officers and in 1949 returned to flying as an instructor with the Volunteer Reserve, undertaking a fortnight's annual training with 1 Reserve Flying School that year and again in 1950 and 1951. He was transferred to the Emergency List in 1954 and retired officially from the RAF in 1959.

The instructor's job had its own hazards. Falkus spoke of having narrowly escaped disaster while instructing a promising young trainee. When the pilot touched down some way from the main building, implying a long walk for both of them, Falkus suggested that he take off again and deposit them slightly nearer. The young man did so, but as they circled to prepare for their second landing he froze at the controls and the aircraft began to dive towards oblivion. Falkus pulled at the joystick, bracing his feet on the instrument panel to pull it out of the dive. The plane began to level out, but

Falkus' intervention had been too late to avoid an impact and the aircraft hit the ground and disintegrated. Falkus and his pupil were thrown out of the cockpit and deposited on the ground some yards away, bruised and shocked but not seriously hurt. Hugh would talk later of his extreme irritation that this youngster had so nearly killed him.

One of Falkus' pupils in these post-war years was Brian Sack, who, with his partner Francis Coulson, went on to own and run the Sharrow Bay Hotel on Ullswater. The Sharrow Bay has one of Britain's most exquisite restaurants (film stars and prime ministers patronise it; Paul McCartney proposed to Heather Mills there). Years later, when Falkus and his friend Bill Arnold visited the Sharrow Bay, Sack gave them a complimentary bottle of wine which Arnold recalls had a price tag of £150. Falkus asked for a second bottle, and Sack obliged.

Although it was to Eskdale that Falkus now turned for recreation, fishing and shooting were incidental to his life in these post-war years. His central passion was for something he had discovered in prison camp: the stage.

On 7th October, 1944, Falkus had written his last letter to Doris, or at least the last which has survived. After an unusually cheerful opening, he went on to give her some news which he had clearly been saving for some time:

'I have been working very hard for months now in the one outlet I have got here - the theatre. I have spent the last two years producing and acting - it has kept me sane through some very difficult periods and makes the time go quickly. Although I can't say much now, I think I have advanced sufficiently to turn professional after the war.

'I am fortunate in having a friend here who is an experienced and really fine actor and I spend hours with him practising . . . I have played a lot of panto. All this probably surprises you - it surprised me. I haven't mentioned it before because I wanted to make sure that I could really do it. I can, what's more I can produce.

'Although you may somewhat naturally incline to scepticism, I can say that I've found at last what I've been looking for all my life - something creative which makes me really happy. I have obtained a large number of useful contacts and got things more or less planned out. If you're prepared to take the risk, I'm going to do a year with the best repertory company I can get into, six months with a Shakespearean, and then run my own repertory theatre.

'You always had confidence in me in the past when I had nothing - now I have really got something and I want your help, darling. I am tremendously sincere about this - I know I can do it and I'm longing to see you so that we can plan everything out. I'm going to be very happy very soon darling, in a new life in a new world. "What's past is done with me".'

So what had begun in Stalag Luft III as a diversion from the tedium of captivity had blossomed into a plan for a full-time career, and in putting it into action Falkus moved with remarkable speed. On 26th June, 1945, barely seven weeks after his return to England, he was welcoming guests to the first night of his first peacetime play.

The setting, unsurprisingly, was a prisoner-of-war camp, and the story, equally unsurprisingly, concerned an attempt to dig a tunnel out of it. Entitled *Oflag 3*, the play had been started back at Sagan by Falkus, Flight Lt Douglas Baber and Squadron Leader D. L. Armitage. Falkus, who played the ironically-named Happy, told the London *Evening News* that they had written it in the winter of 1944-45 on 'scraps of paper anxiously concealed from German prison guards' and that Armitage had written down the ideas and Baber had done the dialogue while he had 'polished it up for the theatre'. At one point their work had been discovered and they had managed to persuade the guards not to destroy it only by assuring them that Shakespeare had been German.

The trio had concealed pages of the script inside their clothing or in their packs for fear of confiscation. Work on the play had continued on the march from Sagan and it had been finished during the final hungry weeks at Westertimke.

Oflag 3 ran for six nights, with two matinées, at the Q Theatre in Kew, and was well received, one paper reporting that it was 'a very creditable dramatic effort by these young men'. The director was Charles Hawtrey, the comedy actor who worked with Will Hay and went on to become a household name in the *Carry On* films.

Doris' youngest sister, Daphne Crutchley, remembers going with her to see it, and enjoying it. 'Not a bad play, though Hugh was far too busy with his theatrical friends to bother to talk to us' she says.

Fortunately for posterity, Falkus assiduously saved his programmes and press reviews. They show that he stayed true to his prison-camp plan to go into rep. In August and September 1945 the Buxton Spa Repertory Company put on two plays in succession by J. M. Barrie, the author of *Peter Pan*; they were *The Boy David* and *What Every Woman Knows*. Falkus, returning to the town where he and Doris had honeymooned, played supporting roles in both. 'Hugh Falkus gives us another fine performance as John Shand' said the local paper of the latter production. Next in the

programme was a play called *Crooked Sapling*, in which Falkus played a
Hitler Youth leader called Phillip Hans Joachim Fassbender - a chance to
draw on his encounters with the originals of such men in those weeks in
Hamburg before the war.

It was followed by Edmond Rostand's play *The Fantasticks*, in which Falkus
played Straforel, *Outward Bound* by Sutton Vane and Mary Webb's *Precious
Bane*. 'The role of Gideon Sarn, the self-confident, hard young farmer who,
having become "maister" through a contract with the supernatural, drives
all on with his lust for power and wealth, sacrificing everyone and laughing
scornfully at fate until fate strikes him, is played with power and conviction
by Hugh Falkus' wrote the local theatre critic (name unrecorded).

Poor receipts forced the Buxton company to shelve plans for further
productions at the end of 1945, a decision which met with great
disappointment among the townsfolk. Repertory companies would sign up
new members at the start of each year, rehearsing a batch of plays which
they would then take on tour, so Falkus had to look for a new posting. In
January he signed up with the Malvern Theatre Company.

In the spring of 1946, Bill Fowler took Toni Briar to see Falkus in a
Malvern Company production in Torquay, of a play called *It Depends What
You Mean*, by James Bridie. It had been directed in London by the acclaimed
stage and screen actor Alastair Sim, who visited the company several times
to oversee the production. Here Toni was introduced to Hugh's girlfriend,
a fellow member, who had 'hair like spun gold'. She was Stella Andrew, in
the part of ATS Private Jessie Killigrew. Andrew went on to play a starring
role in a successful 1950 war movie called *They Were Not Divided*, with
Michael Brennan and Helen Cherry, and enjoyed a brief stage and television career in the USA. The director and screenwriter of *They Were Not
Divided* was Terence Young, who later made his name with *Dr No*, the first
James Bond film. Desmond Llewellyn, who played Q in all the Bond films
until his death, also appeared.

Falkus appeared with Stella in several Malvern Company productions,
including Shaw's *Pygmalion* and Noel Coward's *This Happy Breed* and *Blithe
Spirit*. He earned consistently good reviews (any of the other sort may not
have been kept, of course) from the theatre critics of the provincial press,
and seems to have exhibited some versatility; a critic in Cambridge praised
his 'dithering and havering' in the role of the Oxford professor in *It Depends
What You Mean*, and remarked that his 'wonderful adenoidal accent' in
We Took A Cottage had 'brought hearty laughter almost every time he opened
his mouth'.

Among the junior members of the company that year was eighteen-year-old Margaret Preece, a newcomer to the professional stage. More than sixty years on, Margaret is still producing plays on the amateur stage. She remembers Hugh Falkus very well.

At that time we'd had to put up with a lot of second-rate men in the company, because of the war. Some of them were real weirdos and a lot of them were not ladies' men at all. Hugh was very different. He was all man - big wide shoulders and hands, a deep chest, tall, very strong and a big handsome face with wavy brown hair, and he had that lovely rich voice, so distinctive. I can't say I liked him exactly - he was very arrogant and hardly spoke to the likes of me, I was far too junior - but I did find him very attractive, all the girls did. You couldn't help it.

He got on well with the company as a whole, and we thought he was a very good actor. But it wasn't long before we realised something was going on between him and Stella. She was a real stunner and all the men fancied her, but she was smitten with Hugh and the relationship became quite intense. They even moved into digs together, quite openly, and he spent all his time with her after that. Living together was not the sort of thing you did in those days, but Hugh didn't care what people thought.

Falkus with a group of theatrical friends in Torquay in the late 1940s.

Margaret's brightest memory of Falkus is of a summer's day in Torquay when he took some of the company out for a cruise in his father's boat. When the boat ran aground Falkus simply jumped over the side fully clothed and pushed it into deeper water, drawing admiring gasps from the women on board.

Falkus' next move was to the Wolverhampton Repertory Company, whose brochure of 1947 offers a paragraph on each of its players. 'This handsome young man . . . has had considerable acting experience both in repertory and on tour, and is also part author of *Oflag III*, which has had excellent notices' it says of Falkus. A report in the *Express and Star* depicted

Falkus with an unknown companion, late 1940s.

Falkus and others of the company going down a real mine a few days before the first night to 'obtain local colour'.

Falkus also served the company's cricket team, as wicket keeper. The game must have been important to him; although his relationship with Eskdale was still that of a visitor, he felt sufficiently at home there to join Eskdale Cricket Club at its inception in March 1951, though his appearances on the pitch were at first irregular.

In 1948 Falkus returned to the scene of his maiden success at the Q Theatre to appear in a play called *Poisoned Chalice*. Later that year the Globe Players in Penge presented the first play known to have been written by Falkus alone, though the author did not appear in it. Entitled *Touch and Go*, it was a farce about an 'atomic disintegrator', and it earned good reviews. Some way down the cast list can be found the name of Alec McCowen, playing a schoolboy - a very early appearance by a young man who would become one of our most respected actors.

Another new play by Falkus called *Come And Join Us* was premièred at Richmond's Theatre Royal in January 1950. At around the same time he appeared with Alastair Sim in *Ten Little Niggers*, the play of the Agatha Christie 'whodunnit', at the Miniature Theatre, Sidcup, playing Philip Lombard.

A man of many parts.

Directing an Edwardian production.

The actor Frederick Treves, a familiar face for over half a century to theatre, film and television audiences (usually in the role of a country gentleman or upper-crust military man), shared lodgings with Falkus and another actor, Harold Jameson, at 3 Seymour Place, Marylebone, in the late 1940s. According to Treves, Falkus enjoyed considerable success at the time, though more as playwright than actor.

'I liked Hugh very much' says Treves. 'He was good company and we had some very pleasant times together. He once borrowed my 8-bore to go shooting on Romney Marsh. I have to say though that as an actor, I found him rather wooden. He took himself quite seriously and lacked a sense of the ridiculous.'

When Treves read the novels of Ernest Hemingway, there came a moment of recognition. 'The style of the books was familiar' he says. 'I realised that Hugh had quite deliberately modelled his own style and personality on Hemingway. I used to tell him he was the British Hemingway - I think he liked that.'

By 1949 Falkus had begun to make his mark in broadcasting. It was in this year that he began presenting live television from Alexandra Palace and writing and narrating for the radio.

On 8th May that year he made a rare appearance on television, still in its early days. He was billed in *Radio Times* as playing a part in a BBC production of *Whiteoaks*, adapted from the Mazo de la Roche novel.

In July 1950 Falkus read a short story of his own on the BBC Home Service. Entitled 'How To Escape', it was a light-hearted treatment of the issue which had so preoccupied him and his fellow captives during the war years. 'Falkus talks more knowledgeably and amusingly than the so-called experts' commented the *Sunday Pictorial*.

Another short story, entitled 'Dawn Tide Flowing', was not broadcast but submitted to an agent, Curtis Brown, at the end of 1950. Their New York man rejected it for the American market, but not before remarking that its author wrote 'wonderfully well'.

In 1950 he secured a regular slot, reading stories on BBC *Children's Hour*. He would collect his pay cheque (a chit he saved from April 1951 gives the amount as six pounds, one shilling and one penny) the moment the programme was done, cash it at the pay desk, then take the midday train from Euston for the seven-hour journey north to Eskdale. There he would pick up the bicycle he had left at Ravenglass station and cycle up to Eskdale Green to join Bill Fowler for supper and the night's fishing. The following morning he would ride back to Ravenglass and take the train south again to read the next day's broadcast.

The previous night's catch would often go with him to London, to be sold in a local pub. On one occasion, according to a favourite Falkus story, one of the regulars accused the fish of being roach. A Welsh voice piped up from the bar: "Roach? Those are not roach, they're sewin." 'My first meeting with Dylan Thomas' as Falkus put it to *Shooting Times*. He never recorded another.

Not all travelling was by train. There were cars too, when cash allowed - several open-top sports models and at one time a superannuated London taxi, which Falkus said gave him reliable and cheap transport. A mark on his forehead was the result, he said in later life, of an accident in a Mini when he had lost control and driven into a ditch.

Among Falkus' theatrical friends was Niall McGuinness, a prominent screen actor of the 1950s and 1960s who appeared in several major films including *Edge of the World, Night of the Demon* and *Helen of Troy*. Like Frederick Treves, McGuinness, who enjoyed a parallel and rather longer career in medicine, shared with Falkus a love of wildfowling - in the 1950s and 60s the pair would regularly go shooting on the Wash - and an equal one for drinking. McGuinness married a German girl and bought a farm in County Wicklow, where Hugh visited them. His success enabled him to help Falkus out financially. McGuinness died in 1975.

Toni Briar meanwhile had found solace with an electronics engineer called Peter Ades, whom she married in March 1947, in due course bearing him two daughters. Marriage did not put an end to her dalliance with the irrepressible Fowler, who took to visiting the Ades' home in High Wycombe under the guise of innocent friendship. Toni was furious when Bill announced the following year that his marriage to Mesnil was over, feeling that they had missed the opportunity of a legitimate life together. Their affair was stepped up a notch, though it was several more years - and several more affairs on Bill's part - before Toni finally left Peter Ades to be with him.

Falkus loved the stage and the business of acting and producing, but the countryman in him despised the city. Later he told friends that he could not stomach the superficiality of some of the people with whom he came into contact. He was clearly frustrated too by his failure to make as good a living from acting as many of his London friends had done; no big parts came his way. And his heart was still of course in the country, and particularly now in Eskdale.

Sailing remained a passion, though one of several. According to a half-page feature about him in the *Paignton Observer* dated 14th December, 1950, Falkus ('tall, muscular, slightly bronzed and handsome . . . one of the most promising actors of radio, television and the stage') was to be found almost every weekend working on his 20-foot boat *Quest*, which, said the paper, he was planning to enter in Torquay's Corinthian Yacht Club regatta the following summer.

In an attempt to find a less urban way of supplementing his theatre and broadcasting income, he joined Fowler in a dabble in the pleasure-cruising business. The pair acquired and refitted a series of boats operating out of Brixham - Toni remembers some names; the *Princess Elizabeth*, the *Princess Mary*, the *Billy*, the *Eileen* and the *Surf*. Probably the venture lasted as long as it did more through Hugh's passion for boats than from the commercial reward. A man with no teeth called Berwick was employed to run the business when Falkus and Fowler were away; he managed to siphon off a large chunk of the profits.

In 1950 Falkus made his first venture into the film-making business. He teamed up with Sam Lee, an established London-based producer and director, to make a thirty-seven-minute travel feature about Devon and its history called *Drake's England*. Lee had earlier gained a formidable reputation as a stunt man, having worked on many films made in the golden years of the Ealing Studios, including *Tower of Terror* (1941) and Hitchcock's *Jamaica Inn* (1939); he can be spotted jumping off trains in several of the classic comedies of Will Hay. Possibly he was introduced to Falkus by Charles Hawtrey, who knew them both.

Lee produced *Drake's England*, while Falkus narrated. Falkus also appeared in front of the camera as a young man showing the sights of the West Country to a visitor from the United States (young, female and attractive, of course). 'The beautiful panorama of the English Riviera at Torquay and its surrounding districts, the wild fascination of Dartmoor, country of mystery and legend, the old Plymouth and many other interesting and historical places are shown and described by a

A studio portrait of Sam Lee.

Hugh with Diana Vaughan.   *Diana with Hugh's father.*

commentary which is full of humour and witticism and blends to make a novel, unusual and highly entertaining featurette' gushed the promotional blurb from Anglo Amalgamated Film Distributors. *Kinematograph Weekly* liked both the film and its presenter, though it noted 'self-consciousness occasionally overtakes the speaker during close-ups'. It was not a problem which would trouble Falkus for long.

In 1949 or 1950 Falkus fell in love once again, with a young writer and editor he had met at the BBC. Diana Vaughan was pretty, vivacious, clever and well-bred. Her father, Rowland Vaughan, was a schoolmaster in Shrewsbury, and Diana had read English at Oxford. She had so impressed the publishers of *Argosy* magazine that she had been made its editor while still in her twenties. She heard Hugh's voice on the radio and contacted him at the BBC to ask if he would like to contribute to *Argosy*.

Generally credited with being the first true pulp-fiction magazine, *Argosy* has an illustrious history. Originally published in 1882 as *Golden Argosy*, it was a paperback-sized vehicle for short stories and poems, often written for the magazine, by the greatest names in fiction, from Dickens to Graham Greene and from Sir Arthur Conan Doyle to John Steinbeck.

In the January 1951 edition, *Argosy* published a five-thousand-word short story by Falkus called *There's Rosemary, There's Rue*. Set in London's theatreland, it was a piece about a fading actor called Julian Verlayne who is persuaded by his agent, Napoleon Barr, despite his lack of the necessary youth, to play

Hamlet. The chief difficulty is the casting of the ghost of Hamlet's father:

Rosencrantz and Guildenstern - Osric - His eyes continued down the list until, at the very bottom, heavily underlined, he came to the word Ghost. *There was a blank space opposite, with several question marks. Julian eyed it unhappily. Who the dickens was he going to get to play the Ghost?*

He sat back in his chair and began to think about it. Who could play it? He thought back carefully over many performances. No one that he could remember had ever given the part just that tone of unearthly quality it required. No one had conjured up that essential lightness of touch; that ethereal quality of voice; that strange suspension between two worlds. Wearily, Julian realised there wasn't anyone who could play it as he wanted - there never had been. Perhaps it was an impossible part to play. How could anyone play a ghost?

But then Verlayne is visited by a strange little man, a theatre-lover whose sepulchral voice and appreciation of the role are so impressive that Julian and Napoleon give him the part, despite having no idea who he is. The production is a dazzling success, but the next morning the mysterious actor turns out to have been less than solid flesh, off stage as well as on. The story, well constructed and rich in theatrical detail, could only have been written by someone who was deeply involved in the world of the stage.

There's Rosemary, There's Rue is the only Falkus story to be found in *Argosy*, but the April 1951 edition features a poem:

THAMES BARGE

Lying off the fairway, waiting for the flood
Anchor chain aquiver as the ebb runs fast
New tanned spritsail the colour of dried blood
And a halo of dawn mist hung about her mast.

Loaded to the gunwales, a light wind flawing
Ghosting through marshes where the wild duck flight
Leaning up the river, her topsail drawing
Through star-silvered waters in the dark of night.

Faded old staysail with a torn foot flapping
Snowstorms glooming and a falling glass
Sneaking up the shallows, a short sea slapping
And a wash of water as the big ships pass.

Dreaming on the saltings, her black ribs showing
Green weeds hanging from a nameplate proud
The mournful dirge of an east wind blowing
With cormorants and white sea birds her lonely shroud.

Though they met and married in London, Hugh and Diana spent much of their time in Devon, where they both played hockey, she for the county and he for a team called the Devon Dumplings. There were also visits to Shrewsbury. One day during their courtship, he performed a victory roll (severely frowned upon by the RAF) over the town to impress her. As the aircraft turned upside down, a wrench fell out of the cockpit and smashed a window in the town.

The couple married at Holborn on 22nd December, 1950. After a honeymoon spent partly at Waterside, near Paignton, they moved into a flat at no. 2 St Stephen's Gardens, Notting Hill Gate.

Falkus told Tim Thomas that soon after their marriage, he and Diana had resolved to abandon the London social whirl in favour of the peace and seclusion of Eskdale. It seems unlikely that Diana would have signed up to this plan before she had seen the place, but the fact remains that no one alive today can remember Hugh ever bringing Diana up to the Lakes.

Any long-term plans the couple might have made were, however, put on hold. In the winter of 1950-51, Falkus hatched a new plan; a scheme which would bring together his appetite for performing with his love of the sea, and, he hoped, make him and his new wife some money into the bargain. They were going to Ireland, to make a film.

Falkus with the 'Devon Dumplings' (fourth from left, top row).

V

Shark Island

The first basking shark of which one has a clear and entire view is terrifying. One may speak glibly of fish twenty, thirty and forty feet long, but until one looks down upon a living basking shark in clear water, the figures are meaningless and without implication. The bulk appears simply unbelievable - it is not possible to think of what one is looking at as a fish.

GAVIN MAXWELL, *Harpoon at a Venture* (1952)

SEA TROUT and salmon had lured Hugh Falkus to Eskdale, but it was a shark that took him to the west coast of Ireland and the adventure that would change his life; the basking shark, the second largest fish in the world.

This monstrous but harmless plankton-feeder - reaching forty feet in length and five tonnes in weight, it is beaten for size only by the whale shark of the Pacific - is common around the coastal waters of western Britain, where it migrates inshore each summer in pursuit of seasonal concentrations of plankton.

Today the basking shark roams our waters undisturbed (other than by the cameras of tourists on whale-watching cruises), but it has not always enjoyed such freedom from persecution. Back in the eighteenth century, someone discovered that the creature's outsized liver is packed to the gunwales with oil - up to a hundred gallons of it. The oil is rich in a substance called squalene, which helps deep-sea fish to absorb oxygen and men to make money. Basking shark oil has been exploited for countless purposes over the years, from cosmetics and health tonics to engine lubricant. Uses have been found for the rest of the shark, too, for by-products such as fish meal, bone manure and glue.

During the nineteenth century a fishery grew up on the Irish west coast

Basking shark.

which saw several thousand sharks butchered each summer. The shark's particular fondness for the shores of Mayo was much appreciated by the fishermen of Achill Island in the far west of that county, who earned a good living by slaughtering them with hand-held harpoons thrown from curraghs (small boats). The sharks took such a pasting that by the start of the twentieth century the population had fallen below an economic level. By the 1940s, however, numbers had recovered, and the industry began to enjoy a revival.

The author Gavin Maxwell was one of those who tried (and ultimately failed, in his case) to make a living from hunting basking sharks; he even bought a Hebridean island, Soay, for the purpose. Maxwell went on to tell the story in his first book, *Harpoon at a Venture* (1952).

In the summer of 1946, when Maxwell's enterprise was still struggling to show any sign of return on a considerable investment, he was approached by Charles Osborne, an engineer from Milford, County Donegal, recently settled on Achill Island. Osborne had joined forces with Joe Sweeney, the 'King' of Achill and a businessman with interests in every aspect of the island's economy, who had asked him to help establish a shark-fishing business there, the first attempt at such a thing for half a century. Osborne was hoping for Maxwell's advice on this enterprise. The two men went on to meet many times, and in return for a consultancy fee of £100 the author told Osborne all he knew of the catching, handling and processing of basking sharks.

Osborne told Maxwell that the Achill sharks were so numerous that they were severely testing the patience of the local salmon fishermen, whose nets they could wreck with a sweep of the tail. The writer, whose fishery had at this stage cost him more than £15,000 with very little to show for it, regretted not being able to transport his own business to Achill. 'I realised with a pang that were it not for my island factory I had but to transfer the boats and all the catching equipment to Ireland to feel sure of the capital support I required' he wrote.

Osborne was by nature an enthusiast and a free spirit who had been fascinated by the ocean, boats and fishing from an early age. The son of a Donegal solicitor, he had studied law before answering the call of the sea. He was also a qualified mechanical engineer. His interest in basking sharks had been sparked off by the accidental capture of a young specimen in his nets when he was out after herring off the coast of Donegal.

On moving to Achill, Osborne found himself an old ship's lifeboat and single-handedly converted it into a shark-fishing vessel, which he named the *Pride of Cratlagh* after an area of Mulroy Bay, near his home. The Achill men say the craft, which had an aluminium hull, proved a little too buoyant, so Osborne poured concrete into the stern to keep the propeller below the waterline.

The four-month sharking season did not provide a living on its own, so when Osborne was not busy with the fishery he would take tourists for trips around the bay. He was a generous man, according to later tributes, and would refuse to take their money if rough weather made the trip uncomfortable.

Osborne was also an engaging and articulate personality, so he was soon in demand by radio producers as a guest speaker on maritime matters and, particularly, on the shark-fishing business. In 1950 he took part in a broadcast on that subject on BBC Radio. Among his enthralled listeners was Hugh Falkus.

Falkus immediately saw the potential for drama in a film about the rigours of harpooning sharks from small boats, and made contact with the man from Achill with whom he seemed to have so much in common. The director would be Sam Lee, with whom Falkus had worked the previous summer on *Drake's England*. Lee's career had made him a substantial amount of money; it appears to have been his capital that funded these ventures.

As their cameraman, Falkus and Lee hired a young man called Bill Brendon, from Bude in Cornwall. Bill's father, Rundle Brendon, combined farming with running the Falcon Hotel in Bude, with his wife Dorothy. The couple had two daughters and three sons; Bill, at twenty-six, was their youngest. Still undecided on a career, he had discovered an interest in photography and filming. *Shark Island* appears to have been his first commercial assignment.

Together, Hugh and Diana Falkus, Sam Lee, Charles Osborne and Bill Brendon set out to make an early example of the kind of film that today would be billed as a drama documentary. The idea was to examine the business of hunting sharks through the eyes of the hardy types who did it, and the star was to be Falkus himself, in the role of 'Peter', a ready-for-anything young Englishman who unexpectedly inherits a share in a shark-fishing venture and moves out to Achill to learn the ropes under the guidance of 'Sean O'Donnell', a local expert.

'Peter' is in shot almost continuously, his character clearly modelled on Falkus' own self-image as a man of enterprise, determination and fearless athleticism. We see him taking to the sea as if he had been a sailor all his life (which was pretty much the truth), turning strong and capable hands to the arduous work of launching boats and fixing nets, hurling practice harpoons with deadly aim and hijacking a passing cart because 'he hadn't the temperament to wait for a bus'. Just in case the character might seem a little too heroic, much is made in one scene of his fear of heights and clumsiness as a climber.

Filming began in the last week of April 1951, the team staying with Anthony and Delia Gielty at the Clew Bay Guest House in Dooagh, the last port of call on the road that winds along Achill's precipitous south coast towards Keem Bay and Achill Head. Diana, Falkus' bride of four months, wrote the script. Claire Mullen from Dublin, a twenty-one-year-old Irish Tourist Board employee, appeared in the decorous but homely role of O'Donnell's sister Kathleen. There are documentary-style shots of Kathleen and Sean cutting turf (peat, as we know it in the UK), grinding corn, gathering seaweed for fertiliser and washing laundry in a stream.

We see the fishermen preparing their nets in the little harbour at Purteen Pier, the headquarters of the Achill sharking business, and later butchering the carcasses (it would be a record year - 1630 sharks were killed from Achill

Falkus the shark hunter - a promotional shot for Shark Island.

Gielty's in the village of Dooagh, formerly the Clew Bay Guest House.
It is promoted nowadays as 'the most westerly pub in Ireland'.

alone). But much of the footage had to be shot afloat, in fresh winds and tricky seas. These sequences were filmed from the *Pride of Cratlagh*, Osborne's recycled lifeboat. Space for equipment was at a premium, so the buoyancy tanks were removed.

Falkus threw himself into the role of the keen-as-mustard young apprentice, fearlessly hunting the great beasts for the camera from a bobbing skiff. By 1951 most of the real shark hunters had turned to nets (to use a harpoon, you first have to find a shark on the surface), but Falkus recognised that harpooning would yield much more dramatic footage. He went further, inventing an exploding head which would kill the shark on impact and save a long and hazardous fight.

The enterprise encountered mixed weather, but the second week of May was settled and fine, culminating on the Friday in a day of glorious sunshine. Whit Saturday, 12th May, dawned fine but cloudy. The morning tide had begun to ebb by the time the party cast off from Purteen Pier and motored out into a rolling swell. On board were Hugh and Diana Falkus, Charles Osborne, Sam Lee and Bill Brendon.

Falkus told friends afterwards that he had at first prevented his wife from joining them that day, because he had felt that it would expose her to danger unnecessarily. But at the last moment she had recognised his motive for leaving her on land and had run down to the harbour, demanding to be allowed on board.

Claire Mullen was not with them. Miss Mullen, according to most of the newspaper accounts, decided at the last moment to take a detour to the chemist's to buy some sun lotion (though the *Irish Press* had her taking time off from filming because she was not feeling well). Some of the islanders believe she had found the filming and its brushes with danger rather too nerve-racking, and had been looking for an excuse to drop out.

Presumably the rest of the team were unable or unwilling to brook any delays. By the time Claire Mullen reached the harbour a little after eleven, the boat and its complement of five had left without her.

She would not have needed the lotion. The sun did not appear that day; in fact the temperature did not climb above 55° Fahrenheit (13°C). The morning stayed dry, with broken cloud and a light to moderate wind from the west. By the time the tide turned at a little after three, the breeze had gathered strength and an intermittent drizzle had begun to fall, the prelude to a fresher wind from the north.[6]

Late that afternoon in the shelter of Keem Bay, three miles west of the harbour, the Achill fishermen were preparing to wind up the day's proceedings

Purteen Pier today. Most of the buildings erected for the shark-fishing operations were destroyed by a storm in 1991, but traces of the industry remain, including the huge iron drums, once used to hold shark oil.

and head for home. Several dozen boats lay at anchor or drawn up on the sand under the shadow of Moyteoge Head, which cuts off the western end of the bay. The largest of them was Joe Sweeney's vessel, the 65-foot *New Choice*; her crew had spent the day in the pleasant task of rendering down shark livers.

As a group of the men began to plod their way back up the cliff road towards Keel, one of them, Paddy Kelly, heard a faint shout. He called to his companions to stop and listen. They looked up at the clifftop above them, thinking perhaps that the cry had been a shepherd calling his flock, but could see nothing.

The shout came again, and this time the men realised it was coming from somewhere in the bay below them. They looked down at the flotilla of boats. To their astonishment, they could make out, clinging to the anchor chain of the *New Choice* a few hundred yards out from the shore, the figure of a man. Even at that distance they could see in the clear water that he was naked.

Without hesitating, the fishermen ran back down to the cliff path and on to the sand. Two of them, Hughie O'Malley and Thomas McNamara, seized a two-man curragh, pushed it out into the surf, jumped aboard and rowed as fast as they could for the *New Choice*.

The man was barely conscious and stiff with cold, and it took some effort to lever his fingers off the anchor chain. They could see that he was too big and heavy to lift on board without capsizing their little boat, so they ran a rope around his body and towed him back to shore, trailing in the water as helplessly as a slaughtered shark.

By the time they hauled the man up on to the sand, he was unconscious and deathly white. He wore not a stitch of clothing, nor any watch or jewellery; if, as they feared, he was past help, it would be hard work identifying him.

At first the fishermen thought that they had captured a French poacher, and there was a certain amount of good-humoured banter about the merits of rescuing him. But among the group on shore was eighteen-year-old Michael Gielty, son of Anthony and Delia at the Clew Bay Guest House. Michael knew immediately that the man they had fished from the sea was their guest, Hugh Falkus.

Michael still lives behind Gielty's.

When I realised it was Falkus I told the others that the rest of the film crew must be in the water as well, and we had better start looking for them. So four or five of us carried on trying to revive him while the rest of the men went off in their boats to look around the bay for the others.

At first we thought we had a dead man on our hands. He was stark naked and cold as ice. He told us later that he'd taken everything off, even his watch and ring, so that nothing would get in the way of the swimming.

We dragged him up the beach to the fisherman's hut where some of the men would stay during the shark-fishing season. Then we wrapped him up tightly in bedclothes from the bunks and filled seven or eight bottles with some warm tea that was still left. We wrapped the bottles up with him and took it in turns to massage him, to try to bring him back to life.

One of the younger men, Michael Dominic, was despatched up the cliff path to get help. He headed for Corrymore House, the home of Major Dermot Freyer, a retired British Army officer and by chance a friend of Osborne's; it was the nearest place with a telephone. The house was the best part of two miles away and several hundred feet up the hillside, so the climb took quite a while.

Major Freyer called the local doctor, Edward King, who drove immediately round to Keem. Dr King started to inject Falkus with a stimulant, but by now the patient was sufficiently recovered to wave the needle away (it was not the last time Falkus would refuse an injection).

'They're out by the Daisies' he managed to stutter between fits of violent shivering. The *Pride of Cratlagh* had gone down to the east of the Daisy Rocks, he explained, and his wife and the rest of the crew were still out there in the water, awaiting rescue.

That was not what the men had been expecting. The Daisy Rocks lie out beyond the mouth of Keem Bay, more than a mile from the shore. It had not occurred to them that the man they had rescued could have swum so far.

More to the point, it meant the boats were searching in the wrong place. One of the men, Charlie O'Malley, was sent up the steep flank of Moyteoge Head to signal to them by waving his jacket, a technique the islanders used when directing the pursuit of sharks. O'Malley had to climb several hundred feet before he and his signals could be seen against the skyline. Once he had managed it the boatmen got his message quickly enough, and they all headed out at full speed towards the Daisy Rocks.

Down on the beach, the rest of the men helped Falkus into a three-man curragh - he was able to walk by now - and rowed him back along the shore to Keel.

The redirected fishermen did not have to search for long. They found Diana Falkus and Sam Lee drifting on the tide a few hundred yards to the west of the Daisy Rocks, supported by rubber inner tubes; Falkus later explained that these were part of a makeshift raft he had rigged up to help them to stay afloat. But Diana and Sam had by now been in that bitterly-cold sea for, at Michael Gielty's estimation, a good four hours. It was much too late. They had both succumbed to exposure.

There was no trace of Charles Osborne or Bill Brendon. The boats searched the area through the rest of that afternoon and into the following day, but all they managed to find was Osborne's blue seaman's jersey.

The Daisy Rocks ('dysaghy' in Gaelic) earned their innocent-sounding name from the floral pattern made by the spume when the sea breaks over them in rough weather. They are a familiar landmark for the local fisher-men, who take care to keep them at a respectful distance; at low tide they are conspicuous enough, but at high water they recede to barely-visible pinpricks of black, jagged teeth on which an unsuspecting craft can all too easily founder. (The Irish fishermen did not, and do not, believe in learning to swim. Knowing that if they fall overboard their chances of survival in these cold Atlantic currents are minimal, they apparently prefer to encourage a quick and merciful ending.)

Falkus' swim must have been quite a feat. There is a mile and a quarter of open Atlantic ocean between the Daisy Rocks and the bay where the *New Choice* was anchored. He and his companions must already have begun to drift west with the tide out past the tip of Moyteoge Head before he struck out, so to reach the bay he had to battle a powerful cross-current.

Falkus had proved himself an excellent swimmer at an early age, held a lifesaving medal and was well used to coping with sailing mishaps, so if any of the party were qualified to make such a swim it was he. No doubt his physical stamina, determination and fitness, sharpened by two weeks of daily rowing, helped to give him the strength he must have needed for this Herculean effort. Even so, not even the fittest man can expect to survive for long in the North Atlantic in springtime. Though the sea off the west coast of Ireland is warmed by the Gulf Stream, in mid-May the temperature would have been no higher than 10° Centigrade. Falkus had survived by a very narrow margin.

Falkus did not learn of the fate of the rest of the party until he was safely back at the guest house and well on the way to recovery. The news filtered through that some of them had been found, but at first he was not told of their condition. When at last a Garda officer broke the news that his wife and business partner were dead and that Osborne and Brendon were missing, Falkus went to pieces.

Left: Keem Bay

Below: The Daisy Rocks photographed from the cliff road, close to low tide with a moderate sea running. The two main rocks are about thirty-five yards apart.

Bottom: This picture shows the entire route of Falkus' swim, from the Daisy Rocks (the distant patch of white water at extreme left) to the New Choice's anchorage in the shallow water under Moyteoge Head, a distance of one and a quarter miles (two kilometres). The square building above the middle of the beach, facing the sea on the extreme right of the picture, is the hut where he was revived.

*Above: Corrig More South, where
Charles Osborne and Bill Brendon
apparently hoped to find safety, with
the Daisy Rocks away to the right.*

*Right: Michael Gielty by the hut
where he and his fellow fishermen
revived Hugh Falkus.*

'The poor man was in hysterics' says Michael Gielty. 'He was in a terrible state for quite a while. He really had thought that we would be in time to save them.'

Besieged by newspaper reporters the following day, Falkus - the only witness, of course - explained that the boat had been sunk by a 'huge wave' that had come from nowhere. 'Everything was so sudden' he told the *Irish Times*. 'One minute we were sailing along, the next everybody was in the water.' To the *Irish Independent* he said: 'I have no idea how the tragedy occurred. We were sailing safely near the rocks - the next minute we were all in the water.' The *Irish Press* reported him as saying that a wave had swamped the boat and smashed it against the Daisies, whereupon it had immediately sunk (helped, no doubt, by the concrete in the stern). In those less safety-conscious days, none of the occupants had been wearing life jackets.

The *Irish Independent* followed the story up on the Wednesday, reporting that the bodies of Osborne and Brendon had still not been found. Falkus estimated the height of the wave at twenty to twenty-five feet and said that it had come from nowhere in a calm swell. It had struck, he said, as they were setting up the camera tripod, throwing them all overboard. The water had been intensely cold. He urged that no blame should be attached to anyone for the tragedy.

Falkus said he had gathered everything from the boat which was still floating - inner tubes, empty petrol cans and a plank of wood - to help the rest of the party to stay together and keep their heads above water. (Later he gave Sam Lee some of the credit for this.) Then he had shed his watch and clothes and begun the swim of his life. As he drew away from the party he had looked back to give a final wave of reassurance. Diana and the men had waved back and called out words of encouragement.

Many years later he told his friend Tim Thomas that there had been considerable deliberation about this decision; it had been touch and go whether he swam for it or waited with the others in the hope of rescue. From what quarter rescue might have been expected is unclear, given that they had not long been away from harbour and no one on land had any reason to miss the party or worry about their safety.

Although it did not emerge from the press reports, the local fishermen understand that Falkus was not the only one of the party who elected to swim for it. While he made for the shore and Diana and Sam stayed with the wreckage, Osborne and Brendon apparently struck out for Corrig More South, a 250-metre-long slab of rock a short distance offshore which constitutes the nearest piece of dry land to the Daisies. Both men were apparently strong swimmers. Corrig More would be an inhospitable place to make landfall, but it would at least keep them out of the water until rescue could be summoned. Falkus told the fishermen that he had decided to try to make it all the way to the shore because he feared no one would notice a human figure on an offshore rock.

He told the press that Diana and the three men had appeared cheerful when he left them, and confident that he would soon secure their rescue. 'I never thought for a moment that I wouldn't see them again' he added.

Could a 'huge wave' coming from far out in the ocean really have sent the *Pride of Cratlagh* to the bottom without warning? It is quite possible. Freak waves with crest heights two or three times bigger than the norm are a recognised phenomenon in every ocean of the world, and they are entirely unpredictable.

But there is a more likely explanation. It is the opinion of locals who know the bay and the moods of this part of the ocean that the sinking was directly related to the proximity of the boat to the Daisies - not because it struck them, but because of their influence on the sea's behaviour.

Anthony Gielty, Michael's younger brother and a professional fisherman for many years, says Charles Osborne had told the locals that they were going out to the Daisies that day specifically to capture footage of the waves breaking over them. On hearing this, the fishermen advised Osborne to stay away from the eastern side of the rocks. To the west of the Daisies lies a submerged ledge which can push a rolling swell from the west up into waves several feet high. These waves then break violently over the rocky pinnacles on to the eastern side. A small boat which ventures too close on the east would be directly in their path - and a bigger-than-average wave would be more than enough to send it to the bottom.

'None of our fishermen would go close to the Daisies' says Sheila McHugh, a cousin of the Gieltys, whose family have been fishing off Achill for decades, and who (entirely by coincidence) has for some years been a friend of Falkus' daughter Mary. 'A rolling swell like the one they had that day can look harmless, but it can be more dangerous than a rough sea.'

The Sailing Directions of the Irish Cruising Club give this warning for the area:

Between Achillbeg and Achill Head 13m NW, all dangers are above water except for the drying ledges 0.5m off Ashleam Point and a breaking patch 1.5m W of Dooagh Head. The Dysaghy Rocks, 1m SSE from Keem Bay, are awash at high water so care must be taken to avoid them, especially in poor visibility; they are not far inside the direct course from Achillbeg to Achill Head.

On the evening of the tragedy the Coroner, Mr C. K. Heneghan, held an inquest at the Achill Head Hotel in Keel into the deaths of Diana Falkus and Sam Lee. Falkus paid tribute to his colleagues, calling Osborne 'a magnificent fellow and a magnificent seaman'. But he was still exhausted and in shock, and apparently not up to confronting the bodies of his wife and business partner, so it was Claire Mullen who gave evidence of identification.

The Coroner's verdict of accidental drowning[7] allowed Diana and Sam to be taken home. They were put into coffins and on Monday, 14th May, two days after the tragedy, a local businessman named Quillan (according to the papers) chartered a plane and pilot so that Falkus could fly them back to England and their horrified families.

The Achill Head Hotel, where the inquest was held.

The bodies of Charles Osborne and Bill Brendon were never found. If they had indeed attempted to swim for Corrig More they would of course have had to jettison any buoyancy aids.

Falkus' state of mind during the journey to England can only be imagined. He later told Fred Buller that though he felt he had done everything in his power to save the rest of the party, he was still haunted by the memory of his last view of Diana and the three men and of their shouts of encouragement as he swam to get help. To Tim Thomas he said he had never felt a greater sense of loneliness and desolation than the moment when he swam away from his companions, leaving them clinging to their collections of flotsam in open water downtide of the Daisy Rocks.

Falkus told Thomas that Diana's family had responded to the shock of the tragedy by calling him a murderer, while to his friends Mike and Val Kendall he once said that Rowland Vaughan had accused him of saving himself rather than his daughter. Such a response from a bereaved parent would hardly be surprising; to have deliberately taken himself and his companions so close to such a notorious hazard must have seemed foolhardy in the extreme. It should be remembered, however, that the boat was under the command of Charles Osborne, not Hugh Falkus, and that the weather and sea conditions had given no one on board any reason for concern.

There is one piece of evidence that the Vaughan family did not in fact

Above: The propellor and keel assembly.

Left: Sheila McHugh with the remnants of the Pride of Cratlagh. *All that the sea has left is the propeller and its housing and the rusted iron keel and frame around it. The aluminium hull would have corroded away after half a century in the water.*

banish their son-in-law. It is the address on a letter to Hugh from his parents, dated Monday, 14th May, 1951, two days after the drowning and the day before his thirty-fourth birthday - 'c/o Rowland Vaughan Esq, Shawbury, Salop'. (Coincidentally, it was at RAF Shawbury that Falkus had gained his pilot's licence.) In its entirety, the letter, in his father's hand and written from Cliff Park House, Paignton, reads:

My dear Hugh, we are heartbroken. What dreadful news. How terrible it must be for you and your darling's father and mother. God help you to bear it.

You will not want me to try to say what no words can express, but you know you have our very deepest sympathy in the loss of your loved one. We are grateful that you yourself were snatched from death after exhausting yourself in an effort to get help.

Your loving Father & Mother.

There is a postscript to the tragedy. A few summers ago, two Achill men out fishing on the eastern side of the rocks dragged up a severely bent and corroded propeller and shaft, still fixed to part of the iron framework of an aluminium hull. Almost certainly, given that no other boat has been lost on the Daisies in living memory (let alone one with an aluminium hull), it is from the *Pride of Cratlagh*. This relic is now in the keeping of Sheila McHugh.

In London, Falkus turned to the practical ramifications of the tragedy. The cover from the insurance, he hoped, would soften the blow a little and tide the families over. Sam Lee was forty-nine and married with two young children. Charles Osborne was fifty, with four. Only Bill Brendon, at twenty-six, had no dependants, though he left a fiancée. Diana too was just twenty-six years old.

But when Falkus returned to the flat in Notting Hill Gate he found that the insurance documents were still lying on the desk. They had never been posted. Two families had lost their breadwinners, and Falkus could do nothing to help them.

In later life Falkus never spoke or wrote explicitly about the events of May 1951, though he occasionally made oblique references to them. In the closing pages of *The Stolen Years* - the book he said Diana had urged him to write - he wrote: 'In later years, my own narrow escapes and a world crashed into ruin put me beyond wonder at the mystery of life on this spinning planet. We cling by our fingernails to the rim of a great wheel, and some of us give up and slip off; and some cling for a time, and some stick. Although sooner or later all visions fade; the most tenacious grip loosens.'

VI

'A World Crashed into Ruin'

Life is a chamber of horrors.
THE STOLEN YEARS

WHEN a man's great adventure has ended in unimagined tragedy, when his young wife and three of his friends lie cold in the ground or at the bottom of the sea, when he feels the finger of blame for their loss silently following him; what does he do next?

Falkus knew that before he could continue with his life, he must do all he could to try to make amends. With no insurance payout to look forward to and little money of his own, the only way of doing that was to finish the film, and then to cash in on its success in the names of the lost and their next of kin.

Three-quarters of *Shark Island* was already safely in the can before the tragedy, but Falkus had planned a climactic action sequence showing 'Peter' harpooning and subduing a big shark from a single-handed rowing skiff. Without this, he felt the film would be nowhere near as successful as it deserved to be. He recruited a new cameraman, William Pollard, and in early June 1951, three weeks after the *Pride of Cratlagh* had gone down, he returned to Achill to shoot the missing scenes.

They are dramatic. We see Falkus rowing out alone in a choppy sea to harpoon his quarry. After several near misses he finally spears an enormous shark, which proceeds to drag the little skiff under by the bow, Falkus clinging on for dear life. Just as the bow dips under the waves, he manages to saw through the rope with a knife. Then he rolls overboard and is rescued by his islander guide, 'Sean'. There can have been little fakery

Hugh captioned this picture 'Hugh Falkus with shark approx 5 tons, caught off the island of Inniskea [sic] 7th June, 1951. Harpooned by hand from dinghy.'

involved - we frequently see the shark, the boat and the man all in shot together - and it must have been absurdly risky to stage and shoot. One wonders what Falkus must have felt at having to go back into the cold Atlantic such a short time after his ordeal, and so near the scene of his wife's death.

A framed photograph in the possession of Toni Richards shows Falkus posing with harpoon in front of the tail of a huge shark. On the back Falkus has written: 'Hugh Falkus with shark approx 5 tons, caught off the island of Inniskea [*sic*] 7th June, 1951. Harpooned by hand from dinghy.'

There was some press attention for the shoot, not all of it well-informed. A report in the *Schweitzer Illustrierte Zeitung* of 25th July, 1951, informed its readers that Falkus had returned to avenge his wife by killing the shark that had eaten her - the reporter did not know very much about basking sharks. It is accompanied by a publicity shot of Falkus hurling a harpoon into the flank of the ten-metre shark.

Somewhat more revealing is a short passage about the filming of the final sequence which Falkus wrote for his autobiography. It was eventually published half a century later in *Some of it Was Fun*.

I sat apart from the film crew, alone on the cuddy hatch, nursing my aching body, staring out across the darkening sea and trying to revive my leaden spirit with gulps from a bottle of Scotch. I thought of that poor great harmless creature we had made fast alongside, dying in a welter of blood and foam. For what? To provide a vicarious thrill for a peanut-crunching public sitting in a cheap-scented cinema.

To do it, I had risked my life. One mistake could have drowned me. A loop of rope catching on an ankle when the shark was running would have wrenched me overboard and dragged me down . . . but I had got the dramatic scene needed to complete the story.

Oh, the film would sell now, there was no doubt about that. It would make money, perhaps quite a lot of money, which would be shared between two shattered women whose children could be looked after, fed and clothed and educated. In the state of mind I was in, it was an achievement that left me feeling empty and sick, and, in a strange way, ashamed.

Sam Lee's widow Pippa struggled throughout her life to come to terms with her loss. For years she refused to talk about the tragedy, and would even pretend to friends that Sam was still away on location. Consequently five-year-old Michael and three-year-old Tessa were left to work out for themselves how to adjust to the death of their father.

Tessa even imagined that she herself had been responsible. 'The night before it happened I had a nightmare' she says. 'When my mother woke me I told her "Daddy's at the bottom of the sea with worms". Then a couple of days later, when she told me he had actually drowned, I thought it was the dream that had made it happen.' To this day Tessa cannot bear to be within sight or sound of the Atlantic.

The loss of Sam was a financial shock as well as an emotional one. The family had been living in some style. Their chauffeur had to go, and the Lees' stylish Kensington home was split into flats to help the family to make ends meet.

Shark Island was distributed by Anglo-Amalgamated Productions, which had also looked after *Drake's England*. It was then a new company, set up by Nat Cohen and Stuart Levy to make B movies for showing alongside feature films; it would become better known in later decades for the *Carry On* films. Falkus persuaded Anglo-Amalgamated to give the entire proceeds of the film to the families of the lost men. Most of it was used to help pay for the education of Michael and Tessa Lee and of Charles Osborne's four young children (Osborne's family left Achill after the tragedy, and his wife apparently later moved to Canada). Falkus added his own savings to the fund, leaving himself effectively penniless as well as widowed and unemployed.

The film was premièred in the West End on 25th October, 1951. A promotional poster promised 'thrilling adventures in a shark-infested sea!' and rather oddly named Falkus' character as John Travers, not Peter as in the film. A ticket for a trade screening shows that the film supported *Mystery Junction*, starring Barbara Murray and Sydney Tafler.

Falkus did what he could to help to promote his film, giving press interviews and attending the September première at the Hammer Theatre in Wardour Street. He and Lee had intended to make a follow-up, a drama about smuggling, to be set on the rocky Devon coast he knew so well, but that plan was now dust. For the time being *Shark Island* would be Falkus' last film.

Tessa Lee felt considerable gratitude towards Falkus for looking after her and her brother in this way, as well as great sympathy for his own loss. For many years, at her mother's insistence, she made no contact with him. After her mother's death she finally telephoned him and was invited to visit, but he died before it could be arranged.

Apart from his evidence to the coroner and contemporary comments to the press, Falkus does not appear to have spoken to anyone in detail about the tragedy. Mike Daunt recalls that Falkus once announced that he was going to tell him the story, and told him to bring a notebook. But at the last minute, his eyes brimming with tears, he backed off. "I can't do it, Daunty," he said. "It's just too difficult."

Troubles piled up. On 26th June, days after his return from shooting the final reel, Falkus woke up in the bedroom of the flat in St Stephen's Gardens to find the place on fire. According to press reports, he threw blazing furniture, curtains and bedclothes out of the window and had managed to extinguish the flames by the time the fire brigade arrived. The burns to his hands were severe enough to require hospital treatment.

After the London launch, the film and its aftermath dealt with as well as they could be, Falkus felt a need to be alone with his despair, and, from his own account, his guilt. He decided to live alone for a time, out of contact with civilisation and entirely dependent for survival on his own skills and resources.

So he returned to Ireland, to Mayo, and to the sea. He arranged to be put ashore on a 'treeless, humped splinter of Atlantic rock and sand and grass' off the coast, equipped with basic rations and clothing, fishing tackle, his gun and a supply of cartridges. The 'splinter' was the low-lying double island of Inishkea, the scene of his last shark hunt, three miles off the Mullet Peninsula on the far west coast of Mayo and some eight miles due north of Achill. Abandoned in the early twentieth century when the turf ran out, the islands cover about 1500 acres and are the haunt of many rare seabirds; they have become the most important wintering site in Ireland for the barnacle goose.

This adventure nearly ended in disaster before it had begun. As he was ferrying provisions from the trawler which had delivered him to the island, Falkus inadvertently knocked the bung out of the bottom of his dinghy, so that it slowly sank under him as he rowed ashore with the final load. He had to light a fire to dry his clothes, then salvage the boat, his possessions and his load of precious turf from the sea naked and in darkness.

He stayed on Inishkea until Christmas, living in a one-roomed hut used periodically for shelter by the shark fishermen and existing largely on what he could gather, catch, snare or shoot, his only company a donkey of unexplained provenance.

On his return Falkus wrote and narrated three radio talks about his time on Inishkea. They were broadcast on the BBC Home Service on 26th February, 4th March and 11th March, 1952, under the title 'An Amateur Hermit'. The scripts were unearthed at Cragg Cottage after his death; this is an abbreviated extract from the first part, 'The Island'.

Outside, the wind howled and whined among the empty ruins. Rain lashed the window. Waves swept across the tiny harbour and thundered down on to the strand within a few yards of the door, so that the cottage was enveloped in a mist of spray; but inside it was snug and warm and the light was soft and cheery.

Solitude closed around me. I felt relaxed and happy, with a great sense of peace and contentment. I was alone on a tiny island far out in the Atlantic, cut off from civilisation, from the Irish mainland, by miles of heaving water. It was a splendid feeling. No telephone to ring; no traffic. Only the sound of seabirds crying, of the wind and the sea and the rain.

At midnight I made up the fire, took my gun and left the cottage. The rain had stopped and the clouds had drifted northwards. To the south-east was a misty circle of pale moonlight, and in the west stars were snapping out of a blue-black sky.

It was the hour for fancy, when ghosts might pop out and spirits fly around - and it occurred to me that even if I saw no geese, I might perhaps be rewarded by some unearthly visitation. From where I stood, among the little stone dwellings of the deserted village, the sound of the swell beating on the shore seemed far away and detached. I felt an atmosphere crowding on my senses and heightening my imagination. Here in these sand-filled ruins, people had lived and died. For centuries they had beaten out the barest life on this little island, from the thin soil and from the sea. Now they were gone, and where they had lived and worked and made love the rabbits scampered; and where they had slept there was only the moonlight lingering. Who were they? What had been their loves and thoughts and beliefs? Had they really possessed a carven image around which they sang and danced; a home-made God that calmed the sea and darkened the waters of the bay with herring shoals, from which they drew their life's blood and made the wind sing softly? I didn't know; I don't know now. But standing where I was, alone in the moonlight, it seemed wholly believable.

I was alone, but very far from feeling lonely. The air seemed full of voices unheard, of people unseen. I looked out to where the waves broke in a silver line against the dark rim of the sea, and in my imagination their totem stood up in the white sand - a wooden Aeolus leaning with the wind, black in silhouette against flickering driftwood firelight. Snatches of wild chanting rose above the surge of the sea, and in the red glow from the blown flames, bearded figures danced and sang, their shadows weaving strange patterns on the trampled sand.

As I stood there, above the sound of the wind and the sea, I heard, faintly, a distant murmur in the sky. Far out across the water the barnacle geese were flighting under the moon.

They came with the rushing sound of wind blowing in autumn reeds, and flew fast and low over the ruined harbour. A great patchwork shadow swept across the sand; white feathers shone briefly in the moonlight; a fast-beating shape loomed dimly overhead and I swung with it and fired, and it crumpled and fell with a thud on the grass behind me. At the sound of the gun the geese banked with sudden clamour and climbed up over the grey ruins with a great flutter of wings, and their harsh music diminished as they flew on towards the far end of the island.

The second episode dealt with 'Housekeeping', and Falkus described how he had shot rabbits, geese, curlew, snipe, plover and even (by accident) an oystercatcher, and cooked them with varying degrees of success on his stove or over the embers of his fire. He also told how he had put bread out for some friendly choughs, and found it mysteriously taken. When he lay in wait for the culprit he was astounded by the appearance from nowhere of the donkey. (By the time the island adventure had been written up for what later became *Some of it Was Fun*, the donkey's début had been rescripted; it was now first observed at Falkus' window, stealing paper which he had used to plug a window-pane.)

Falkus gave no dates for his stay on Inishkea, but his accounts (he talks of his fears of being stuck on the island 'for weeks') imply a stay of no more than a few weeks with a planned return for Christmas; in the event this was delayed by bad weather.

He often talked in later years of his island adventure. He never talked, or wrote, of what happened on his return.

Hugh's close friends knew he had fathered not one but two sets of twins, the second being the outcome, they understood, of his brief reunion with Doris in the spring of 1945. In fact Rowena Mary Falkus and her brother Anthony David were born on 30th September, 1952, more than seven years after his return from the war. In the early days of that year, after his lone island adventure, Hugh had sought comfort once again with Doris.

Whatever solace he may have found with his first wife, this second reunion seems to have been even briefer than their first. It made so little impact on Christopher and Malcolm that in later life they had no recollection that their father had ever been to their home.

Doris, already bringing up a brace of ostensibly fatherless boys, now faced the more serious stigma of two genuinely illegitimate children. As a Catholic she considered herself still married, but she knew others would see things differently. She bowed to her priest's advice that she should have Mary and Anthony adopted. As a prelude to this being arranged, they were sent at three weeks old to Nazareth House, an orphanage in Yelverton.

Anthony Falkus' story is a sad and short one. A sickly baby, he died in the orphanage in February 1953, at less than five months old, of pancreatic failure. The following January Doris, who knew by now that she could not go through with adoption, brought Mary back home.

Soon after Anthony's death Doris and Mary moved to Plymouth, the result of an appeal by Doris to her parents for help - Christopher and Malcolm hated boarding so much that on one occasion they had run away. Harold and Eileen Walter sold their retirement bungalow in Christchurch, Hampshire, to buy a terraced house in Neath Road where the family could all live together. Their new home did not last long, literally. One night Doris set fire to it. It was an accident of course, but she did a thorough job; the family were lucky to escape with their lives. After renting for a while, Doris, Mary and the twins moved to another terraced house, in Holland Road.

Mary, separated from her brothers by more than twelve years, spent her early years unaware that she even had a father. Effectively brought up as an only child, she developed a habit of wandering off alone, frequently seeking sanctuary from the local bullies in St Edward's, the local Catholic church. Her disappearances would send her mother frantic with worry, and Christopher and Malcolm would be despatched on their bicycles to look for her.

One day towards the end of 1960 Mary, rummaging in the larder, found a bundle of letters. They were from Hugh to Doris. She had heard Hugh referred to casually by her brothers and mother, but had not realised who he was. Now it hit her that he must be her father.

'It was a terrible shock' she says. 'My mother wouldn't explain - I don't think she could bear to talk about it. It was my brothers who filled in the blanks, years later.'

When Mary took the decision to enter an enclosed convent, Malcolm felt it was time to explain to her about her twin brother. They met for tea at the Royal Festival Hall; it was a tearful discussion. 'I always felt Mary's wandering away as a child was a kind of innate searching for a twin she knew nothing about' he says. 'I wanted to suggest to her that perhaps her "vocation" was a similar searching for something to fill the same void.'

Malcolm conveyed his suspicions that their father had put Doris under pressure to have the pregnancy terminated; as a Catholic, of course, she would have refused to consider such a thing. Mortified by the shame of being pregnant while unmarried, she had asked Hugh's parents to pay for the family to move to a guest house in Totnes while she prepared for the birth. Malcolm assured Mary that she had not been deliberately kept in the dark about their father, explaining to her: 'The whole experience was so painful, especially as it covered Anthony's death, that it was simply blotted

Mary Falkus and (inset) a youthful photo-booth portrait.

The house at Holland Road, Peverell, Plymouth, where Doris and her children lived in the 1950s and 60s.

out . . . There was so much love and so much tragedy in Mummy's life and we were all a part of it. Now you can understand why I have so vehemently rejected my father.'

Doris never opened up to her daughter in any depth about Hugh, though others were more communicative. 'My Aunt Daphne told me he hadn't given a damn about anyone' says Mary. 'He expected pampering, meals when he wanted them, talcum powder in his slippers. He didn't enjoy the twins' company at all - he just wanted them to run away and play.'

The twins' later achievements would have delighted most fathers. They were gifted young men, both in the classroom and on the sports field, and made the most of the opportunities provided by the post-war welfare state. Both went on to play tennis for their county (Mary too became a talented tennis player, once tipped for Junior Wimbledon), and captained their university tennis teams. After St Boniface's, Christopher Falkus won a County Major Scholarship to University College, London, where he took a First in history and won the Derby Prize for the subject. From his father he inherited a talent for the stage; he took the lead in many school plays and performed at university, even considering, for a time, a stage career.

Malcolm, as able as his brother, won a prestigious state scholarship to the London School of Economics. Like Christopher, he left university with a First and the prize for the best degree.

Christopher did make one or two attempts to get to know his father. In about 1960 he went up to see him in Eskdale, where they shared a cricket field. 'Hugh captained the third or maybe the 13th XI of some quaint local underwater team and we played against a team consisting mainly of sheep on a steep slope' he wrote later.

One evening in 1979, Christopher and Malcolm met their father for dinner at the Flyfishers' Club in St James. According to Malcolm:

Christopher, who brokered the meeting, said Hugh really wanted to meet me. After all he never had met me in any proper sense of the word, either as child or adult. This was, in anticipation, a momentous meeting for me.

In the event it was a complete anti-climax. Christopher valiantly led the conversation, telling Hugh how well I was doing and what a wonderful thing it was to be a university lecturer, and so on. Hugh showed not the slightest interest and kept moving away to chat to acquaintances. I made an excuse to leave early, angry, nearly in tears, and humiliated. Chris, bless him, was completely comforting and understanding and left with me.

Malcolm's last memory of Hugh is of an encounter some years later, over tea at his Aunt Elsie's house in Croydon, when his father sat playing a ukulele and 'croaking' songs he said he had written. 'He seemed from another era, strumming an old-fashioned song on an old-fashioned instrument and imagining it would have commercial appeal. I felt he was living in a Wodehousian world that entirely ignored the present' says Malcolm.

Falkus understood enough about a child's experience of rejection to write a sensitive and moving chapter in *The Stolen Years* about it. 'The Day' concerned a friend of his called Richardson (we will never know what basis he might have had in reality) whose parents were separated; he lived with an aunt and was able to see his mother only on special occasions. Falkus wrote that on the day in question Richardson was meeting his mother for tea (taking Hugh in tow) and had bought a cheap necklace in an attempt to please her. Richardson's anguish as he finds it cast aside with the table litter is observed with subtlety and compassion. One wonders if Falkus was ever conscious of the irony - and perhaps, if he himself knew what it was like to feel rejected as a child.

Malcolm Falkus still finds it hard to understand why his father behaved the way he did.

The war disrupted many families and relationships, and it must have been difficult for Hugh to return to civilian life without a job, to five-year-old twin sons he didn't know and to an older wife, now past thirty and perhaps somewhat careworn. I'm sure Hugh had money worries - there was not much help to be had on the Falkus side, and if Hugh left Mum with virtually nothing and made his own life, that can be understood perhaps, given the circumstances.

But my mother was a remarkable and wonderful person. I remember her at this time as still lovely and vigorous, and nearly always happy, despite everything. She had great talent - she was an excellent artist, and could play the piano well. Above all she devoted herself to her children and made every sacrifice for them, to the exclusion of much of a life for herself. She deserved so much better than she ever received, from him or indeed from us, her sons. I can feel pride in my father for much of what he achieved professionally, but not for the way he behaved as a husband and father.

The hurt Hugh had caused the family could never entirely quench Doris' feelings for him. Through the 1950s and 1960s she continued to follow his exploits at second hand, watching his films on television and saving newspaper cuttings.

In 1963 or 1964, Mary met Hugh for the first time.

'My mother went to see him while he was filming in Bristol and he came back to Plymouth so that we could meet. I remember being annoyed that he sat as if by right in my mother's chair. He talked about his work, his films, his books - he didn't seem to want to know about us and what we were doing. I have an image of him struggling endlessly to light his pipe.'

The visit was awkward and brief; there were long silences. Finally Hugh said he wanted to see the local barracks before driving back to Bristol, so Mary rode in his car to show him the way, then walked back alone. 'When I got home I noticed the ashtray he'd been using, full of dead matches. I remember feeling that the matches were all he had left us.'

Mary attended Notre Dame prep school in Plymouth before transferring at twelve to Merton House School for Girls in Sussex, where her mother had taken a post as matron. Meanwhile Christopher, with his wife Margaret, had moved to Brisbane, Australia, to take up a lecturing post in British and European History at the University of Queensland.

In January 1966, Doris and Mary joined them. But Doris found life in Australia a lonely business and a little over two years later she returned home with Mary to Plymouth.

On his own return to the UK Christopher Falkus entered a career in publishing, pioneering the concept of the partwork before becoming head of the Art and Illustrated Book Division at Weidenfeld & Nicolson, and then, while still in his thirties, its managing director. His brilliance and wit won him the friendship of many leading intellectual figures, including Sir Harold Pinter and Lady Antonia Fraser. When David Burnett, then at Book Club Associates, had the idea of publishing a heavyweight series on the Kings and Queens of England, Christopher took on the editorship, helped by Lady Antonia. They were outstandingly successful, not one of the thirty titles selling fewer than 200,000 copies. Falkus himself wrote the volume on Charles II, while his second wife Gila did Queen Anne.

Christopher Falkus - who is remembered for an acute sense of humour as well as a fierce intellect - was one of the first to see the commercial potential of books linked to television programmes, particularly light entertainment. He looked after titles by John Cleese and Eric Morecambe, virtually wrote the *Goodies Annual,* and published novels by Leslie Thomas, Jilly Cooper and Sue Townsend. After a less happy interlude in 1988 with Robert Maxwell's Macdonald Group, during which he worked on the notorious tycoon's authorised biography, he accepted an invitation to return to Weidenfeld & Nicolson.

'Chris was quite simply the most brilliant person I have ever encountered' says his brother. 'He had an incisive mind and an extraordinary memory.

Above: Doris Falkus (second left), with her children and daughters-in-law. Left to right, Malcolm, Doris, Mary, Margaret (Christopher's first wife), Christopher and Judy (Malcolm's wife).

Right: Christopher Falkus and his first wife, Margaret, with Kathleen at Cragg.

Below: Mary (Sister Julian) with Christopher (left) and Malcolm.

Even on the most mundane matters he would have something perceptive and original to say. It is not surprising that so many among the great and the good found him fascinating company.'

In late 1991, Christopher suffered a heart attack, at first undiagnosed. After that he worked from home, but his health did not improve and he died on 29th March, 1995, at the age of only fifty-five.

It was Christopher who gave Hugh Falkus his only grandchildren. With Margaret he had a son and a daughter, Justin and Sarah, while with his second wife, Gila, he fathered Helen and Thomas.

The focus of Malcolm Falkus' career ultimately moved to the other side of the world. In 1987, after twenty-five years teaching at the London School of Economics, he took the Chair in Economic History at the University of New England in Australia, specialising in the Far East. He was Director of the Asia Centre at UNE from 1991-97 and a Committee Member of the Australian National Thai Studies Centre. On his retirement in 2000 he became Emeritus Professor at UNE. After working in Cambodia on a World Bank project, he retired in 2002. He now divides his time between Thailand, Cambodia and Australia, with occasional visits to England.

In the mid 1970s Malcolm persuaded Doris to sell the cramped little house in Holland Road, feeling that she would benefit from country air and a proper garden. Doris and Mary moved to a country home in Bardwell, Suffolk. After two years in teaching, Mary entered Stanbrook Abbey near Worcester, an enclosed Benedictine monastery, where she became known as Sister Julian, or, more correctly for a Benedictine nun, Dame Julian. She later took a degree in psychology.

Within a few years of the move to Suffolk Doris became ill with cancer, and exceptionally Mary was allowed leave to care for her mother in her last months. Doris Falkus died on 31st March, 1980, at the age of sixty-seven; her grave is at Bury St Edmunds, close to Hugh's old school. Mary returned to Stanbrook Abbey, where she still lives, works and studies. Her main responsibility is the management of St Mary's House, the Abbey's guesthouse and retreat.

VII

Lady Margaret

Miggy, as she was usually known in the family, was warm-hearted, very pretty,
great fun, mildly eccentric . . . a dazzling sight on her bright chestnut thoroughbred,
its glossy coat and silky mane the exact colour of her own long tresses.

ANNE DE COURCY, *Society's Queen: Edith, Marchioness of Londonderry*

CHARLES Stewart Henry Vane-Tempest-Stewart, seventh Marquess of Londonderry, was a central figure in British politics in the years before the Second World War. As Viscount Castlereagh, he served as Unionist MP for County Down from 1931 to 1945. As Air Minister in Ramsay MacDonald's coalition government, Londonderry was an outspoken champion of the Royal Air Force. In the years before the war he tried urgently to persuade Parliament to reverse the disarmament programme that had been set in motion by public reaction to the horrors of the First World War.

Edith, Lady Londonderry, a central figure in London society for more than thirty years, is remembered as the last of the great political hostesses. Each year on the eve of the opening of Parliament, the Prime Minister of the day at her side, she would greet up to two thousand eminent guests to Londonderry House. Their circle included politicians (Winston Churchill, Neville Chamberlain and the Asquiths) and writers (John Buchan and Sean O'Casey), as well as royalty. Yet she was a woman of conscience who fought for the suffrage movement and founded the Women's Legion.

Ramsay Macdonald was devoted to Lady Londonderry; she became his closest confidante. He warned her that as soon as Stanley Baldwin succeeded him as Prime Minister her husband's forthright approach to the disarmament issue would cost him his job.

Lady Margaret Vane-Tempest-Stewart.

In May 1935, an ill-considered remark in the House about the activities of British bombers in keeping order on the troubled borders of India and Iraq - the bloody results of which had caused deep concern at home - gave Baldwin (who had not forgiven Lady Londonderry for once describing him as 'that common little man') the pretext he needed. On Baldwin's succession, Londonderry lost the Air Ministry to Philip Cunliffe-Lister. As consolation prize he was made Lord Privy Seal and Leader of the House of Lords, but within a few months he was stripped of those titles too. All this despite the fact that the Government, in belated recognition that Londonderry had been right about the threat from Nazi Germany, was now wholeheartedly embracing its former Air Minister's call to re-arm. Londonderry was devastated.

At the beginning of the 1930s, Charles Londonderry had demonstrated that his interest in his job was practical as well as political by learning to fly. In 1932 he had a landing-strip built at Mount Stewart, the family's country seat on the shores of Strangford Lough in County Down, which enabled him to fly across to England whenever he wanted to. He owned two planes, a single-engined Gypsy Moth and a larger Monospar for occasions when the family needed a flying 'people carrier'.

But Lord Londonderry was not the first of the family to get his pilot's licence. That honour fell to his second daughter, Lady Margaret Frances Anne, who beat her father into the air by three days.

Margaret - 'Miggy' as she was known in the family - was an enterprising and highly intelligent young woman. As a child she made a great impression on the Churchill family's governess, who somewhat tactlessly told Winston's wife Clemmie that she had a 'remarkable brain' and was far ahead of the Churchill children. According to Anne de Courcy in *Society's Queen*, her biography of Edith, Marchioness of Londonderry[8] (to which the author is indebted for much of the information in this chapter) Margaret was 'warm-hearted, very pretty, great fun, mildly eccentric . . . a dazzling sight on her bright chestnut thoroughbred, its glossy coat and silky mane the exact colour of her own long tresses. She was a talented painter, a good tennis player, a good rifle shot, a natural pilot who flew solo after only six and a half hours' instruction.'

Margaret's parents had high, even royal, marital hopes for both Margaret and her younger sister Helen, considered the beauty of the family, but the girls turned their noses up at all suggested suitors. Margaret's first serious affair, with a man called Bunny Phillips, came to a humiliating end when her father called Bunny in and told him he would disinherit his daughter if she married him.

In 1934, again very much against her parents' wishes, Margaret married Allan Muntz, an aircraft entrepreneur who had become friendly with Lord Londonderry through a shared love of planes and flying. The fact that Muntz was a divorcé with a wife still living guaranteed this grand Catholic family's disapproval.

Lady Margaret had a colourful war. After the marriage to Muntz ended in 1939, she became a war correspondent and lived for a time with an Australian newspaperman. She was with the invading US forces when they landed in Normandy on D-Day.

In the middle years of the war, according to later press accounts, she met and fell in love with the pioneering French airman Antoine de Saint-Exupéry, whose books about flying - *Night Flight, Wind, Sand and Stars* and *Flight to Arras* - are acclaimed as among the most evocative ever written on the subject. In the summer of 1944 Saint-Exupéry was attached to a French Air Force base in Sardinia, from which he was flying daily missions to take covert photographs of occupied France. In the wake of a series of errors attributed to his age - he was well into his forties, considered virtu-ally senile for a serving pilot - his colleagues were planning to get him grounded, for his own safety. But on 31st July, 1944, the day before he was to be told this news, Saint-Exupéry was returning from one of his missions when his Lockheed F5 photo-reconnaissance aircraft disappeared some-where over the French coast. He was never heard from again, and no trace of the plane could be found.

In the summer of 1998, a fisherman working his nets near the island of Riou, off the coast near Marseille, dragged up a silver chain bracelet; examination revealed that it was engraved with the name of Saint-Exupéry's wife Marie. A search began and two years later divers discovered the twisted wreckage of the Lockheed lying on the sea bed. Examination revealed no bullet-holes, and the Germans had recorded no planes shot down that day. A technical failure of some kind has been blamed; or possibly Saint-Exupéry ran out of oxygen - he was known to be careless with it - and passed out. There are those, however, who believe he guessed that he was about to lose his wings, and deliberately flew into oblivion.

After the war Lady Margaret teamed up with an RAF pilot she knew, Richard Rumbold, to write a biography[9] of her late lover. Rumbold was fascinated by the Saint-Exupéry legend and had been hoping to meet his hero after the war. The pair did much of the travelling for their research in Margaret's plane, a Miles Whitney Straight, one of the first light aircraft equipped with a side-by-side cockpit. 'Together we flew all over France collecting our material, mainly from interviews with Saint-Exupéry's relations, friends and fellow airmen' wrote Rumbold in his introduction.

The book was preceded by a fifty-minute radio play about the life of Saint-Exupéry, entitled *Portrait of an Airman*. It was broadcast on the BBC Third Programme on 14th February, 1951, the play's co-author discreetly billed as M. F. A. Stewart. Alan Wheatley, who went on to become a familiar television face in the 1960s as the Sheriff of Nottingham in ITV's *Robin Hood*, provided the voice of Rumbold as author and narrator.

According to a later report in the *Evening Standard*, Hugh Falkus met Margaret Stewart as a result of his playing a role in *Portrait of an Airman*. The *Radio Times* for that week gives a full cast list, but Falkus does not appear in it; perhaps their paths crossed because they simply chanced to be working at the BBC at the same time.

Whatever may have happened between Margaret Stewart and the newly-married Falkus in early 1951, it seems he did not wait long after the Achill Island tragedy that May before embarking on a relationship with her. Barely six weeks after the death of Diana, Hugh received a postcard, postmarked 25th June, 1951, at the flat at St Stephen's Gardens. It was from his sister Elsie in Paignton, and read: 'When are you bringing Stewart down? Your room quite free after this week as bookings fell through. I have not taken anyone else. Love E.'

If Falkus and Lady Margaret were indeed an 'item' as early as the summer of 1951, the relationship must have gone on to survive both his self-imposed exile on Inishkea that winter and his brief return to Doris at the beginning of 1952.

The couple were married at Caxton Hall, Westminster, on Friday, 18th July, 1952. The newspapers reported that the bride wore a bronze silk suit with a bronze and yellow cap and gold shoes and carried a cluster of orchids and lilies-of-the-valley. The witnesses were Lady Margaret's sister, Lady Helen, and a Mr Timothy Craxton, described as an RAF friend of the groom.

Falkus' broadcasting career was now well under way. A cutting from *Radio Times* for the week following the wedding advertises '*Summer Parade* . . . an open-air magazine for under-twenties' on the BBC Light Programme, and adds 'Paddle your own canoe . . . Hugh Falkus joins some enthusiasts on the river Brathay at Ambleside, Westmorland'. It went out immediately before *The Archers*.

This was part of a *Summer Parade* feature called *Out and About*, presented by Falkus. 'We hope the new signature tune "Holahi, Holaho" sung in parts by the Aberkenfig Youth Centre Choir, will make them itch to be *Out and About*' beamed *Radio Times*. No doubt it did, in those unworldly days. 'Hugh Falkus has accepted invitations from young people to go gliding over Dunstable Downs, exploring Swildon's Hole in the Mendips, climbing in Borrowdale, canoeing in Westmorland, cruising with the Girls' Nautical Training Corps at Plymouth, scrambling up Kinder Scout and ambling round Flatford Mill studying natural history' the article elaborated. The gliding programme did not go too well - according to the reviewer for *The Bulletin and Scots Pictorial* 'It was most unfortunate that Mr Falkus' interview in a glider should have been made completely unintelligible by noise, from the take-off to the landing'.

The following year Falkus narrated a BBC television series called *Britain in the Skies*, chronicling our contribution to the story of flight and airborne warfare. This was quite a success - Emery Pearce of the *Daily Herald* went so far as to call it 'the finest TV documentary ever shown'.

Very little is recorded of the married life of Hugh and Margaret, or of his relations with the Londonderry family. The couple's base was their marital flat in Londonderry House in Mayfair; Falkus told friends that a favourite diversion had been popping champagne corks on to the heads of passers-by below (Margaret apparently loved champagne - one society friend nicknamed her 'Lady Flushbucket'). Otherwise he hardly spoke of this time, alluding only to the plethora of angling and shooting opportunities which had been available to him. He told his friend Bill Arnold that he had once caught twenty-three salmon before breakfast, and on another occasion had shot ninety-three pheasants with a hundred cartridges on a single drive. On many of these ventures Margaret was presumably very often with him - in addition to writing, painting, shooting and flying, she and Hugh shared a love of fishing and wild places.

A contemporary press photo of the newly-wed Hugh and Margaret.

Hugh and Margaret with a large sea trout. The location is unknown, but is probably somewhere in Scotland.

Hugh (left) in full shooting dress with a party of well-heeled sportsmen. This and the picture above (right) were found among Hugh's papers. Very likely it was taken during his years with Lady Margaret.

Malcolm Falkus remembers going with his mother and brother once to take a look at Londonderry House; this was in September 1953, after they had been to watch a Test match at Lords. Doris referred to her ex-husband's new wife rather bitterly as 'Lady Horseface'.

Falkus would not have met his noble father-in-law. Lord Londonderry died in 1949, to be succeeded by his son, Edward Charles, as eighth Marquess and leaving Lady Londonderry as Dowager Marchioness. Lady Londonderry bought a house for Margaret and Hugh, Rathmullan in County Donegal (it was later sold, and is now an upmarket hotel).

According to Margaret's youngest sister, Lady Mairi Elizabeth, now Lady Mairi Bury, Falkus never once visited Rathmullan; indeed the couple seem to have spent hardly any time in Ireland. As it happens Rathmullan is only a few miles from Charles Osborne's home town of Milford, and one wonders if Falkus had his reasons for keeping away from the area. Lady Mairi, who still lives at Mount Stewart - she is the last of Charles Londonderry's family still surviving - recalls that instead her sister had been planning to buy a house on the Isle of Lewis for herself and her new husband.

Among the few clues to the couple's activities is a postcard from Margaret dated 7th July, 1953, and postmarked Stornoway, in the Outer Hebrides. It is addressed to Hugh at Knott End; presumably he was intermittently using Bill's home as a rural retreat. The card reads: 'Masses of sea trout, bags of sand eels and whisky galore - Maggie.' There is a row of kisses and a crude drawing of a large fish, captioned 'the big lie', alongside a little one, labelled 'the small truth'. Apparently Margaret was quite prepared to go fishing under her own steam, and to some far-flung spots at that.

Three letters from Margaret found at Cragg Cottage reveal something of her personality. Two of them contain essentially lovers' nonsense; in one of these, on Londonderry House notepaper, she addresses Hugh as 'Dadsie' and signs herself 'Tick Tock'. The second is typed, with many mistakes, and purports to come from 'Ticktocknadrochit Lodge, Hertford Street' (the address of Londonderry House). It is written as if by a dog, and signed with an inky pawprint.

The third is more conventional, apart from the addressee - 'McHugh of Glenlivet and Tomintoul, Lad of the Isles and Fishes' - and reads in its entirety: 'Sweetheart, all the best over the border. Good luck, good health and *all* my love, Maggie.'

That letter was dated 8th August, 1954. If all was well between the couple at that point, it did not remain so for long. Something seismic seems to have happened between Hugh Falkus and his third wife in the autumn or winter of 1954. By spring 1955, once again apparently penniless, Hugh had returned to Eskdale, moving in full-time with Bill Fowler at Knott End. There seems to have been no further contact between the couple, and Hugh and Margaret were divorced in 1958.

Lady Mairi believes it was her sister who ended the marriage because 'she simply could not stick him any more'. She does not remember Falkus with affection.

'I met him first at a cocktail party' she says. 'I thought he was very good-looking, but extremely arrogant. During the time they were together he came to Mount Stewart only once, one Christmas. My mother was not impressed by him - frankly, none of us liked him. My sister was a wonderful person, but he did not treat her well - I believe he bullied her.'

The present Lord Londonderry, Alastair, the ninth Marquess, barely met Falkus when he was married to his Aunt Margaret, but by chance he did get to know him briefly a few years later. In a letter to the author, Lord Londonderry revealed that in 1957 he was sent to the Outward Bound School in Eskdale as a punishment and spent one 'cheerful' lunch with Falkus 'reminiscing about drunken escapades at Londonderry House'. 'I never saw him again thereafter' he says. 'I meant to write to him after watching his superb wildlife films, but sadly I never got around to it. However, I do have a tape of *Self Portrait of a Happy Man* and still watch it with the greatest pleasure.'

Lady Margaret died in October 1966 of cancer, aged fifty-six. A review of Anne de Courcy's book was found among Falkus' papers; he had scrawled upon it 'My mother in law! Late and unlamented', further evidence that he had not exactly hit it off with one of the grandest families in Britain.

VIII

The Cottage on the Fell

Where these rocks and hills have been scattered over the plain of the vale (as in Grasmere, Donnerdale, Eskdale &c), the beauty which they give to the scene is so much heightened by a single cottage, or cluster of cottages, that will be almost always found under them, or upon their sides; dryness and shelter having tempted the Dalesmen to fix their habitations there.

WILLIAM WORDSWORTH, *Guide to the Lakes* (1810)

CRAGG COTTAGE sits grey and foursquare in a corner of the lower north-western slopes of Birkby Fell, the granite stump of Raven Crag at its back, Eskdale spread out before it. Even today, when you stand in the lane by the cottage and survey the valley, no other building is in sight. The landscape is a muted weave of birch woodland and cultivated pine plantations, tussocky bog and green pasture, rocky prominences and centuries-old stone walls. Walk up past Cragg Farm on to the slopes of Raven Crag and the blue thread of Hugh's river appears in the middle distance, winding and widening as it passes Muncaster Castle on its way down to Ravenglass and the Irish Sea.

In the 1950s Cragg was a substantial Lakeland hill farm, with grazing over all the land between Raven Crag and the Esk as well as a larger area of 'intake' on the north side of the river. The bulk of its income came from a flock of a thousand or so Herdwick sheep - said to be the hardiest of all breeds - supplemented by shorthorn cattle, pigs, hens, ducks and geese and an annual hay crop. It was enough to provide a comfortable living for Benny and Anne Armstrong and their children, Benny junior, Marjorie, Leslie, Kenneth, Kathleen and Bruce.

Benny Armstrong was a First World War veteran. He had served as a stretcher bearer with the Coldstream Guards on the Somme and had been

Hugh's valley, looking down from Raven Crag. Cragg Farm is in the right foreground, with Cragg Cottage the building next to the road, separated from the farm by a clump of trees. Inset: View of Cragg from Whin Hill in late May.

invalided out, his face smashed by shrapnel. The wound partially blinded him and left him with a speech impediment which made it hard for people who did not know him to understand what he was saying.

For years after Benny and Anne Armstrong took Cragg Farm on in 1933, it did not have running water; all the water for cooking and washing had to be drawn from the beck that tumbles down from Raven Crag.

All six children worked on the farm, the men looking after the stock and seeing to the outdoor work while Anne and her daughters milked the cows, fed the hens and attended to the cooking, washing and cleaning. Life was lived out more or less entirely within the valley, with trips to neighbouring Whitehaven or Millom on market days and the occasional cycle ride to a dance or social gathering elsewhere in the valley. Motor vehicles were still a rarity and horses a necessity. Cars did not provide a great advantage for everyday transport; the Birkby road which serves the valley from the A595 was still unmade, gated in places and in such poor condition that driving up it was scarcely quicker than walking. An occasional country bus passed the end of the track up to Cragg and the family relied on this for most of their expeditions away from the farm.

Kathleen Armstrong as a young girl, with her brother Bruce.

Kathleen with milk churns in the lane below the farm.

Kathleen Armstrong, the fifth child, was born at the Armstrongs' first home at Gill Bank, on the banks of the Whillan Beck high up in Eskdale, on 10th October, 1932. She was six months old when they moved down to the gentler terrain of Cragg.

'Kath was a lovely girl' says Marjorie. 'She was the racehorse, I was the Clydesdale. She had wonderful, sensitive hands and loved dressmaking. She was very outgoing - sometimes she acted with the drama group in Ravenglass.'

As children, Kath and Marjorie had to walk the best part of three miles each day to the local junior school in Muncaster, crossing the river by the iron bridge at Hinning House and taking a short-cut through Low Eskholme Farm. If the Esk was in flood they would walk down to the A595 and cross the river by the road bridge. There were no school dinners; lunch was sandwiches, carried in a backpack.

Marjorie was the first to leave home, in 1946 at the age of twenty, though she would return each summer at haymaking time to help out. It was a decade later, when she was back home on holiday from her nursing job in Manchester, that Kathleen told her about Hugh Falkus.

The bridesmaid and the bride - Kathleen and Marjorie at Marjorie's wedding in 1957.

A young Kathleen Armstrong.

'Hugh had come to the farm to talk to Dad about the fishing' Marjorie remembers. 'That was how they met. I wasn't too sure about him. He was much older than my sister - she was still in her early twenties and had led quite a sheltered life. She had never been away from home. She didn't tell me until later that he had been married before and had children.'

Nor did Kathleen tell Marjorie - if indeed she knew - that Hugh was still married to Lady Margaret Vane-Tempest-Stewart.

The contrast between Hugh Falkus and Kathleen Armstrong could scarcely have been greater. For Kathleen, the arrival in her life of this worldly, supremely confident man who had known the thrills and the hardship of war and already had marriages to three very different women under his belt was an enormous adventure. For Falkus, Kathleen and Cragg were the opportunity to make a soft landing at last. And a romantic one, as he indicated in the opening lines of his 1976 film *Self Portrait of a Happy Man:*

Thirty years ago I was on this riverbank exactly where I am now. I'd just come back from the war, and I'd come up here for a night's sea-trout fly fishing on this enchanting little river. And at daybreak I sat and watched the sky catch fire behind Scafell. I had never seen anything so beautiful, it was all so quiet, so peaceful - just as it is now; for me, the most beautiful valley in England. At sunrise I sat here and watched the sunlight winking on the windows of that little cottage up there on the fellside, and I thought, the man who lives in that cottage could be a happy man. And I suppose you could say that I'm a happy man, because that's where I live and do most of my writing.

The Armstrong clan were sceptical at first about Kathleen's new paramour. 'Hugh wasn't from our world at all' says Marjorie. 'We thought he was very full of himself, and in our world drinking was very much frowned on, though Dad got on very well with him. But there was no point in trying to get Kath to change her mind. She was hooked.'

Falkus had become very nearly the Armstrongs' next-door neighbour. Around 1950 Bill Fowler had begun an affair with Dorothy Kennedy, who with her husband Nigel owned several properties in the Lakes. One of these was a mixed farm at Knott End, a mile or so upriver from Cragg. Dorothy let Bill have the place for a peppercorn rent, and in 1954 Bill moved in with his mother Beryl (his marriage to Mesnil having ended) and son Timothy. In 1955, on the demise of his relationship with Lady Margaret, Hugh joined them.

The trigger for this was a new venture. Bill Fowler had heard that the mink-farming industry, established in the UK around 1929, was making big money, so he and Falkus set out to try it for themselves. On flat ground between Knott End Farm and the river, Bill and Hugh constructed rows of makeshift wood-and-mesh cages, each on legs made from sawn-off lengths of timber gathered from the woods. They bought in the initial breeding stock from Canada and Norway at considerable expense - £35 per animal, Falkus told the *Cumberland Star's* reporter when the paper visited the farm to do a feature.

The animals would be mated each spring, then just before Christmas the fully-grown young would be slaughtered and skinned and the pelts sent to the Hudson Bay Company in London to be cured and sold on to the fashion industry. The going rate was £8-£10 per pelt, a month's wages back then for some people, but no profit could be expected for the first three years.

In 1958 Toni Briar, still irresistibly attracted to Bill, finally left her family to join him and the trio worked together on the enterprise. But mink farming proved an uncertain business. The breeding process was inherently unpredictable, the success of each mating being unknown for several weeks after the animals were paired. Once the kits were separated from their

The ranks of mink cages at Knott End in early 1958. Inset: Falkus feeding the mink.

mothers, each needed a separate cage. The animals did not take readily to confinement and would sometimes attack and injure each other, or eat their newborn.

At its peak the farm had a breeding stock of about sixty mink, producing a hundred or so young animals each season - just about enough to make two mink coats.

The task of killing and skinning the animals proved repellent. Though Falkus and Fowler were well used to handling what their guns brought to hand, they were at heart, like most field sportsmen, animal lovers. The killing took place over a few days each December, using the gas from a vehicle exhaust pipe. A sliding panel would be inserted into the cage to confine the animal to its living quarters while a length of rubber pipe was connected to the exhaust. It was a final solution that proved cheap and effective, but it was nearly as unpleasant for the perpetrators as for their four-legged victims.

Bill did the skinning. For some reason the males proved particularly hard to kill, and the result of handling an animal that still had life in it was usually a badly-bitten hand. At the end of the day Bill, Hugh and Toni were bleeding from their injuries and reeling from the effects of the carbon monoxide, to say nothing of the feelings of revulsion induced by the business of slaughter. However thoroughly Bill showered and bathed afterwards, Toni could always detect the smell of mink on his RAF moustache.

The Armstrong family were sceptical about the mink venture, and even more so about Kathleen's new paramour. But if Kathleen had any doubts about Hugh's suitability as a partner, her own qualifications were very clear to Hugh. Here was a girl who was not only youthful, attractive and warm-hearted; she loved and understood the natural world, and knew all about fish and fishing. Indeed, she was capable of enjoying it almost as much as Hugh. 'When my wife goes fishing, time takes on an entirely new dimension' he said, fondly watching her trotting off with her spinning rod in *Self Portrait*.

To Kath, Marjorie and their brothers, the Esk had been a playground since childhood. In summer, when they were not busy on the farm, they would go swimming or fishing in the river. Although Kath's father Benny Armstrong was a skilled angler - Falkus would later hail him as 'Master of the Esk' - the standard local method for procuring a sea trout or salmon for the table was to use a spear fashioned for the purpose, and his younger daughter knew how, and where, to use it.

There were certain spots under the bank where salmon liked to lie, and the Eskdale farmers knew how to take advantage of them. The local technique was to weave a 'hodd', a kind of elongated cage three or four feet long and open at one end, from alder roots lashed together with cord. The hodd would be left anchored in the current. To a running salmon it would appear the perfect place for rest and refuge - until the farmer came back with his snatcher or spear.

Kath knew all about the lies and how to get salmon and sea trout out of them, by fair means or foul. And of course, her father owned a useful stretch of the fishing. In the circumstances, perhaps it is understandable that Hugh felt able to overlook the differences in social class and background.

After the two began courting in 1956, they saw each other whenever Hugh was in Eskdale. Bill and Toni married on 25th October, 1958, and Hugh and Kath were their witnesses. Three weeks later, on 15th November, two months after Hugh's divorce from Lady Margaret, the Fowlers did the same for him and Kath. The ceremony took place at the Register Office in Whitehaven. It was a simple wedding, with the guests mainly from Kathleen's family and their friends in the valley.

The newly-weds on the doorstep at Cragg Cottage, probably in the summer of 1959.

The reception was even simpler. The couple booked a room at the Pennington Arms in Ravenglass, built and owned by the Pennington family of Muncaster Castle. Their host and hostess for the occasion were Harold and Eileen Tonge. Harold died a few years ago, but Eileen still lives next door to the Pennington.

'I've done a few wedding receptions in my time but this was about the smallest' she says. 'There were only the four of them - Hugh, Kathleen, Bill and Toni. They ordered a round of drinks and one of my home-made pasties each and that was it. They didn't stay long.'

Not long before this the Muncaster estate had put Cragg Cottage, immediately below the farm, up for sale, and Benny Armstrong had taken the opportunity to buy it. Probably he intended to retire there eventually, but his daughter's needs changed all that. A few weeks before the wedding, Benny sold it to her - discreetly, to avoid family dissent - for £800. Kath could not possibly have found such a sum in hard cash, but it seems that she came to an arrangement with her parents to pay them in kind over the years that followed by providing a cooking and laundry service to the farm. Hugh may have contributed something from his income.

Falkus and 'Uncle Benny' shared a mutual respect which lasted many years - they got on 'wonderfully well', according to Marjorie - but the rest of the family regarded the new son-in-law with scepticism. And Hugh was never likely to blend in with the modest rural culture of Cragg Farm. Though the cottage had always been considered a part of the farm estate, the marriage of Hugh and Kathleen ever after marked it out as a separate territory.

By now Marjorie had married Geoff Mallinson and settled in Workington, further up the coast. At first Kath would cycle up from Cragg to see them, but her own marriage put an end to that. Marjorie missed her sister badly. She and the other Armstrongs were rarely invited to the cottage, and she did not feel comfortable dropping in on them casually. Her brothers were not much impressed by Hugh's outspoken and self-confident manner, but being steady and peaceable men they did not clash openly with him.

Benny and Les, the two oldest, still live at Cragg today. 'Falkus didn't have much to do with us' says Benny, now eighty-two. 'They had their life and we had ours. I never knew what all the fuss was about him.' The pair continued to farm at Cragg until 2001, the year foot-and-mouth disease swept rural Britain (though FMD was not the cause of their retirement). Today all the land is let out to neighbouring farmers for grazing or fodder crops.

The little slate-roofed cottage, 'very ordinary-looking on the outside and very snug on the inside' as Falkus later described it to *Cumbria Magazine*, was built along with the farm in the nineteenth century. It was plainly equipped and furnished and lacked an inside toilet or any form of heating. But Falkus was very happy to live simply, and he was not a man to concern himself with home improvements. It was not for some years that the income from his writing and broadcasting would allow for the installation of a modern kitchen for Kath, and later a fitted study for Hugh, paid for by the proceeds from his film *Signals for Survival*. The luxury of a garage did not follow until 1980, funded by the success of *Nature Detective*.

Marriage to Kath was the catalyst for Falkus' final break with his life in London. After 1958 he visited the capital only when his writing and broadcasting career demanded it. For the first time since boyhood, he had a permanent home. His social life, like his leisure life, now centred on the Esk and the friends who came to visit.

Falkus' enthusiasm for the theatre had not died. On settling in Eskdale, he transferred it to the amateur stage. In December 1958 he put on a production for Gosforth and District Amateur Dramatic Society of *See How They Run*, a farce by Philip King, in the Public Hall in Gosforth, playing the part of Lance Corporal Clive Winton. The following April he was the producer of *Sailor Beware* at Gosforth, along with three one-act plays for Waberthwaite Drama Group.

Hugh and Kathleen spent many of their evenings in the Pennington, the King George or the Bower House with the Fowlers, Bill and Sheila Barron and other members of their circle. (Bill was another RAF man; the Barrons, who lived at Linbeck, just above Knott End, were among Hugh and Bill's closest friends).'Kath was a lovely girl' remembers Toni. 'She used to call Hugh 'Huge'. He and Bill would patronise her dreadfully - often they behaved as if she was only there to cook and get the drinks. But she was quite capable of standing up for herself. She could give as good as she got.'

Kathleen never learned to drive. In the early 1960s Hugh started giving her lessons, but a mishap put paid to this plan. 'Kath was in the early stages of learning - she had only been out a few times - when she crashed the car in the lane' recalls Marjorie. 'There wasn't too much damage, but Hugh shouted at her and upset her so much that she told him she was never going to drive again.' For this reason, throughout their life together, it was Hugh who did the shopping.

Not that Hugh's driving was any better - he was notorious for the speed at which he would pilot his car around the narrow Cumbrian roads. A cutting from the local paper from the early 1960s reports that the presenter of *Five Minutes with Falkus* had overturned his Mini Van and hit a telegraph pole, badly injuring his wrist.

There is no trace of any contact with James and Alice Falkus in this new life their son made in the north of England. If they corresponded or visited, there are no letters or postcards, diary entries or old photographs left to document it. They were of course already in their seventies by the time the war ended. In their last years the couple returned to Surrey, where James died in 1957 at the age of eighty-two. Alice followed in 1960, aged eighty-six.

Neither do Arthur or Elsie figure in Hugh's post-war life. The only recorded contact is a letter from Arthur sent in May 1980, *à propos* the death of Elsie, enclosing a cheque for £285.90 in respect of Hugh's share of the remainder of her estate. The letter bore the address of the house in Cambridge where Arthur was living with his second wife Kay, but he wrote that they were about to move to Corfe Mullen in Dorset.

If Kathleen hoped for a family with Hugh, she never said so to her sister, or later to Bill and Marie Arnold, who became the Falkuses' closest friends. The Arnolds believed Kath was not much interested in children, other than her own nephews and nieces, and never wanted to raise any of her own. There is little doubt about Falkus' views on the matter - he had offspring already whom he neither discussed nor visited, and would quickly make himself scarce on the odd occasions when visitors brought their families to Cragg.

Hugh and Kath began a life of great simplicity. The cottage had no electricity - they depended on Calor gas for both cooking and lighting - and in winter they lived in two rooms to conserve heat. Hugh's old van was succeeded by an ancient Austin which had once been a London taxi. It was used mainly for shopping; they rarely strayed far from home and lived mainly on the fish and game provided by Hugh and on vegetables raised by Kath in their kitchen garden (Hugh's only interest in the gardening was to insist that Kathleen collected the worms she dug up). 'I can honestly say that my wife is a wonderful cook and a wonderful gardener, and a very good naturalist' Hugh said later of his wife in *Self Portrait of a Happy Man*.

Kath had learned from her mother how to run a tight ship at home, and nothing was wasted. She baked bread and cakes and made pies, soups and jams. Hugh's main contribution was the weekly shopping run to Seascale, a modern expression of the hunter-gatherer role which had always fitted him so perfectly. If there were problems with the car, Bruce, the youngest Armstrong and still in his teens, was handy with mechanical matters and more than willing to help out.

Marriage and the move to Cragg coincided with the end of Hugh's involvement in the mink farm; Toni believes he could stand the hard work, the smell and the slaughter no longer. It did not survive long after Falkus pulled out. Problems began to mount. The slaughterhouse which supplied the farm with waste offal and scraps to feed the mink began to charge for the privilege. The *coup de grâce* came in 1962, when the Ministry of Agriculture, concerned at the increasing number of escapes from mink farms, introduced security legislation. From that year on, every mink farmer was obliged by law to sink a continuous fence three feet into the ground to prevent the animals from burrowing their way out.

The money from the skins had proved enough to keep the farm going and provide a tiny income, but it was nowhere near equal to funding the installation of several hundred yards of fencing deep underground in the boggy terrain of Knott End. It was time to 'pelt out'. The farm was abandoned and the mink slaughtered. To try to destroy those that had escaped and bred over the years, the Ministry led a blitz, setting traps all the way up the valley. They managed to trap thirty-three mink, but eradication was out of the question. Twenty years later, when Bill Arnold moved into Knott End, one of his first jobs was clearing and burying the remains of the cages and the associated rubbish; it filled sixteen trailers.

At least Fowler was now a man of property. In 1959 there came a parting of the ways with the Kennedys after a neighbour blew Bill and Toni's cover by introducing Toni to Dorothy as Bill's wife. Dorothy was ready to wash her hands of Knott End and sold it to Fowler for, as Toni remembers, £2000. Bill still also owned Long Yocking Cottage.

In 1957, the nuclear reprocessing plant at nearby Windscale (now

Sellafield) suffered an accident which at the time was the world's worst nuclear disaster. This shameful event was a direct result of unreasonable Government pressure on the operators to demonstrate to the USA that Britain could hold its own in the development of atomic weapons. A fire in the core led to the escape of radioactive gases which contaminated hundreds of square miles of Cumbria; later it was found that the fallout had travelled much further, across the North Sea to Germany and Scandinavia.

Falkus never took the threat of radioactivity from Windscale too seriously. At the foot of its report on this disaster in October 1957, the *Daily Mail* reported that he and Fowler were hoping that society women would soon be wearing entirely new shades of mink fur. 'I'm told that radioactivity makes hair grow' Falkus told the reporter. 'We may get new colours and mutations because of this. If we do we may be producing unique new pastel shades - isotope pink and gamma blue.'

Barely a year later, Windscale and its problems must have seemed rather less amusing. In 1959, after pulling out of the mink farm, Falkus was forced through economic necessity to take a job there himself, as a health physics monitor.

This was a scarcely more salubrious way of earning a living than slaughtering mink. His duties entailed patrolling the plant, which then employed three thousand people, with a Geiger counter, to check that radiation levels were safe.

'At that time working at Windscale was considered a last resort, even more menial and less rewarding than going down the mines' says Tony Corkhill, who does the same job fifty years on and has known retired employees who remembered Falkus. 'Apparently his RAF background was very much in evidence. He was not at all well liked and treated his workmates as underlings, talking down to them and addressing them as "my good man". He managed to upset quite a few people.'

This was perhaps the briefest of all Falkus' money-earning ventures. According to an anonymous source - a local man who wrote to the author to say he had worked with Falkus at the time - he was sacked after a few months for producing a play in Gosforth while on sick leave. On his departure he had told his colleagues that the Government owed him a great deal of money for the time he had served as a prisoner of war, and that to help him to get some of it back they should throw any public property they could find lying around - clothing, boots, tools or other equipment - into the back of his van. They duly loaded the little van to well above the windows with anything they could find. When it refused to start and the duty policeman strode up to see what was going on, Falkus loftily summoned the officer to help him push the van through the gates and out on to the road.

Bill Arnold remembers Hugh's bitterness at the way prisoners of war and their families were short-changed by the Government after the war. The families received money, but only in partial lieu of servicemen's pay. 'Hugh always said that they should have had post-war tax credits, like non-service people who had been taxed with the promise they would eventually receive their contributions back' says Arnold.

The play that got Falkus sacked must have been his 1948 farce *Touch and Go*, which he put on in revised form for Gosforth Drama Society in January 1960. It would hardly be surprising if the suits at Windscale had failed to see the joke, sick leave or not - it was a slapstick little number whose plot concerned the shenanigans that ensue when a scatterbrained inventor comes up with an 'atomic disintegrator'. The critic from the local paper wrote: 'Author and producer Hugh Falkus, who is on the staff of the Atomic Energy Authority at Sellafield, first presented his lively farce in London . . . he has modernised the plot specially for this Gosforth production. In doing so he has undoubtedly given the society their brightest success for several years.'

In addition to producing the play Falkus played the leading role of Charles Bandersnatch, 'artful colleague of the professor', and was praised by the newspaper for 'inspiring the less experienced members of the cast'. Among the players was thirteen-year-old Timothy Fowler, Bill's son.

By now Falkus must have accepted that his hopes of a lucrative career in show business were not to be realised. Comments he made to friends at various times in his life indicate that he saw himself always as the actor, or perhaps the theatrical impresario, *manqué*. But he took to the amateur stage with goodwill. His next play, *Charlie Takes a Chance*, was given its première by the Renaissance Players in Barrow in August 1960, attracting the first full house Her Majesty's Theatre had seen for some time.

As he approached forty Hugh was calming down a little, but he was still operating simultaneously on several fronts. He spent a summer in the late 1950s working for Richard Waddington, author of *Salmon Fishing: a New Philosophy* (1947) and *Fly Fishing for Salmon* (1951) and the inventor of the treble-hooked shank that bears his name. Waddington enjoyed the sporting rights across the entire Glenlivet estate, including a stretch of the river Avon (pronounced A'an), the main tributary of the Spey.

The value of what Falkus could learn from a man who had effortless access

Hugh (top right) with the cast of Touch and Go. *Young Timothy Fowler is in the centre of the group.*

to so much sport presumably made up for the pride he had to swallow to take a pay cheque again, having sworn at the end of the war to remain his own master. He worked as a loader and beater for Waddington on the moors and as a gillie for him on the Avon, looking after the guests and acting as a guide.

Falkus was not a fan of the Waddington mount which is still so widely used as a basis for salmon and sea-trout lures, but he is said to have rated its inventor highly as a fisherman. It is surprising that no mention is made of his friendship or apprenticeship with Waddington in *Salmon Fishing*, though he did quote a passage from what he called Waddington's 'thoughtful' book, on the subject of the absolute necessity of not striking when a salmon takes.

Waddington's widow Janet, who met Falkus when he fished with the family in later years, remembers him as charming and very good-looking, but rather vain. 'He would always have a comb with him, and he would keep taking it out and combing his hair. It made us laugh. But he was a very personable man. He was the most compelling story-teller, he would have you on the edge of your seat. Not always a new story, but he told them so well that we never minded.'

Hugh and Kathleen in the garden at Cragg in the 1960s.

Falkus with dog and gun by the river, 1960s.

By 1960 Hugh and Kathleen were taking in paying guests in the summer to help make ends meet - country-lovers and walkers at first, rather than anglers. Kathleen told Jeremy Barkworth-Edwards when he visited her decades later for an interview for *Salmon, Trout and Sea Trout* that guests had often been astonished when they asked about her husband's whereabouts and were told he was out night fishing. He had not yet begun to rescue it from its popular image as an aberrant pursuit, practised only by eccentrics and poachers.

Falkus liked to present Kathleen as a match for his own intellect, saying that she was well read and had a good mastery of written English. Kathleen was certainly bright, but according to David Burnett, her skills with a pen were very limited. Among the papers the couple left behind was an article by her entitled 'I Married A Lunatic', rather disappointingly corrected in pencil to 'I Married A Writer'. A cheerful account of life at Cragg in the early years, it bears the stamp of Hugh's agent, W. G. Benson and Campbell Thomson, so presumably some attempt was made to get it published. At face value the piece has an authentic feminine ring, but the text displays an easy descriptive touch and a love of the semi-colon which

135

Falkus with fishing boat at Ravenglass - date unknown but probably 1960s.

point to its likely true provenance. What follows is an abbreviated extract.

There's no television, and rarely a battery for our radio, but there's no smog either; no crowds, no roar of traffic - just the wind in the trees, and the river, and the fells.

Hugh is a writer - very poorly paid, I might add, for the amount of work he does - but I've never quite got used to our working hours. It's nothing for him to write all day and night, then go off duck shooting at dawn; and then, with renewed inspiration, start writing again when, wet and muddy, he returns for breakfast in mid afternoon. I've known him work on an 'urgently needed' script for three days and nights on end, stopping only for meals, and then rush off to London with it, only to find that the powers-that-be didn't want it after all!

Often I'm woken at some unearthly hour in the morning: Hugh - with a cup of tea in one hand and a new script in the other. "What d'you think of this, sweetheart?" he asks with enthusiasm, seating himself heavily on my feet. "Listen while I read it, and tell me what you think." Think - at five o'clock in the morning! Well I try - the trouble is, he

Hugh and Kathleen on the Esk.

sleeps at the oddest times. If he's not rattle-tattle-pinging on his typewriter all night, he's out on the marshes shooting under a winter moon; or playing some table game he's just invented; or twanging away on his banjo, working out a new song! He writes nice songs, but I must be alone in thinking so, for no one ever buys them.

In the summer, Cragg Cottage becomes a haven for fishermen whom we take in as paying guests in a hopeless effort to pay off the winter overdraft. So far as I know, my husband is frightened of only two things in this life - spiders, and letters from the bank manager.

At this time of year, everything revolves around the fishing. The sitting room looks like a tackle shop. In the kitchen there's a jumble of wet boots beside the stove; trousers hang dripping from pegs - someone's always falling in - clothes, nets, bags, stockings, lines and rods are drying; the precious fish hang in the larder, away from the cat, waiting to be cooked for breakfast - but not until they've been most carefully weighed, of course!

Hugh is on the river day and night looking for poachers, or fresh-run salmon and sea trout; helping the guests to catch fish, or fishing himself.

Sometimes, when the cottage is empty, Hugh and I spend all night on the river. As the sky darkens the river becomes mysterious and wonderful, and suddenly we're in another world - a world of mystery and enchantment, with bats flickering over the tree tops; owls hooting; and the scent of honeysuckle, and the sound of the water.

Winter is usually mild in our valley; but it can be severe and the lane blocked with snow for weeks. To prepare for this we lay in supplies of tinned food and flour and heap fuel high against the cottage wall. When the north-east wind raves down the valley from Scafell, we cover the cracks in the doors and pile logs in the open hearth - and let it rave. We're snug enough.

We go out very seldom; but perhaps once a year we make a quick visit to London on business. Usually it's a wild goose chase over one of Hugh's scripts that someone's interested in but never seems to buy! We enjoy these jaunts, which at least give us the chance to see old friends again; but infrequent though they are, we're always glad to leave the bustle of the crowded streets and the rush of traffic and get back to our lonely cottage among the fells - to the sound of the river, and the plovers and the curlews crying.

Kathleen (presumably, again, with her husband's help) made at least one attempt at fiction. It was a short story (undated) entitled 'The Winds of Love', about a young woman going for a screen test and finding romance. The manuscript indicates that she had some fun deciding on a *nom de plume*. 'Roma Dawn' has been crossed out in favour of 'Elsie Cumberland', then 'Kathleen Arthur', before she has finally thought better of all the pretence and changed it back to 'Kathleen Falkus'.

In the 1950s almost all Hugh's work had centred on the theatre or broadcasting. But by the end of the decade, his passion for his river and its fish had begun to take him in a new direction. The more he learned about the sea trout and its ways, the more he began to feel that he had something to share with the wider angling world. So it was, at the start of the 1960s, that he began to write about fishing.

IX

The Green Bible

I don't think I've ever enjoyed anything so much. It was a time when I was living
in a little cottage in the back of beyond, trying to write, and I had
discovered the sheer delight of catching sea trout.

INTERVIEW ON BBC RADIO BRISTOL, 1976

THE twenty-first century sea-trout angler may be excused for envying those who fished the North Country rivers in the years after the war. The runs of sea trout and salmon were generous enough for those who pursued them to be able to fill their baskets relatively easily, when conditions were half decent and the fish were running. With more fish and fewer anglers to educate them, there was no need to run through every trick in the book to avoid a dry net, as we often must today.

All fly fishing was, of course, done with a silk line - which meant a floating line, unless you neglected, accidentally or on purpose, to grease it - and sea trout were generally pursued with conventional wet-fly patterns tied in biggish sizes.

The sea trout were many, but the Esk's night fishermen were few. Falkus shared the river with a handful of devotees. Among them were his father-in-law, Benny Armstrong; George Jackson of Cropple How; Brian Heath, a vet, who lived at Cragg Cottage before the Falkuses and specialised in Herdwick sheep; and Geoff Rivaz, of the rod-making firm of Caudle and Rivaz. None were more dedicated than Richard Woodall from Waberthwaite, whose ancestor of the same name founded the family firm; it is now one of the country's most respected processors of traditional ham and bacon products. Two of Woodall's sons, Bar (Richard Barnes) and Joe, still fish the Esk today.

139

Bar, the eldest, went to school with Kathleen Armstrong in the 1930s. He first fished the river with his father around 1940, on the water the family owns between Knott End and Cragg. 'There were many more fish in the war years and after' he says. 'In July and August every pool was packed solid with sea trout. There were times when we would get twenty or more each in a night.'

Perhaps, given such plenty, most anglers simply did not need to worry about reaching a deeper understanding of their quarry. The conventional methods worked well enough, as they had for decades.

It had been known for centuries that sea trout go to sea to feed and return to spawn, but the angling world seems to have given very little thought to the significance of this. To be fair, the picture was muddied somewhat by local variations in feeding habits. While in sparse rivers like the Esk the sea trout undoubtedly give up feeding, this is by no means the case everywhere. Fish that do feed can be caught using imitative fly patterns, exactly like brown trout, a fact which allowed even the wisest of angling writers to continue to bracket the sea trout with the brown.

Certainly the nineteenth century angler made little, if any, distinction. The sea trout is alluded to only briefly in Stoddart's famous 1847 work, *The Angler's Companion: a Popular and Practical Handbook to the Art of Angling*. W. C. Stewart, in that much-loved work *The Practical Angler*, subtitled '*The Art of Trout-Fishing, More Particularly Applied to Clear Water*' (1857), deals in great detail with all the methods of taking trout from rivers and streams but does not mention the sea trout at all, either by name or implication. Neither does Francis Francis, in his compendious work *A Book On Angling* (1867); a brief section on night fishing for 'trout' makes the usual assumption that the quarry are taking natural flies.

A journey through the late nineteenth century and into the twentieth reveals a slow awakening. John Bickerdyke in *The Book of the All-Round Angler* (1888) recognised the sea trout's status as a separate quarry, though his brief advice on fishing methods continued to treat it as another form of trout.

At last, in 1917, comes a book which deals both exclusively and explicitly with our fish. *The Book of the Sea Trout* was written by Hamish Stuart, though it had to be completed by someone else - the novelist and angler Rafael Sabatini - and was published posthumously after Stuart's untimely death at sea. Stuart stated confidently that 'the sea trout feeds in fresh water in all its stages and at all periods of its sojourn'. Although he wrote enthusiastically of the joys of fishing through the night, he offered no advice on the subject other than an assumption that the fly will be fished deep and slow.

Next came another Scot, R. C. Bridgett, who in 1929 published *Sea-Trout Fishing*. Bridgett's book is wide-ranging and more practical than Stuart's, but his chapter on night fishing (one of the first, if not the first, in the literature) is written off the back foot throughout, as if the author were apologising for suggesting so unsporting a way of filling one's creel. Bridgett went so far as to admit that his night-fishing experience was 'not extensive, conditions having only infrequently been of the nature which makes the practice, in my opinion, allowable.' In 1929, you could still be an expert on sea-trout fishing without having done much of it at night.

Bridgett's attitude indicates that he was writing in a climate of opinion which viewed night fishing as vaguely disreputable. 'When the river is by reason of long drought reduced to a level which makes the capture of a sea trout almost impossible of accomplishment by day, then to take advantage of [the darkness of] a July night seems to me not only legitimate but entirely sportsmanlike' he writes in its defence. 'But it is not to be thought that night fishing is either coarse or easy.' He was on to something there.

Two little-known books published in the 1940s display a continuing negative attitude to the nocturnal approach. *Catching the Wily Sea Trout* (Herbert Jenkins, 1946) was written by A. R. Harris Cass, who lived and fished in Devon. Cass opened by saying: 'Night fishing for sea trout seems to me to be more of a business of catching fish than pleasant sport' and went on to claim that taking fish betray themselves by feeding on moths, and that if there were no moths there would be no fish. In 1949 H. P. Henzell, writing from the other end of Britain - he was a loch angler first and foremost - published *Fishing for Sea Trout* (Black), in which he complained: 'So far as I am concerned fishing for sea trout with the fly has the great disadvantage that, except in unusual circumstances, it is almost entirely confined to the hours of darkness.'

Kenneth Dawson, writing in 1938, embraced night fishing, while acknowledging that it can be a tricky business. His chapter on it in *Modern Salmon and Sea Trout Fishing* makes level-headed reference to the problems of invisible tackle and snags. Dawson, who fished mainly on the rivers of his native Devon, was one of the first to point out that pool tails are great places to find sea trout in the dark, though he assumed that this was because they found them good places to feed. He knew what he was fishing for, but did not appreciate how different his quarry was from its non-sea-going cousin. He was in good company.

Hard on the heels of Dawson came William Lawrie, whose *Border River Angling* appeared in 1939. At last we meet an author who is prepared to sound a positive note. 'There would appear to be an opinion held by a certain class of angler that to take trout at night is a matter so simple in its execution as to be unworthy of the name of angling, and that those depraved persons who are wont to practise such deeds of darkness cannot be considered sportsmen' he wrote, going on to assure us that on the contrary 'to be a successful night fisher, considerable knowledge of the feeding habits and feeding grounds of trout is necessary'.

The advice that then follows echoes our modern wisdom: the value of night fishing in producing the best sport and often the best fish, the need to concentrate on the deep, shaded pools and glides and the merits of keeping the fly well sunk and moving it steadily and slowly.

Yet there is not one reference in this chapter to *sea* trout. Lawrie, like most of his contemporaries, was still fishing for 'trout' and freely using the term for both forms.

Those of more scientific inclination understood the difference well enough. *The Sea Trout - A Study in Natural History*, by Henry Lamond (1916), appears to have been the first to offer a scientific account of the difference between the sea trout and the brown, though there is little evidence that the angling world took much notice.

G. Herbert Nall, who took up biology as a retirement pursuit, becoming a Fellow of the Royal Microscopical Society told the sea trout's story in great detail in *The Life of the Sea Trout* (1930), which remains the only popular scientific work devoted entirely to the fish. Falkus later called Nall's book 'the greatest work on the sea trout ever written' - not that it has had much competition.

Nall, by studying and explaining the sea trout's feeding and spawning habits, had given us anglers all the evidence we should have needed that while sea trout are anatomically and genetically identical to brown trout, their way of life is so different that from the angling point of view they are effectively another species. But Nall's book was weighty and technical, and too academic to interest the average angler.

It was left to Hugh Falkus to spread the gospel to the wider angling world. He developed a passion for his beautiful, wild, mercurial quarry, a passion which was to burn for the next two decades. 'For me, of all fish and fishing, this is the very top' he proclaimed in *Salmo the Leaper*, his 1977 BBC film.

Ever the enthusiast who must undertake everything that was worth doing to the limits of what was possible, Falkus was not content to stroll down to the waterside and cast a line for an hour or two, accepting with good grace whatever the river happened to throw his way. He entered into this new sport with the zeal of a missionary. He did not simply want to find out about sea trout; he wanted to find out *everything* about sea trout.

Falkus was the perfect man for the job. He was a shrewd and fascinated observer of wild creatures, a quick learner and an instinctive challenger of received opinion. He walked the banks of the Esk through the seasons, learning to understand the river and everything that swam in it, scuttled beside it or flew over it. In particular he monitored the sea trout and salmon as they journeyed in their thousands upriver in the summer and autumn and drifted back down to sea again with the first frosts. He watched them lashing their way upstream over the shallows, hanging ghost-like in the deep pools and shuddering in the throes of spawning.

Falkus' enthusiasm and skill as a naturalist were at the heart of his success as an angler. He told BBC Radio Bristol in 1976: 'The best angler is the best naturalist, because a really good naturalist must be a good hunter, whether he hunts with a camera, a rod or a gun . . . the art comes in studying nature, studying the environment in which your quarry lives.'

In his study on winter nights, he consulted the literature. Lawrie does not get a mention in *Sea Trout Fishing*, though Falkus is known to have read his book. Nall's findings, however, are reported extensively, while both Stuart and Bridgett are credited in the bibliography which was added in the second edition.

One book which helped and inspired Falkus, according to David Burnett, his later publisher, was a modest little work called *Fishing for Trout and Salmon* (1944), by Terence Horsley, who like Falkus had served as a wartime pilot, in his case in the Fleet Air Arm (most unfortunately, he was killed in a gliding accident not long after the war).

'Those who believe night is the time for sleep will never catch as many sea trout as the rest of us' wrote Horsley. 'If you know where the fish are lying, go down to the river as the sun dips below the horizon and make your first cast as the brighter colours fade from the sky. Between then and dawn you will catch trout which, during a visit to the river in daylight hours, you were prepared to swear didn't exist.'

As an angler, Falkus would have gone along with all that. As a naturalist, meanwhile, he appreciated that the study of behaviour was more revealing than the study of morphology. Nall's book had confirmed to him that as far as behaviour was concerned, the sea trout had more in common with the salmon than with the brown trout. The earlier writers' work simply revealed that they had not read Nall, or at least not fully appreciated the importance of what he was telling them.

Falkus with a good sea trout, 1960s.

Falkus by the river, 1960s.

Marriage to Kathleen and a new base at Cragg gave Falkus the opportunity to fish one of the most productive stretches of the Esk whenever he wanted to. He could fish further afield if he wished - in practice, he had access to most of the river - but the focus was on the water from Knott End down to the tide. In the early years he continued to go out with Bill Fowler, but after the move to Cragg he would more often fish alone except for his beloved dogs. Kathleen would often join him, though to bring food and act as his gillie rather than to fish; she preferred the spinning rod and the light of day. Sometimes she would bring a sack of hay down to the river to sit on. She confessed to Jeremy Barkworth-Edwards of *Salmon, Trout and Sea Trout* that when Falkus waded out to share a 'half-time' break and a Gaelic coffee, they would often use the hay's comfort for more than sitting; *piscatur non solum piscator*, as Falkus was fond of saying.

Fishing alone was a vital part of the Falkus approach. When he began to invite guests to Cragg they were expected to station themselves well away from each other and refrain from idle chatter while fishing, a sensible plan on a river as narrow and clear as the Esk. Falkus was a great champion of man's natural hunting instinct, and believed it was a great mistake to compromise it by fishing in company. Writing of his ability to sense when a fish

A later picture of Falkus steeple casting on his river.

is about to take (a skill which Fred J. Taylor, for one, witnessed at first hand), he said: 'This intuitive faculty is, I believe, an atavistic survival; a part of man's hunting instinct. Although it has been long submerged, I feel certain that with help it can be brought to the surface. We must learn to use our eyes and brains in a new way - or rather, in a very old way: the way of our ancestral hunters.'

There is no doubt that in those early, hungry days Falkus caught an awful lot of sea trout, including some big ones. In July 1957 he landed a giant, an Esk record of 15lb 6oz[10]; its outline was traced on a stone slab which for many years was on display at Knott End. The story of its capture first appeared in *The Angler's Bedside Book* (1965), an anthology of original fishing stories edited by Hugh's friend Maurice Wiggin.

In the early 1960s Falkus acquired a new fishing companion. Brigadier George Wilson, from Keswick, had retired from the Army to take a management job with the National Trust at Windermere, and to go fishing as often as he possibly could.

The Woodalls remember 'Briggy' Wilson as a charming companion and an outstanding angler. He was also dedicated in the extreme. Fishing on the last night of the season one year, Briggy, then well into his sixties, fell in. He plodded back up to the cottage, changed into dry clothing, and went straight back to the river to fish through the night.

Falkus first met Briggy Wilson salmon fishing on the Dunthwaite beat of the Derwent. 'That magnificent fisherman', as Falkus referred to him, soon became something of a guest of honour on Hugh's river. Falkus, who freely admitted in later years how much he had learned from Briggy, would give him VIP treatment, always ensuring that he was on a good pool and that his creature comforts were met. Everyone in the Falkus inner circle discovered at some time or other what it was like to be scorned or abused by their host, except, apparently, Briggy Wilson.

As the seasons passed, Falkus drew together the threads of what he had learned, added in what the literature had taught him and began to assemble a theory of the game. By the end of the 1950s he was ready to start sharing it with a wider audience.

Falkus' decision to go into print on the subject of sea-trout fishing was in part provoked by the writings of F. W. Holiday, a regular contributor to that fondly-remembered weekly *Fishing Gazette* on the subject. Kathleen told *Salmon, Trout and Sea Trout* that an article by Holiday in *FG* had made Falkus 'hopping mad'. A perusal of *FG* archives reveals the likely culprit, published in September 1959; among other heresies (as Falkus would have seen it) the piece asserted that an hour before sunset was 'not too early to start' and that nine feet was a good length for a sea-trout rod. The following year Holiday published a book, *River Fishing for Sea Trout*, which stated: 'Night fishing, generally speaking, is between the hours of sunset and midnight. Very occasionally you may fish hopefully all night . . . [eg] when a hot day is followed by mist or low cloud. You may be lucky enough to hit on two or three such nights in a whole season.' Elsewhere he claimed: 'Almost all fly fishing for sea trout is now done with a greased or floating line, and this is the only method which will be discussed.'

Holiday could not go unchallenged. Falkus' first article appeared in the *Fishing Gazette* on 7th January, 1961. Entitled 'Sea-Trout Fishing CCSP' (you have to read on to discover that this stands for the Falkus edict of 'concentration, confidence, stealth and persistence'), it covered two full pages without illustration - quite a long piece for the *FG* - and focused on the need to adopt the right approach and the right philosophy in pursuing sea trout at night. In keeping with the style of the period, readers were told nothing of the man behind the byline, or how and where he had learned his fishing. Though confident in tone, the article did not go so far as to express any dissent with previous contributors; this was a gentler age, and *Fishing Gazette* was not in the business of fanning the flames of conflict between its correspondents.

Fishing Gazette's Editor, A. Norman Marston, must have been pleased with his new contributor. He commissioned a series of six articles from Falkus under the title 'Sea-Trout Night Fly-Fishing Strategy' and ran them from late March 1961 until the end of April. The pieces, simply numbered 1 to 6 without separate titles, were structured and businesslike in approach and written in typically assertive tones. This was no tyro author tentatively offering his first contribution to the body of angling doctrine but a man with complete confidence in his own knowledge, from opening sentence to closing full stop.

Part 2 was illustrated with a pencil drawing by the author of an angler sheltering from a rainstorm, while later ones included diagrams explaining the correct relationship between fly and line and showing how the angle of presentation affects fly speed. 'The fly cannot work properly unless the line is entirely free from grease' wrote Falkus. 'Let the beginner burn that on his memory with letters of fire.' After taking us through the correct approach to the water and presentation of the fly, the final piece in the series touched on the location and capture of big fish.

Falkus was back in the *Fishing Gazette's* pages a few months later with a second series, which fleshed out the philosophy he had outlined with more detailed guidance on matters of practical procedure. This time the title was 'Sea Trout Night Fly-Fishing Tactics'. The first piece, published on 5th August, 1961, examined the question of how to strike a sea-trout take, while the second and third covered greased-line fishing and the fourth dealt with the sunk line. Falkus then went on to devote the whole of parts 5 and 6 to the fly-maggot - a reflection of how important the method was to the North Country fishermen.

In January and February 1962 two more articles followed in the *Fishing Gazette*: 'Sea Trout Fishing - Failure: 1' and 'Sea Trout Fishing - Failure: 2', outlining the mistakes anglers make at night and how they should be avoided. There was also a piece for *Trout and Salmon* (November 1961) which explored the conundrum of the feeding habits (or lack of them) of migratory fish, and suggested that the root cause was the physiological change that drives the urge to migrate.

Taken together, these early articles are a coherent expression, almost fully-formed, of the Falkus philosophy as we later came to know it. And of course they were the prelude to a much more lasting piece of work; a book.

Given that many passages from his magazine writing correspond closely with the eventual text of *Sea Trout Fishing - A Guide to Success*, it seems the two must have evolved in tandem. During the winters of 1960-61 and 1961-62, Falkus spent night after night in his study at Cragg Cottage working on an old Smith Corona typewriter. He would stick sheets together in sequence to form a long scroll, a method he was to use for many years. Kathleen would often help.

'We used to call it "rattle-tattle-ping"' she told *Salmon, Trout and Sea Trout*. 'He would say, "Pot, I'm off to do some rattle-tattle-ping," and I'd hear it through the bedroom floor for hours.' Falkus would often wake his wife in the small hours to seek her opinion on newly-written passages.

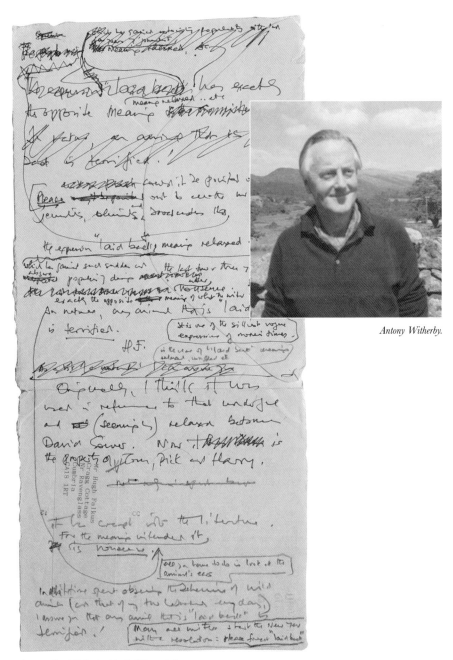

Antony Witherby.

An example of Falkus' original editing technique
(by courtesy of Malcolm Greenhalgh).

Falkus never did embrace modern technology. His friend and co-author Malcolm Greenhalgh remembers the day a well-meaning friend brought him an electric typewriter. He started to type 'sea trout', but his touch was too heavy and the machine immediately produced an incontinent string of s's. That was enough for Falkus. 'You can take that f . . .ing thing away' he told his benefactor.

Kathleen's contribution to her husband's fishing and writing exploits was not always given the credit it deserved. One magazine article began: 'When preparing a list of tackle requirements for a night's sea-trout fishing, you would be wise to omit your wife. This axiom might be called the Falkus Golden Rule for Sea Trout Success . . . after dusk she can see neither to read nor knit, nor even to admire your casting skill. And what will she do? Sooner or later she will start to chatter.' The piece concludes with a paragraph which Falkus presumably intended as redress: 'In Cragg Cottage during the summer months, there are many men but no women. Except, of course, for Kathleen, my wife, who cleans the place up and does the cooking and makes the beds and bakes the bread and fetches the milk, and feeds the cat and fills the stove and does the washing, and digs the garden, and mows the lawn, and listens to all the fishing stories.'

The book that had so inspired Falkus, Horsley's *Fishing for Trout and Salmon*, had been published by H. F. and G. Witherby, a sporting and country book specialist well known to Falkus. In an account published in 1992 in *Salmon, Trout and Sea Trout*, later recycled as a chapter in *Some of it Was Fun*, Falkus claimed that it was a direct approach to Witherby's that had led to the publication of his book. He recounted how he had taken the train up to London to meet Antony Witherby (the nephew of the founder, Harry Witherby) to ask him not just to publish it but to keep it in print for ten years, because he felt it would need that long for his methods to be discovered and adopted by anglers.

David Burnett reveals that this account is one of Hugh's fireside stories. In fact the introduction came through his literary agency, W. G. Benson and Campbell Thomson, who had been engaged by Falkus to market his plays (he appointed several agents during his early writing career, though none lasted very long). They approached Antony Witherby, who was impressed enough to take it on, though no undertakings were given about keeping it in print. The first edition of *Sea Trout Fishing - A Guide to Success* appeared in June 1962. It cost sixteen shillings. Among the fishing titles advertised on the back cover was Terence Horsley's book.

Falkus went much further than any of his predecessors. He drew together the strands of what was then known about the subject and presented them in the context of a proper understanding of the fish. He did not content himself with the odd chapter about night fishing; almost the whole book was devoted to the subject.

In his *Fishing Gazette* articles, Falkus had dealt with the hows and whys of sea-trout night fishing. In his book he opened from a wider viewpoint, examining the biology and character of the sea trout itself before going on to tell us how much we had all been missing by failing to give either the fish, or the sport of angling for it, the recognition they deserved.

The Falkus doctrine as outlined in *Sea Trout Fishing* was founded on three central principles:

1. The sea trout is a different creature both from the salmon and the brown trout and must be angled for as a 'species' in its own right, taking account of its different biological agenda and its consequently different travelling, feeding and fleeing propensities.

2. Because mature sea trout do not normally feed after they enter the river, they should be angled for with lures which resemble the prey they were last pursuing at sea, rather than the riverborne insects on which conventional fly patterns are based. Since such prey are much larger than the patterns conventionally used in fly fishing, many more and bigger fish will be caught by the angler who uses large lures.

3. Night fishing should be regarded not as a subsidiary branch of the game but as the *principal*, and by far the most rewarding, sporting technique for catching sea trout.

For the first time, the concept of *choosing* to fish at night for sea trout - and right through the night at that - was both presented to the sportsman, and fully developed from first principles. And it was done clearly enough for every angler to follow, from the beginner to the experienced game fisherman.

The lesson that the sea trout is a fish in its own right and must be angled for accordingly is the most important single contribution Falkus made to accepted wisdom on sea-trout fishing. It became the cornerstone of a popular revolution.

Close behind is the insistence that sea trout can be pursued with advantage in the watches of the night when surface activity has ceased. While

Falkus agreed that most sport with sea trout could be expected in the hour after dusk, he asserted that many more fish, and very often the biggest, could be caught by the angler who persists when fellow fishermen and wildlife alike have gone home to bed - provided he turned to the sunk lure on a sinking line. 'On many nights the fisherman who through lack of equipment or experience cannot fish a sunk fly properly will catch very few fish' he concluded.

A pity perhaps that Holiday never noticed a correlation between his own adherence to the floating line and his failure to catch fish late at night. In fairness it must be said that Horsley too had missed this trick, while Dawson had entirely discounted the sunk line.

Not that sunk-line fishing was new; certainly Falkus did not invent it, any more than he invented night fishing, which, in its widest sense, must date back to the first fisherman who ever went out in the dark with hook of bone and line of twisted hair. Those who remember how sea-trout fishing was done in the post-war years, both in Wales and the North, attest to that. It was an open secret among the more serious anglers that going along with nature and letting your silk line fish ever deeper as it became waterlogged often resulted in the best fish of the night.

Moc Morgan, who began serious sea-trouting on the Welsh rivers in the 1950s, kept records which showed that the average weight of fish caught in the small hours was substantially higher than those taken in the first two hours of the night.

'There were plenty of people fishing for sea trout in our rivers back then, but not many would fish through till dawn as I did' he says. 'After a couple of hours the line would get waterlogged and become a slow sinker. After three hours you'd have a fast sinker. There was nothing particularly secret about what we did, but Hugh was the first to put it all in writing.'

Perhaps we should not be surprised that it took so long for rank-and-file sea trout anglers to wake up to the fact that their quarry stays open for business through the night. No one who has tried his hand at night fishing can have failed to experience the powerful desire for bright lights and warm linen that creeps upon the angler during those moments after midnight when he realises he is alone on the riverbank with only the dew and the stars for company and the river winding black and lifeless around him. Even today on our great sea-trout rivers, many an angler may be encountered trudging back to the car park at half past midnight, complaining that the fish have stopped taking and sport is over for the night.

Falkus taught us that more often than not they haven't, and it isn't. He

dissected the night into four convenient portions, using footballing termi-
nology; the first half (dusk to around midnight); half-time (midnight till
1am); the second half (1am to daybreak); and extra time (first light).
(According to Malcolm Greenhalgh, 'half-time' is a quirk of the Esk,
caused by high tide backing up the flow for a short period.) He talked of the
wonderful bags of fish he had taken during all these periods, and described
how he had done it. And of course, he did so with such style, charm and
vigour that it was hard for the most sceptical reader not to share his confidence.

In short, Hugh Falkus taught us what we had all been missing; and he did
it wonderfully well.

'The sun has dipped behind the distant fells, whose eastern flanks are now
a dark purple in the afterglow' he writes in Chapter 7, *à propos* of the opening of a night's campaign. 'A gleam of light springs from cottage windows
far across the valley. A moth flutters over the pool and falls spinning on the
surface, already ringed by the splash of a jumping fish. A white owl glides
silently across the water meadows; the faint night wind flutters the leaves;
the fascination of a darkening river deepens, and where the current chuck-
les against mossy stones beneath overhanging branches, all is shadowy and
mysterious.'

Night fishing for sea trout became a little less shadowy and mysterious once
Falkus had written about it, but its magic did not lessen. Rather, it increased.
The wider angling world began to see the game for what it was; not the next
thing to grave-robbing but a glorious, thrilling sport in its own right.

The beauty of the lyrical passages in *Sea Trout Fishing* is matched by the
thoroughness and clarity of Falkus' practical advice. He was not the first to
attend to the knots and wrinkles of night fishing - Horsley, for one, had
engaged briefly with that in 1944, exhorting the reader to reconnoitre
during the day and never to go out at night without a torch and a spare cast
- but he was certainly the first to do it properly. Where earlier authors had
dipped a toe into the water and wiggled it about a bit, Falkus worked out
the rules of engagement and laid them out for us, systematically and in
great detail.

Sea Trout Fishing appeared at a time when tackle technology was opening
up new possibilities - possibilities which would soon remove for ever the
angler's dependence on silk lines, with their insistence on floating when
they were newly dressed and sinking when they were not. In the 1960s, the
river's third dimension was placed within the control of every angler, and it
was Falkus who mapped it for us.

Despite all this, the first edition of *Sea Trout Fishing* seems to have dropped into the waters of angling literature with the gentlest of splashes. *Trout and Salmon* gave it a favourable but less than feverish review ('a book to be recommended') in October 1962, four months afters its publication. It was not until December that the *Fishing Gazette* got round, rather apologetically, to mentioning it:

Of the dozens of fishing books published every year, it is inevitable that a few fail to receive the mention they deserve in the columns of the angling press. One of these is Sea Trout Fishing, *by Hugh Falkus. Published during the early summer, it has gone comparatively unnoticed, yet it is one of the best books on sea trout to reach the book departments for some time.*

Hugh Falkus is well known to Fishing Gazette *readers. Perhaps the most important point he makes is that sea-trout fishing is a sport of its own - too often it is regarded as merely something halfway between brown trout fishing and salmon fishing.*

A reader cannot fail to be caught up with Falkus' enthusiasm . . . Sea Trout Fishing *is full of simple yet important lessons. I am a great believer in starting the newcomer the right way, and this is a book to do just that. But it is also a work which any game fisherman would be delighted to have on his bookshelf.*

This was not the view of a critic signing himself 'PB', who reviewed the book in *Creel* magazine. PB took great exception to Falkus' contention that night fishing must be practised alone and in silence, and asserted: 'His philosophy of sea-trout fishing is extremely faulty, as are most of the arbitrary assumptions he makes.' Attacking Falkus' belief that the angler should use a rod of not less than ten feet, he concluded: 'His hermitical fishing must be responsible for his failing to know how few anglers can fish at all with such a rod, let alone enjoy it.'

Falkus could not let that pass. In the next edition of *Angler's Annual* he responded:

Although in many ways I am a vain and boastful fellow, my intention is not to plume up my will, but to inform of my fishing credentials. And in my opinion it would be a splendid thing for the sport generally if all other fishing writers, reviewers and editors were made to do the same. Certainly those who seek to proselytise.

. . . I don't have to write about fishing. If I choose to do so it is only fair that the buyer should know something of what he is buying - caveat emptor notwithstanding.

As a sad little example, there is a piece in my book urging the sea-trout fly fisherman who wishes to retain his sanity to avoid fishing in the still watches of the night with voluble companions. Sound enough advice, if somewhat obvious. Well, one idiot reviewer signing himself 'P.B.', who evidently knows as much about sea-trout fishing as I do about horse racing, took it upon himself to treat this with derision. In his view, it seems, the only reasonable approach to night fishing is via some sort of midnight barbecue!

But surely, any technical writer who wishes to burst into print, whether as author or reviewer, has a certain moral obligation. If someone comments on something he knows nothing about, and he makes a public idiot of himself, that is his affair only up to a point.

There are of course certain people who just can't help it; who do this sort of thing to draw attention to themselves. The psychiatrists have a name for it. And if this 'P.B.' happens to be one of them, as I suspect he must be, he has my pity and I take no offence at the rubbish he wrote. But the unhappy truth is that there are simple, honest souls, thirsting for knowledge, who may believe some of the nonsense written by these impostors; who may, for instance, really think that the way to set about fishing for sea trout is to assault the river en masse *and wait hopefully for a feeding fish!*

The standard of much of our fishing literature today is abysmal. A few thoroughly sound and experienced fishermen battle bravely on writing good sense in English, and doing their best not to repeat what has already been written a thousand times. Alas, they are all too few; and almost invariably their work is sandwiched between slabs of drivel.

It has been said that anyone who reads the fishing press these days deserves what he gets. A cynical view, but understandable. Editors should employ someone of experience to check the copy they publish, or learn enough about fishing to enable them to do so themselves.

The Editor of *Creel*, incidentally, was that sainted angler and writer Bernard Venables, who never became a member of Falkus' circle.

There is no sign that the 'idiot reviewer' ever replied to this fusillade. One wonders if he ever dared to write a fishing article again.

Curiously enough, F. W. Holiday reviewed *Sea Trout Fishing* kindly, approving almost everything Falkus said and reserving criticism only (again) for the author's choice of the long rod and for the over-confident claim that sea trout do not feed in fresh water. There are plenty who would agree that he had a point on each count.

In general *Sea Trout Fishing* was quietly approved by the angling *cognoscenti*, presenting as it did an excellent curtain-raiser to the sport, at least to those outside the world inhabited by those North Country and Welsh anglers who specialised in sea trout and already knew of these techniques.

'Falkus did for sea-trout fishing what Halford had done for the dry fly fisherman seventy years before' says David Burnett. 'He drew together all the available knowledge, wisdom and experience and produced a comprehensive book, one that would show the beginner how to catch sea trout in many different situations. He didn't actually invent any of it, but his contribution to the game was immense.'

Unfortunately, the originality and freshness of the text was not matched by the book's presentation. It was a drab little volume, indifferently produced even by 1960s standards, with a crudely-drawn angling scene on its green-and-white dust-jacket and a handful of simple line drawings inside - the surface lure, a worming rig and a couple of diagrams of pools - along with sixteen rather dull black-and-white photographs, mainly showing stretches of water. 'They were in fact deeply instructive, because they showed us how to recognise sea-trout lies, but it took a connoisseur to interpret them' says Burnett.

Despite high praise, the book sold slowly. The original print run of 1500 copies took eight years to sell out (Witherby's never remaindered books) and it was not reprinted until 1971; the new dust-jacket was of poor quality, even compared to the original.

If the book itself was not perfect, neither was its timing. In the early 1960s, there were still so many salmon in our rivers that the sea trout was nothing like as highly valued as it is today.

By the mid 1960s Falkus was absorbed in his burgeoning career as a maker of wildlife films, and he was much distracted. And he had another writing project, which for the time being took precedence; *The Stolen Years*.

Falkus told friends that it was Diana who had urged him to write a book about his boyhood. He seems to have incubated the idea quietly for some years after her death before acting on it; he spoke little about it to his friends. Possibly the death of his father in 1957 gave him the spark he needed to put pen to paper. Kathleen seems to have had little or nothing to do with it and is not referred to in the text, which makes no direct reference to anything that happened in Falkus' life after the 1930s (the first edition does not include the prologue about the events of the summer of 1940). Presumably this was because he had planned to save these for a later volume.

There is evidence that the warm, easy, confident writing style Falkus displayed in *The Stolen Years* owed something to the encouragement of Maurice Wiggin, a friend of Hugh's and an occasional visitor to the cottage. Wiggin was a working-class boy from the Black Country who became a successful Fleet Street journalist, perhaps best remembered as television critic of the *Sunday Times* for twenty years (he retired from that post in 1971 and was, rather cruelly considering his towering skill with the pen, made redundant a few years later), but his books, including several on angling - *Troubled*

Waters, The Passionate Angler, Fishing For Beginners and his best-seller *Teach Yourself Fly Fishing* - stand among the finest in the literature.

Wiggin gave Falkus great encouragement in his writing at the time when he was working on *The Stolen Years*. He wrote to him in April 1964, in response to a letter in which Falkus must have expressed self-doubt.

But you are a fine writer. You are. You are. You must never doubt this. You write very well indeed, and if only you could gather confidence, you would write like a master, like Hemingway and Fleming combined . . . what you whiz down in your letters, without stopping to think about writing, is the stuff of you. And it is what proves you are a born writer. Ergo - write anything and everything as you would write your letters. Don't stop, tremble, and go into a cold sweat. Just press on.

The eventual publication of *The Stolen Years* was secured by Campbell Thomson, the agency which had handled *Sea Trout Fishing*. They managed to place the book with the Museum Press in London, and it appeared in 1965, with a handful of line illustrations by David Cobb. In 1966 the World Publishing Company of Cleveland, Ohio, brought out an American edition.

Many Falkus aficionados view *The Stolen Years* as a treasure of a book, unreliable as it may be on matters of historical fact. 'In my view it can be measured, as literature or short stories, against anything published in the last century' says Hugh's friend and confidant Jo Rippier, a retired English lecturer. Pungent with the smell of the saltmarsh, it evokes Falkus' early years with the skill and passion of a truly gifted writer. *The Stolen Years* is about the pain and embarrassment of youth, the unforgettable thrill of those first hunting triumphs and the drama of taking your life in your hands in a small boat on a big sea, but above all it is a tribute to Hugh's father; and the benign persona of James Falkus shines from every page.

'When I was a boy fishing was the essence of my life, and fishing with Father an incomparable joy' wrote his son. 'His limitless enthusiasm made him the perfect companion - as I discovered when time darkened and we could fish together no longer.'

It is the darker passages (several of which are quoted in the opening chapter of this book) that lift *The Stolen Years* from the picturesque to the powerful; the boy spurned by the mother he was so desperate to please, the abandoned farmstead where once a pretty girl had stood framed in a doorway, the brushes with watery death. But James Falkus is never less than a beacon of life, light and energy. Falkus finished the last chapter, and the book: 'I like to think that he found his lonely creek, and that he lies always by the sea-lavender-covered marshlands, where there is no sound but a distant sea and the curlews crying. He was a very kind man.'

In retrospect it seems astonishing that a man of such forceful character, of such arrogance and, on occasion, such callousness, could have written with so sure and sensitive a touch; a clue to the deep complexity at the heart of the man.

The Stolen Years is very much a collection of reminiscences rather than an attempt at autobiography. Rich in atmosphere and drama, it is conspicuously short of verifiable facts. But perhaps we should not worry too much about that. It is the work of a storyteller, not a historian, and its author never claimed otherwise.

In 1979 Witherby's published a new edition, with forty-nine line drawings by Falkus. This time a dedication was added, to 'three friends', Antony Witherby, David Burnett and Tim Rickett. More conspicuously, the prologue describing Falkus' capture by the Germans in June 1940 made its first appearance.

It was not until well into the 1970s that Falkus turned his attention to a second edition of *Sea Trout Fishing*. In this he was much encouraged by his close friends, particularly Tom Rawling, a Lakeland-born teacher, poet and sea-trout fishing devotee who had got to know Falkus in the 1960s. In the early 1970s, when he was touching seventy years old, Rawling contributed two articles to *Trout and Salmon* which examined the approach presented in the first edition of *Sea Trout Fishing* in detail and extolled its virtues, and those of its creator, with huge enthusiasm. But the principle catalyst to the production of the second edition - and to its eventual success - was the angling writer and historian Fred Buller.

It was Falkus' voice that first attracted Buller's attention. Fred was motoring along with the car radio on one day in the early 1960s when a programme about Grizedale Forest began. The presenter was Falkus, and Buller was much impressed.

'It wasn't just the sheer quality of his voice, but the way he used it and his command of language' says Buller. 'He spoke with total authority. It was compelling stuff - he was in the Attenborough class.'

Not long afterwards an introduction came, through another member of the angling aristocracy, Fred J. Taylor. Falkus had been so impressed by Taylor's writings on fishing in *Angler's Annual* that one day in 1966, travelling between Bristol and London, he had knocked on the door of Fred's Aylesbury home to introduce himself. Taylor was invited to Cragg, and urged to bring a friend. Fred J. chose Fred B.

Fred Buller with Kathleen at Cragg,
around 1969.

Fred J. Taylor with HF in the early 1970s.

'I was going up to Loch Ken to research the Kenmure Pike for my book *Pike*' Buller remembers. 'Fred asked me if I'd like to call in to meet Falkus on the way back. I didn't hesitate. I saw him as a real writer.'

Falkus and Buller had plenty of common ground. They were both skilled anglers with huge appetites for new fishing wisdom, and Buller too had a first book under his belt; *Fred Buller's Book of Rigs and Tackles* had just come off the presses.

Buller left the manuscript for *Pike* with Falkus for comment. Falkus was impressed, though he made some constructive criticisms about the text - notably, that it was too wordy - which Buller was happy to take on board. 'He taught me to read passages of text aloud. If you find yourself coming to a stop, it means something is wrong with the way you've written it. It was a most enlightening piece of advice.'

Pike went on to be a great success - it was acclaimed by the *Sunday Times* as 'the best book ever written about pike and pike fishing'.

Buller for his part felt he could open Falkus' eyes to the value of good visual presentation, in particular the importance of plenty of high-quality drawings and photographs. The feast of illustration in the second edition

Kathleen with an 18lb salmon caught by Hugh after a night's sea trouting.

of *Sea Trout Fishing* is largely due to Fred. In contrast to the first edition, the second is decorated throughout its four hundred and fifty pages with photos and drawings, covering everything from casting and fly-tying techniques to the design of a wormery.

Falkus' enthusiasm for writing books and articles had waned after *Sea Trout Fishing* and *The Stolen Years*, presumably a result of his preoccupation with filming and film scripts. But Buller's ideas were the catalyst to a new motivation, and he worked flat out to complete the new edition.

With so much illustrative material, simply sticking sheets of typescript together was no longer enough. Falkus developed a new assembly technique. Having sketched out the contents, he would prepare a large envelope for each chapter. Material he had gleaned, pictures and finished manuscript were then placed in the appropriate envelope.

He knew that to be truly comprehensive, the book would have to take in ground that had not been covered in the first edition. A new chapter on loch fishing was compiled with the help of Sidney Spencer, whose *Salmon and Sea Trout in Wild Places* had been published by Witherby's in 1968. Spencer, who had the fishing on Lough Esk in County Donegal virtually to himself and spent most of his time in summer afloat on it, is remembered as a skilled loch fisherman as well as a fine writer.

In September 1974 Falkus and Buller took the ferry to Ireland to see Spencer and examine his methods. The trip also provided an opportunity for them to research an additional chapter on saltwater fishing, for which the pair drove across to Donegal to fish the voes for sea trout as Falkus had done in the old days.

The second edition of *Sea Trout Fishing* is twice the length of the first, approaching 100,000 words. While the heart of the book - the chapters on

'The Fish' and those on night fishing that follow - are essentially unchanged (though revised in detail), Falkus slotted in a new opening chapter on sea-trout flies and a much longer one on 'tackle, angling, safety and culinary matters', as well as those on loch fishing and saltwater fishing. The single chapter on daytime fishing was extended to two (dealing with high water and low).

Finally we were treated to a trip into the past through the diaries of a nineteenth century angler called Walter Caddy, the property of Bar Woodall. Caddy's experiences were introduced to remind us of the constantly-changing status of the sea trout, and warn us how much we all stand to lose if we do not safeguard our rivers.

The first edition had contained no introduction, no foreword, no explanation of why or how the book was written. Nor did it feature any credits, bibliography or acknowledgements, except for a brief note thanking two men; Bill Fowler ('Mr W. M. W. Fowler of Eskdale'), and George 'Briggy' Wilson. The second edition put this right with a lengthy preface in which the author paid tribute to the dozens of people who had contributed, directly or otherwise, to the book, followed by a scene-setting introduction which described the capture of a nocturnal salmon, to introduce his thesis about the value of big, sunk flies for sea-trout at night.

There is a small mystery about the dedication of the first edition. Originally there was to have been a third dedicatee, a Mr J. Hatton, described as a fellow of Exeter College, Oxford - presumably the Joe Hatton who appears among the long list of Cragg visitors in the preface of the second edition - but Falkus crossed Mr Hatton out, as witnessed by a printer's proof, still extant and in the possession of the angling book specialist Dave Hatwell. We know neither why he was first included in this select company, nor why his name was dropped; possibly he contributed the rather technical information Falkus included about the solubility of oxygen at different temperatures.

Bar Woodall tied many of the flies illustrated in the book. The caption to plate 2, which illustrates a range of traditional sea-trout patterns, conceals a typical Falkus story. He had mistakenly specified a woodcock feather for the Teal and Green instead of teal, and Bar had followed this instruction. The error was not noticed until the book was in press. According to Bar, the Irish fly-tyer referred to in the caption who 'always tied the Teal and Green with woodcock' never existed. Falkus invented the explanation at the eleventh hour, to avoid the embarrassment of an *erratum* slip.

The second edition of *Sea Trout Fishing* was published in 1975 at £6.50, eight times the price of the previous issue (inflation had arrived). This time it was met with superlatives by the lorryload. Writing in *Trout and Salmon*, Arthur Oglesby acclaimed it as 'a wonderful book . . . a must for anyone who would seek knowledge of sea trout and their capture by rod and line'. Maurice Wiggin called the book 'a wonderfully compelling blend of expertise and enthusiasm - one of the the great fishing books of all time'.

Conrad Voss Bark in *The Flyfishers' Journal* wrote: 'This is the definitive book on sea-trout fishing . . . the text is beautifully written, clear, precise, authoritative and full of good humour and good nature and the feel of the river . . . anglers of many generations to come will treasure *Sea Trout Fishing* and return to it again and again for its knowledge and its wisdom and for the sheer pleasure of reading it.' As indeed they have. In a letter to Tony Witherby, Voss Bark summed up the appeal of the book and its author perfectly: '[Falkus] has a nice sense of humour and and a kind of damn-you-this-is-the-way-to-do-it approach . . . when you read the text you warm to the man who wrote it, irrespective of whether you know him or not. He bursts with enthusiasm, life, energy, enjoyment, and it all flows over you.'

Not surprisingly, the second edition did much better than the first; the initial print run sold out within months. Reprints followed almost every year, with a revision in 1981 to include a handful of colour plates. To date *Sea Trout Fishing - A Guide to Success* has sold some 20,000 copies, a phenomenal sale for a specialist fishing book. The number of anglers who have been inspired to take up night fishing for sea trout, to persist with it and finally to succeed, is legion. Forty-five years after it first saw the light of day Hugh's green bible remains in print, a lasting testimony to his reputation as the father of modern sea-trout fishing.

X

A Light in the Darkness

There is nothing, nothing, *in the whole sport of fishing so enchanting as a sea trout spate river in the drowsy dusk of a warm summer evening.*
SEA TROUT FISHING

S*EA TROUT FISHING* persuaded the many anglers who had never properly got to grips with the business of night fishing for sea trout that they had been missing some of the most thrilling sport it is possible to experience with a fishing rod. But it went much further - it told them exactly how they could put that right. And the detail was as radical as the big picture.

Most writers of how-to-do-it angling books are content to build on the published wisdom that has gone before, reviewing, recycling and reassessing. *Sea Trout Fishing* undoubtedly borrowed from the preceding literature, but most of what Falkus said had never appeared in a book before. In particular, Falkus set out a number of relatively unsung techniques for catching sea trout at night which he had learned and developed on his local rivers, and explained them properly and in great detail.

Chief among these was the sunk lure. Most night fishing up to that point had been done with conventional wet flies, fished down and across as for trout, on a floating line - in the days of silk, it was Hobson's choice. Falkus exhorted us to appreciate that just as night was not a last-resort choice of time for a sea-trouting trip but the *best* time, so the deep-sunk lure should be regarded not as a last-ditch method but very often the *best* method, at least once the 'first half' was over.

The idea that a sunk fly fished slowly through the pools after dark would work well for sea trout had been dimly appreciated for a long time, at least among those anglers who had noticed what happens when a silk line is allowed to sink. Bridgett had hinted at the possibilities back in 1929, observing that 'a fly that is deeply sunk seems to be most effective', advice which was echoed by Lawrie in *Border River Angling* ten years later. But these references are few and scant.

Perhaps the first writer who embraced the sunk fly with real enthusiasm was a Cornish schoolmaster called Jeffrey Bluett, who in 1948 published *Sea Trout and Occasional Salmon*, dealing with his encounters with migratory fish on the rivers of his native West Country, particularly the Tavy. Bluett devotes three short chapters to night fishing, about which he has this to say:

I can never understand the attitude of those anglers who, just because they are unable to catch fish on any particular evening, pack up after say an hour's fishing at one place, saying the fish are not going . . . Realising that the blank evenings frequently occurred when the temperature was low, I decided that there were no moths about, and that consequently the fish were not near the surface . . . As the fish were apparently lying on the bottom, it seemed to me that something might be done by getting down to them. I was amazed at what happened.

Bluett's reasoning might have been suspect (he shared that theory about moths with his fellow West Countryman A. R. Harris Cass, mentioned in the previous chapter), but his conclusion was spot on. He goes on to describe how he learned to fish with his flies almost (and sometimes actually) touching bottom, concluding: 'This slow-working, deep-sinking method is so deadly on occasions - frequent occasions - that I almost questioned putting a detailed description of it into print.'

So Bluett appreciated its value some years before Falkus, even though he was working from the premise that sea trout take our flies because they are feeding. If Falkus ever read *Sea Trout and Occasional Salmon*, neither the book nor its author is mentioned in *Sea Trout Fishing*, nor is it listed in a catalogue of Falkus' library made by Fred Buller after his death.

In 1962 Falkus was writing some years before plastic lines were introduced, so his advice on choosing a line was confined to whether or not to grease it. He recommended having two rods set up, one with a greased line and the other with one that was entirely untreated. This would have given a rather modest sink rate, comparable with a modern slow-sinking line - good enough to get a fly well down in a quiet glide, but nowhere near equal to the job in a heavy flow or in deeper water.

Ironically, the arrival on the market of the first plastic fly lines in the

1960s at first made life more difficult for the night fly fisherman. These first lines were floaters, and float they did - right through the night. Anglers who had been exploiting the tendency of a silk line to sink as the night progressed remained frustrated until sinking lines followed a few years later.

The first hundred and fifty pages of *Sea Trout Fishing* set out a soundly-reasoned and highly-structured approach to outwitting sea trout at night, vastly more detailed and comprehensive than anything that had gone before. The full possibilities offered by darkness to the sea-trout hunter were revealed at last. Earlier writers had peered briefly into the gloom that surrounded night fishing before tiptoeing away; Falkus waded in and switched on the floodlights.

Three principal approaches are outlined: the subsurface fly, the sunk lure and the surface lure. The dry fly, considered very much part of the armoury by earlier writers (they were fishing for 'trout', remember) is not even mentioned (it is granted a brief, dismissive paragraph in the second edition). This attitude no doubt is rooted in the very sparse fly life of the Esk, which produces sea trout that make little or no attempt to feed. Sea trout anglers on larger, more fertile rivers such as the Dee, Nith and Annan have long counted the dry fly a useful part of their armoury.

You would imagine, from the familiarity with which Falkus shoots into the surface lure in Chapter 3, that he is referring to an established method which needed no introduction. You might also imagine, if you had never heard of it before (and few people had), that Falkus had invented it in the first place.

Neither is the case. An appreciation of the origins of this method, now widely accepted as one of the deadliest ways of taking sea trout, requires a little investigation.

The modern surface lure, or 'wake lure' as it is more descriptively known, can readily be traced as far back as 1951. In that year Hardy's catalogue offered two versions, one tied on quill for use with a fly rod, the other apparently on cork (or possibly wood) for use with a spinning rod. No explanation of the tying is given, or of the provenance of these patterns.

Where did Hardy's get them from? No one at the company today can tell us. But it seems very likely that their origin lies on Hugh's doorstep in the Lake District.

As young men, the Woodall family of Waberthwaite, introduced in the previous chapter, knew an angler called Marshall Warhurst, an ironmonger from Ulverston, who regularly fished the Duddon, a few miles to the southeast of Eskdale, in the 1940s. Warhurst told Bar Woodall that one night his fly had caught on a twig on the far bank. He pulled it free and began to draw it across the water to remove it. Halfway across there was a mighty swirl as a sea trout attacked it.

Warhurst was a thinking angler. He went home and tied up a fly which consisted of little more than a length of goose quill and a large single hook. The next night he returned to the pool, where he immediately hooked and landed a large sea trout.

Fortunately Warhurst did not keep this discovery to himself. In 1945 he submitted an article about it to the *Fishing Gazette*, though he did not mention the twig.

'For the past three fishing seasons I have been experimentally catching sea trout at night with a lure I describe as a "wake lure", which name fully explains its special nature' he wrote. 'This method of night fishing for sea trout is incredibly deadly on our local rivers, providing the fish are present and not too stale.

'I noticed that the first few casts with ordinary flies were more than usually likely to bring a rise . . . as a wake seemed to be the answer, I constructed some lures which were almost unsinkable, and, fished on the surface with a well greased line, they produced a super wake. The results were positively astounding!'

Warhurst's lures were made of cork, with a section of goose quill sealed at both ends to create what he called a 'buoyancy tank'. For the spinning-rod user, he recommended a clothes peg with its legs cut off. A few feathers were added, but the pattern was not critical - what mattered, said Warhurst, was the wake.

'The finished article is preposterous in size and appearance, but there is no denying its amazing attraction for the fish . . . the method is to fish down and across a smooth glide, or, in fishing a still pool, to draw the line through the rings, causing the lure to cut a steady wake' he concluded. He reported that on light nights fish would follow the lure without taking it, but that on dark ones they took it savagely.

Marshall Warhurst's exploits were brought to a wider audience by that great Lake District angler Arthur Ransome. In a broadcast on the BBC Home Service in 1956, published in Jeremy Swift's anthology *Arthur Ransome on Fishing*, Ransome explained how Warhurst's 'Zeppelin' was tied with the eye of the hook slightly behind the front end of the quill, so that it would plane across the surface.

'The thing is too big for any fly, but might be the fourteenth cousin of a cockchafer' wrote Ransome. 'All that matters is the V on the water. That

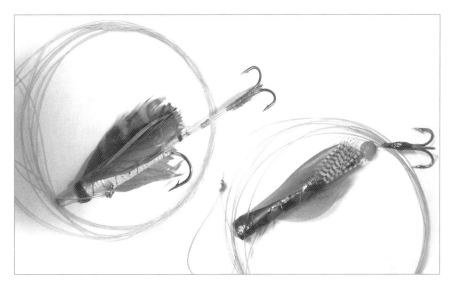

Two wake flies tied by Marshall Warhurst in the 1940s, the property of Tony Barrow (picture courtesy of Paul Hopwood).

triangular wake spreading across the pool first tells the trout that there is something stirring on the surface and then guides them to the apex of the triangle, where they find that something, active and in motion, inviting them to close their jaws on it before it can get away.'

Ransome got the point, though he too glossed over the distinction between trout and sea trout. He reported that by 1948 the wake lure was revolutionising night fishing in the North Country rivers. He described how in that year he had attended a demonstration of the fly by Warhurst, who greatly impressed the author by landing a near double-figure sea trout on it, following it immediately with a salmon of similar size.

Ransome himself ventured out at night only once, for the sake of trying out his friend's invention - getting his fingers badly bruised by the reel handle as a big sea-trout powered off with both lure and cast.

The modern origin of the Falkus wake lure can therefore be dated back with some precision to the river Duddon and the summer of 1942, twenty years before *Sea Trout Fishing* was published. Some anglers on Welsh sewin rivers like the Dovey were apparently using the Mouse, a floating deerhair concoction which is still popular today, by around the same time. But the idea of using drag to entice a trout or sea trout (or indeed any fish that hunts live prey near the surface) is certainly much older.

Back to Bickerdyke and *The Book of the All-Round Angler*. This 1888 classic included a chapter on night or 'bustard' fishing, the bustard being a fluffy moth-like pattern which, as he reported, was then the standard pattern for night fishing for 'trout'. Bickerdyke advocates the use of a brown or white fly, fished only after full darkness has arrived, and gently retrieved. He refers particularly to its use on the Cumbrian Eden.

Ransome, however, leads us further back than this; more than a century further. He quotes *The North Country Angler, or the Art of Angling as Practised in the Northern Counties of England,* an angling classic published anonymously in 1786: 'The body of the fly is at least as thick as a goose's quill, with a great rough head . . . when I have thrown it out to its full length I draw it back by little pulls . . . when I hear a fish break the water and feel my line stop, I generally strike, though great fish hook themselves by closing their mouths and turning their heads.'

It is unlikely that history stops (or starts) there. No doubt someone, somewhere, caught a sea trout on a floating lure, by accident or design, long before the author of *The North Country Angler*. But until Falkus came on the scene it remained an arcane trick. He turned the wake fly into a nationally-accepted technique for catching sea trout, now acclaimed as deadly on rivers the length and breadth of Britain. Anyone who complained that the HF Surface Lure was crude - consisting as it did of little more than a chunk of cork trailing a treble hook - was missing the point. It was all about creating that 'V' on the water.

Technology has moved the wake fly on in the past forty years, of course. Today's patterns are lighter and much more sophisticated (at least to the angler's eye) than the device pictured on page 35 of the first edition of *Sea Trout Fishing*, but it is still the wake that provokes the take.

As to the choice of sunk flies, Falkus exhorted us to abandon the conventional patterns of the past. 'Many years ago the orthodox type of sea-trout fly in general use - stubby, tail-bewhisked, in size little more than an overgrown brown trout wet fly - seemed to me an illogical form of lure for sea trout' he wrote. 'I came to the conclusion that these flies were too small and, in the majority of cases, of the wrong shape.' By which he meant too short, too fat and too heavily dressed. He concluded after much experimentation that the sea-trout hunter's fly box should contain no more than half a dozen patterns, of which the most important was the Medicine Fly, a simple pattern consisting of an ultra-slim silver-painted body, a wigeon, teal or brown mallard wing and a blue hackle.

In the years that followed, this fly continued to be Falkus' first choice for

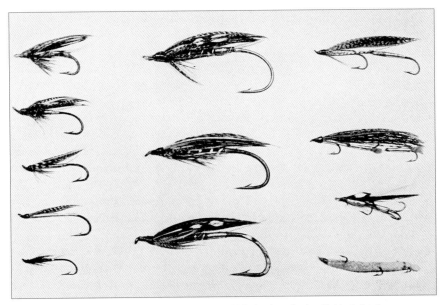

A plate from Horsley's Fishing for Trout and Salmon *(1944) showing a fly virtually identical to the*
HF Medicine Fly (left-hand column, fourth from top), along with several tandem lures.

general sunk-line fishing. For the second edition it formed the basis of a
tandem version with a long peacock-herl wing, the HF Sunk Lure.

Falkus is widely assumed to have created the Medicine. He seems to have
endorsed the claim himself; certainly he signed off a reference to this effect
by the Flyfisher's Classic Library on the imprint page of their 1995 limited
edition of *The Sea Trout*. But fly patterns can be reinvented, renewed and
rechristened at the twist of a hackle, and there are as many variations of
successful ones as there are tyers. In truth the Medicine is indistinguishable
from the Silver Blue and its relations, patterns which had been used on
the North Country rivers for many years. An example appears, unnamed,
in Horsley's 1944 book *Fishing for Trout and Salmon*, complete with the
instruction to paint the shank with silver nail varnish. Only the name was
new, and that, as Falkus himself stated in his book, was suggested by
'Briggy' Wilson.

Tandem patterns play a starring role in the second edition of *Sea Trout
Fishing*, but only one such is referred to in the first. Even then Falkus was
not quite in the vanguard, having been pre-empted (once again) by Horsley.
On the same plate as the Silver Blue appears a double-hooked 'demon' lure

which is all but indistinguishable from the HF Sunk Lure. W. E. Davies, in his little book *Salmon and Sea Trout Fishing* (Elliott Right Way Books, 1957) gives us a page full of tandem 'demons' and 'terrors' which are also very similar, and would fly out of any tackle dealer's shop in Cumbria or Wales as quickly today.

Anglers who tear their hair out trying to get the better of sea trout that refuse to take a fly properly may have recourse to a cunning little North Countryman's wrinkle which was enthusiastically popularised by Falkus - the fly-maggot. As described in *Sea Trout Fishing*, this consisted of placing two or three maggots on the hook of a small, conventional single fly and fishing it very slowly.

This is another technique whose true origins melt into the mists of time. Far from being kept as a trick up the sleeve for those difficult nights when fish will not take conventionally, it seems to have been regarded in the North Country as a standard way of taking sea trout. It was certainly popular on the Esk long before Falkus' day, having been used routinely by the Woodall family and those they fished with before the war. Its earliest mention in the literature appears to be by W. C. Stewart (1857) in *The Practical Angler*, which is listed in the bibliography of *Sea Trout Fishing*. Stewart stated firmly that the method was 'not fly fishing' and claimed that it changed the character of the sport 'from the most clean and pleasant to the most disagreeable of all the methods of capturing trout'. He was referring, of course, to trout in general and was not writing in the context of night fishing.

W. H. Lawrie had no such reservations. *Border River Angling* advised that the addition of a maggot to the bend of the hook would treble the number of 'trout' taken. Lawrie also described a development of his own, to be announced by Hardy in their catalogue of the same year - a double-hook pattern specifically designed for the maggot, which was to be attached to the forward hook, tucked under the body of the fly. In its final refinement this fly had a double hook at the rear and the angler was invited to add a maggot to either or both.

Falkus added little to this advice in 1962, offering no variant on the single hook - again, the Falkus factor was the rationale he built up for the method, coupled with systematic trialling. He challenged earlier writers who had condemned the fly-maggot as too easy and too deadly, pointing out that over many nights of experimentation he had found that the addition of a maggot failed as often as not. He advocated its use on stale, late-season, low-water fish.

Not until the second edition came along did Falkus introduce a refinement of his own to the fly-maggot. This was the famous 'Secret Weapon', a single-hook fly with a tiny flying treble whipped to its shank, a pattern which remains a strong seller in tackle shops to this day. This may be a true Falkus invention, though it had been foreshadowed elsewhere in the literature, ironically by Holiday, who had suggested that the treble at the rear of a small tube fly makes a better vehicle for a maggot than a single hook.

But *Sea Trout Fishing* gave us much more than a list of techniques. It provided a root-and-branch reappraisal of the vital elements of fishing success - including much that applies across fishing in general - and urged the reader to overhaul his entire approach, from rivercraft and knots to wading strategy and the identification of wildlife.

Nor, of course, did Falkus stop at telling us how and when to fish. In contrast to previous writers on the subject, he exhorted us in urgent tones to get out there and get on with it. In fact, he practically drove us to the riverbank at gunpoint.

Don't wait for the perfect night that so rarely comes. Ignore the wiseacre who hangs up his rod and speaks of thunder; let others tap the glass and funk the ground mist; don't worry if the air is dry or the grass is wet or the wind is north, south, east or west, if you want to fish, then fish. And, which is more, go on fishing - however poor the conditions - because you will neither gain experience nor catch many fish if you don't. Fish all night, if free to do so . . . you will get an offer at some time during the night. Nothing must be allowed to undermine your confidence, for nothing can be done on the river without it.

In the second edition, Falkus took the chance to expand considerably on the peripheral issues of sea-trout fishing. He went more deeply into the science of angling, with discussions of issues such as why hooks come out (asserting that they can actually be *too* sharp, a claim which has found few supporters), and dealt in detail with issues such as knots, the choice of nylon and the breeding and management of worms and maggots. There is also much digression into matters which are at best peripheral to the game, such as the identification of animal tracks and trails, the ways of commercial poachers, cooking tips and how to skin an eel. Chapter 5 contains two full pages on the place of the owl in literature.

In the end, those who carp on darkened riverbanks, forty years on, over the detail of Falkus' technical advice are missing the point. Looked upon as a manual, *Sea Trout Fishing* is excellent and comprehensive, but it is not beyond challenge - mainly because the author's experience was largely confined to his beloved Esk and its neighbours, which are very different waters from the sea-trout rivers of Scotland, Wales and south-west England. The King James Bible of sea trout fishing? Perhaps not. But few anglers would dispute the claim that it stands as the most comprehensive, the most powerfully written and the most inspiring book ever written on the subject.

Not the last, of course. Someone had to follow Falkus, and in the event the baton was picked up by those two luminaries of the Welsh sea-trout angling scene Moc Morgan and Graeme Harris, whose *Successful Sea Trout Angling* was published in 1989 by Blandford Press. The authors began by taking full and detailed account of the literature that had preceded their work and giving warm credit to Falkus' book.

Moc Morgan had asked Falkus to write a foreword, to which Hugh at first agreed. The copy was slow in coming. When Graeme Harris pursued him for it, Falkus said that if Harris would write a suitable foreword on his behalf, he would put his signature to it. Harris duly drafted some text, but at the last minute, Falkus changed his mind. Instead the foreword was done by Sandy Leventon, Editor of *Trout and Salmon.*

According to his friend Tim Thomas, Falkus did not want anyone to think he had somehow handed the torch on to another author. 'He felt his book should still stand as the definitive work on sea-trout fishing' says Thomas. 'He did not want to give the impression that he was sanctioning a new work which could be seen as taking over from it.'

Successful Sea Trout Angling, like *Sea Trout Fishing*, remains in print. It is both complementary and complimentary to Falkus' work.

'[*Sea Trout Fishing*] was immediately acknowledged as a modern classic of the angling literature and very soon became a best-seller - quite rightly so, because it broke new ground in both the very high quality of the publication itself and more importantly in the manner of the presentation' say the authors in their introduction. 'Gone was the substantially anecdotal style of writing beloved by earlier authors, to be replaced by the highly-readable instructive prose of a professional writer, who, moreover, knew his stuff.

'Most authors of fishing books eventually tell you what to do. Some may even tell you how to do it. Falkus not only told you what and how, he also explained when, where and more unusually, why.'

The authors went on to explain their decision to embark on a new book about the sport by pointing out, in carefully diplomatic terms, that their own experience, and that of most of their fellow Welsh anglers, was different from that described by Falkus. Anglers in the Principality, they pointed out, had been catching plenty of big sea trout for years with their own approaches and techniques. They explained that they had read *Sea Trout*

Fishing several times and had tested its doctrines, but they had both found, on several fisheries including the Towy, Teifi and Dovey, that they caught more fish by going back to their own tried-and-tested methods.

They do not, for example, support the Falkus view that the angler must refrain from making his first cast until it is completely dark. These Welsh rivers are in general bigger and longer than Hugh's Esk, and because many of them wind for miles through rich dairy-farming country they do not run crystal clear in their lower reaches, even at summer low. It is probably for these reasons that Welsh anglers find a dusk start is no bar to a good night's fishing, as long as the quietest reaches are left until full darkness.

Nor do Harris and Morgan agree with Falkus that if fish are not taking on a known stretch of water, it is unlikely that they will be taking elsewhere. Again, Falkus could speak with authority as far as the stony Lake District rivers were concerned, but it would be a mistake to apply his rules unquestioningly in Scotland, Wales or the West Country.

Unfortunately many of today's anglers appear to have taken these subtle discrepancies as their cue to challenge the whole edifice of Falkusian teaching. The author would very much like to have caught a sea trout for every time he has heard Falkus dismissed during a bankside discussion simply because he tried to deny us an extra twenty minutes of crepuscular sport, or because he stood so confidently by the Medicine and the Sunk Lure - two flies which do not seem to work half so well in Wales as they apparently did in the Esk in its days of plenty.

Indeed, fly choice is a subject on which many Welsh anglers would challenge Falkus. The Welshman's favourite sunk-lure pattern is more often than not a big black one, usually with a garnishing of silver, and maybe a touch of red for luck. Yet the most that Falkus could find to say about dark flies was that they are 'not ineffective'.

Falkus's teachings were detailed, specific, and in places perhaps a little dogmatic. His insistence that sea trout almost never feed in fresh water was certainly an exaggeration. True enough that Esk sea trout scarcely feed after leaving the sea; there is next to nothing for them to eat. It is a lean and rocky river which produces barely enough fly life to see the young fish through their junior years. No doubt, before the days of acid rain, things were better, but not much. The major rivers of Scotland and Wales are different, and so are their sea trout. Hugh himself discovered this when, in later years, he lived in Wales for a while and was introduced to its sewin, not always at such close quarters as he might have expected.

But the dissenters are missing the point. It is not for the technical advice that we continue to read *Sea Trout Fishing;* it is for the inspiration it offers. Could any angler with blood in his veins read the introduction to the second edition without longing for the river? Or leaf through the pages of instruction and encouragement that follow, for the first time or the hundred-and-first, without a soaring of courage and a growing certainty that the fish are out there in the dark, simply waiting for him to play his part?

A degree of technical skill is important in the conquest of sea trout, but without confidence, persistence and determination it is quite useless. Hugh helped us to find those qualities; he is still doing so.

Successful Sea Trout Angling builds on several ideas introduced by Falkus. Harris and Morgan even took the Falkus concept of dividing the night into stages and suggested two extensions - the 'warm-up', the early dusk period when the angler may choose to try out his tackle away from the main fish-holding pools; and 'kick-off', the short period immediately before full darkness.

More valuably, they entered territory unexplored in Falkus' book by pointing out that all sea trout are not the same, because the fish's behaviour changes with time after the migration from salt water to fresh. They offered a fourfold classification: travellers, fish which are passing through a pool en route to a destination upstream; resters, those which are staying put until the following night; stayers, those which remain until a change in conditions (usually a spate) send them on their way again; and stoppers, fish which are already near the redds and will not move again until the time to spawn is near.

According to Malcolm Greenhalgh, Falkus gave a somewhat grudging approval to Harris and Morgan's book and accepted this new classification system.

Curiously, many of the comments we hear today about Falkus simply betray the fact that the speaker has not read him properly. Anglers who know the value of using small flies and fine points on stale fish in low water often comment that this is contrary to Falkus. Not so. Check page 48 of the second edition: ' . . . as July turns to August and August to September, a smaller fly can also be used, and with increasing advantage'.

Some of those who fished with Falkus in later years have challenged his reputation. There have been dismissive comments, and suggestions that he was not particularly efficient at putting fish on the bank.

Those who knew Falkus in his prime will have none of it. 'He was a master at night fishing' says Fred Buller, who fished with him for over thirty years in Eskdale, Scotland and Ireland. 'He got into a rhythm when he was casting a fly. He fished with great concentration, and usually caught more fish than anyone else.' Fred J. Taylor adds: 'Hugh was a wonderful fisherman. He used to believe that you could sense when a fish was about to take. Sometimes he would calculate the precise moment in advance - he would count to six or seven and then strike just as the fish took. It was very impressive to witness.'

What few records survive from the 1950s and 60s bear witness to Falkus' skill at putting fish on the bank. David Burnett has a photograph of twenty-three sea trout laid out on the lawn at Cragg, caught on the night of 31st July, 1965, by Falkus, Peter Dams, Briggy Wilson and Tom Rawling. Falkus took ten of them.

But Falkus had begun fishing seriously for sea trout in 1945, and long before the second edition of *Sea Trout Fishing* was published his hunger for fish on the bank had begun to fade. Never believing it right to kill fish you were not going to eat, and a furious opponent of the idea of catching fish simply to put them back, he began to spend far more time on the bank than in the water. He would give help and advice freely to his friends and guests, yet rarely wet a line himself.

There were fine books on sea-trout fishing before Falkus, and there have been fine ones since. The question of their relative technical merit will no doubt be debated endlessly. But so far, no writer has produced a book anywhere near as inspirational, as moving or as beautifully written as *Sea Trout Fishing - A Guide to Success.*

XI

Holding Court

It was the friendliest little river I've ever known.
I would fish all night, and pray the dawn would never come.
FRED J. TAYLOR

BY THE late 1960s the success of Falkus' writings on sea trout had begun to expand his circle of fishing friends and to draw an increasing flow of visitors to Cragg Cottage. There were many favours to return to those who had accommodated or entertained him during his post-war wanderings. There were also many new-found angling friends and acquaintances who were keen to get to know this new champion of their craft, and to visit the valley where he had learned it.

With income uncertain and money tight, paying guests made a valuable contribution to the Cragg housekeeping budget. The guest roster was managed discreetly through contacts made on the grapevine. Anglers who crossed Falkus' path, usually by writing to express admiration for *Sea Trout Fishing* or through introductions on other rivers, would be invited to come and stay. Hugh issued the invitations and the joining instructions - you fished as his guest, but paid for your bed and board. He would never discuss rates or payment arrangements. Such matters were always referred to Kathleen, who managed the housekeeping throughout their years together.

Those who became friends had the choice of two spare bedrooms, one a double, the other equipped with two single beds. Paying guests were usually annexed to a green caravan parked up on Whin Hill, a low gorse-covered eminence facing the end of the track up to the cottage. This gave slightly more convenient access to the river, which lies several hundred yards from the cottage; Fred J. Taylor and his brother Ken used it from choice.

In the summer months, both cottage and caravan were usually fully booked. No charge was made to friends, but no one would have dreamed of turning up without a few bottles of whisky or wine, or a contribution to the larder.

Hugh would greet newcomers with coffee, whisky and chat on arrival. In high summer Kathleen would serve a gargantuan farmhouse breakfast at lunchtime, after which there would be reconnaissance and a council of war before an afternoon nap and dinner. As the season advanced and night fishing began earlier, the evening meal would be brought forward accordingly. Eventually it would be pushed back again to ten-thirty or so, to allow time for a couple of hours' fishing first.

Fishing was all but compulsory for paying guests, but those who joined the ranks of the Trusties (never a defined group, but the term Falkus liked to apply to those who had won his friendship) would often come to Cragg purely for the social dimension and leave their rods in their bags for the duration - unless fish were running in numbers and the river's call became too strong to resist.

Everyone who visited Cragg agrees on the subject of Kathleen and her cooking; it was straightforward, very English, and absolutely first-class. All the bread served in the cottage was baked by Kath herself in her Aga, and there were joints of roast Herdwick lamb from the farm, sides of beef and her own superlative steak-and-kidney pies. Beans, peas, cauliflowers, root vegetables and herbs came from the cottage garden, as did blackberries, blackcurrants and raspberries, served fresh or in a pie, and with cream by the jugful.

There were sea trout and salmon of course, along with portion-sized brown trout from the becks, and sometimes hot-smoked eels, which Hugh would catch by leaving a worm anchored in a back eddy (he did not hesitate to use a worm for the sea trout too, if fish were needed for the table). The gun brought woodpigeons and rabbits, and the occasional cut of wild venison was supplied by Hugh's stalking contacts. In autumn and winter there were pheasants, ducks and wild geese.

Hugh loved sea fishing: barnacle-fisted sailors' sea fishing, with drift and trawl nets, rather than the rod-and-reel variety, except for the odd occasion when he and his friends might chuck out a lure for mackerel. His favourite shipmate was Paul Pedersen, a full-time professional fisherman who owned a small vessel working out of Ravenglass. 'If they gave caps for inshore fishing, this man would get one' said Falkus of Pedersen in his BBC film *Self Portrait of a Happy Man*. Hugh would join him for a day or two at a time,

Falkus fishing out of Ravenglass on Paul Pedersen's boat (Arthur Oglesby).

returning exhausted but refreshed. He and any friends he took with him would be under orders from Kath to bring back whatever fish she needed for the table. They contributed codling, plaice, sole and turbot, crabs and lobsters from the pots and once a tope (caught by Fred Buller). 'Nothing we buy means quite so much to us as the food we catch or grow ourselves' said Falkus in *Self Portrait*.

None of it was wasted. Kathleen Falkus ran a tight kitchen. She would label each item of food carefully, using everything in sequence. She knew just how long to hang a pheasant or a duck and how to tell a bird that would roast or casserole well from one that was better used in a pâté or soup. A freezer became an early necessity and before long the couple acquired two, one for fish and one for game.

All of this was outside Hugh's province, of course; his domain encompassed the study and the sitting-room. He was happy to do the washing-up, but this was a rare concession from a man who continued to inhabit a highly traditional male-dominated world. Splitting logs for the fire suited him better than any form of work in the house, and he did it with his customary determination and vigour, fashioning a trestle for the purpose and producing vast quantities of expertly-cut firewood.

HF and Fred Buller in Portnellan Bay on Loch Lomond in 1970, a cast away from the spot where Tommy Morgan hooked his 47lb record pike and Buller once lost one at least as big. The small pike was Hugh's only catch that day.

Falkus never fished competitively, certainly not after the early, hungry years were over. Though he would exult in the successes of his friends and pupils, he treated his own catches as of little importance. He wrote in *The Stolen Years* that he had never caught a salmon over thirty pounds (though he told a story of losing a much bigger one on the river Tweed), a sea trout over fifteen pounds, a pike over eighteen pounds or a brown trout over six-and-a-half pounds (a list of conquests which would delight most anglers).

Dogs became an early feature of the Cragg life; always labradors, and always a pair - black at first and later yellow. The affection and indulgence both Hugh and Kathleen lavished on their animals were exactly like that of any other couple who, from necessity or choice, place dogs at the centres of their lives instead of children.

Only the best dogs, of course. Prince, who starred with Stinky Wow-Wow in *Self Portrait of a Happy Man* (it was Hugh who chose the names), had been sired by Sandringham Sidney, one of the Queen's field trial champions. 'My dogs play such a very large and happy part in my life' said Falkus in the film, hugging and patting Prince like a breeder in a dog-food commercial. 'I know there are people who hate dogs, but I feel there's a great chunk of living that dog-haters know absolutely nothing about.'

Winter walk with the dogs (BBC).

Though Hugh and his wife scarcely appeared in shot together in *Self Portrait*, in company he was capable of showing great affection for her, and full respect for her talents. A farm girl with a basic education she may have been, but she was bright, curious and knowledgeable. She helped him in his writing from the earliest days, assembling proofs and on occasion helping him with research.

Like a latter-day Professor Higgins, Hugh did his best to 'improve' his own Eliza Doolittle by correcting her broad Cumbrian speech. The re-modelling job he did on her vowels was obvious to their friends, and can be detected on the soundtrack of *Self Portrait*. Whatever we might think of this half a century later, Kathleen was apparently very proud of the result.

Despite all this, there were times when Falkus would patronise Kathleen cruelly. He did not hesitate to upbraid her in the hearing of the company if a meal was delayed or the care of a guest had in some way been over-looked. Nor was there any question, when it came to Scotch and story-telling, of her ever being accepted as an honorary man. In Kath's company (or that of any woman) Hugh would impose a censor on off-colour material, and when she herself tried to tell some story which he thought inappropriate or insufficiently entertaining, he would cut her off.

Kathleen bakes, Hugh ties.

Hugh and Kathleen in the garden at Cragg, around 1970.

"Daunty doesn't want to hear that!" he told her when she tried to tell Mike Daunt, the man who would inherit his casting-instructor mantle, an innocent joke.

Kathleen was no doormat, and the response could be fiery. But in the early years, at least, their clashes did not get beyond the verbal.

'Their relationship never appeared to be that of husband and wife, more that of gentleman and housekeeper' says Daunt. 'But she was devoted to him and I'm sure could never have contemplated life without him.'

Fred J. Taylor would agree. 'A lovely, lovely girl' is his verdict. 'She was the kindest of hostesses, the finest of cooks, the sweetest woman. There was only ever one man in her life and she would do anything for him. I don't half miss her.' Fred dedicated a cookery book, *One for the Pot*, to Kath.

Kathleen was undoubtedly devoted, and faithful, to Hugh. Bill Arnold remembers her response when an eminent visitor, a biologist, made a pass at her - she kneed him in the crutch. This did not stop her flirting herself with men she liked, though it was always meant innocently.

Hugh continued to display a tendency to reinvent the past quite blatantly, particularly when speaking to the press. Interviewed by John Bield of the *Daily Telegraph* in 1981, he said that in the wake of his broadcasting career he could have become a millionaire. 'We both decided that Hollywood and the bright lights were not worth the price' he said. 'So we came here, and have never regretted it.'

It would be comforting to believe that Kathleen, the tireless cook and home-maker, the devoted wife, the contented countrywoman drawing joy from the fells, the flowers and the butterflies, was happy at the prospect of spending the rest of her life in that idyllic valley, with no cares beyond the domestic. It would probably be unfair. Undoubtedly she was willing to settle for Cragg and Hugh, but she gave hints that she would have liked to see more of the world. After Hugh's death she told a friend, Roland Carson, that she had at first seen his arrival on the scene not as his ticket into Eskdale, but her ticket out.

As hosts, Hugh and Kath undoubtedly made a good team. Their roles were perfectly complementary. Kath ruled the kitchen and all matters domestic, leaving Hugh to revel in his role as lord of the valley and king of the river.

The forcefulness of his personality impressed all who met him. The angling writer Brian Clarke wrote in his obituary for *The Times* that Falkus 'was, with Ted Hughes, one of one of the only two men I have ever met who could fill a room simply by being in it'. Very few stood up to him, or wanted to; fewer still ever got the better of him.

'Imagine that you are fishing with me and staying at my cottage' wrote Falkus in *Sea Trout Fishing*. 'During conditions of low water when night fishing is in force, as it usually is, you will be out from dusk until dawn. After which, we shall sit and drink coffee and whisky, admire each other's catch, discuss the night's events and watch the sunrise. Then, bed.'

And so it was. Visitors to Cragg, whether they were retired military men, captains of industry, consultant surgeons, successful actors or writers or just humble angling novitiates up for a taste of the great man's company, learned the Falkus code and were happy to follow it.

The available fishing tended to vary from year to year, according to Falkus' variable relations with his neighbours. Up to half a dozen anglers at a time would generally be allowed on the river. Fly fishers would get first choice of the pools, but the worm-throwers were welcome if there was space, particularly when turbid water ruled out the night fly.

The pressure on this crystalline little river could be rather too great for good sport, particularly after a prolonged spell without rain. The score or so of named pools between Linbeck and the tide would be fished night after night, and not always by anglers whose touch was as delicate as Falkus'. He believed that it was impossible to overfish a pool if you did it properly, for sea trout as for salmon; Fred Buller disagreed, as would many sea-trout hunters. When there were too many fishermen and too few fish, Fred would sometimes avoid a dry net by working his fly through the tiny dubs and hidden potholes where an untutored fish might be found. Knowledge of the river, as always with night fly fishing, was critical. Our bigger sea-trout rivers have long, deep pools and glides where a careful angler can hope to take fish throughout the night, and even perhaps share his territory with a companion. Not so on the Cumbrian Esk, where a dozen casts will cover a pool and a clumsy one can empty it.

Staying at Cragg was not to be confused with going on some kind of holiday with a little angling thrown in when you felt like it. Rather, this was game-fishing summer camp, with Falkus your commandant and the tireless pursuit of sea trout or salmon (according to season and water conditions) your mission. Woe betide you if you had other ideas.

Few visitors did. Most people relished the experience, feeling only too flattered to be directed in their efforts by the celebrated author in person.

If you imagined that your duties as a guest had been fulfilled once fishing was over, you might well have a surprise in store. Should Falkus invite you to take a Gaelic coffee, a mug of Cragg tea (as much whisky as tea) or a tumbler of malt with him and his friends, no matter that it might be five in the morning and the sun rising, you were expected to join in with a will or give a good reason why not. The same applied at night. 'If he saw you yawning or looking at your watch as if you were thinking of going to bed, he would challenge you immediately, and remind you that it might be your last day on earth' says Fred Buller. 'If you had to be up in the morning, that was fine - as long as you had explained that to Hugh.'

You would be unlikely to catch Frank Plum yawning or looking at his watch. Frank was a physiotherapist from Blackburn, a man who had done well enough in life (having received a large inheritance from his father, who had served as a doctor with the British Army in India during the last days of the Raj) to be able to take plenty of time off for recreation.

Frank was one of those happy men who go fishing and shooting for the *craic* and the company, rather than the desire to prove themselves by contributing very much to the bag. An indifferent performer with rod and gun, he did not much trouble the Esk's sea trout and salmon, or, in winter, its ducks and geese. Although Frank had a left master eye, he shot for most of his life with a gun set up for a right-eyed sportsman. This had the effect of doubling his intended lead when birds flew from left to right and reducing it to zero when they crossed the other way.

Unsurprisingly, Frank rarely hit anything. The effect was all the greater when on one cherished occasion a mallard flew over with a gale behind it at an estimated eighty miles per hour from his left and he knocked it stone dead, in full view of Falkus and the rest of the party.

Hugh, Michael Heaton, Kath and Frank Plum in the cottage in about 1970. Hugh's beloved 4-bore is on the wall.

A natural extrovert, Plum was most in his element acting the fool, playing poker or putting the world to rights over a bottle or two of Scotch with Falkus and fellow members of the inner circle; he was one of the very few men who could drink even Hugh under the table. He was Hugh's host, chauffeur and gillie on countless fishing and shooting trips away from Eskdale, and would take him salmon fishing on the Spey or wildfowling on Lochar Moss in Dumfriesshire, a favourite hunting ground for both men. The Plums even took Hugh and Kath with them on two Continental holidays in the late 1970s, one of them involving partridge shooting in Spain. Ever generous with his money, Frank would help the Falkuses out financially by discreetly settling domestic bills.

Frank was Hugh's comrade-in-arms on many of their less responsible adventures. He was with Hugh one summer day in the 1960s when they took a rowing boat out from Ravenglass for a spot of plaice fishing. The day was fine and the sea calm, so Hugh decided it was safe enough to take the little craft out beyond the sandbar that divides the triple estuary from the open sea; a dangerous thing to do, as he well knew. As Frank was pulling the anchor up over the bow the rope slipped out of the fairlead and slid around the side of the boat, with the result that the dinghy swung broadside on to the tide.

Frank Plum and HF after a successful fishing trip.

Falkus afloat with Frank Plum.

HF, Frank Plum, Michael Heaton and Kathleen toasting the maiden voyage of the Poing.

The next moment both men found themselves in the water, clinging to the upturned hull.

Hugh, who had survived much worse scrapes than this, assured Frank that if they simply held on tight and waited, the tide would carry them safely into the shallows. They waited - and waited. Eventually, realising that the shore was not getting any closer, Frank ventured to remind Hugh of the anchor and to speculate that it might be responsible for their lack of movement. Falkus' response was unprintable. He handed Frank his knife and ordered him to dive under the boat and cut the rope. They drifted to safety, and Frank took great pleasure in relating the skipper's blunder to their friends back at Cragg.

Not all these maritime escapades ended in laughter. David Burnett remembers Falkus' reaction when the Ravenglass fishermen spoke (in rather too much graphic detail) of having brought in a long-submerged corpse.

'Hugh didn't say a word - we drove back from the harbour in complete silence. When we got to the cottage, he went straight into the study, poured himself an enormous tumbler of whisky and downed it. Then he poured another, and downed that. Then he slumped down at his desk with his head in his hands. I might as well not have been in the room.'

One summer Frank was with Hugh, Fred Buller and another Trusty, Michael Heaton, when they launched a new Swedish clinker-built dinghy, christened for some reason the *Poing*. Frank suggested that the new craft should be launched on the river and steered down to the estuary with the current, and, after toasting her in champagne served in paper cups by Kathleen, that is just what they did. Frank was also there when Falkus got into trouble with the Ministry of Defence for sailing his boat into the danger area while firing was taking place from the range at Eskmeals.

Frank's physical prowess and fearless nature - he had been a competitive rugby player in his youth - proved useful when it came to shooting a sequence of still photographs for *Freshwater Fishing* (also used in *Sea Trout Fishing*) to demonstrate how to escape drowning if you are unlucky or careless enough to fall into a river wearing waders. Falkus ordered Frank to model for the pictures. Frank was none too thrilled at the prospect, but earned himself a small role in angling history by pretending to lose his balance on cue and conducting himself as directed while Fred Buller took the pictures.

Frank was also clever and well read, and was well able to hold his own in conversation with Falkus when the talk turned to poetry and philosophy.

'Hugh used to say that he needed to have his brain fed, and Frank was very good at that' says Fred Buller. 'He was one of those who would still be knocking back the whiskies with us at four in the morning.'

Tom Rawling, mentioned in Chapter IX, was not of that company; his qualifications for admission to the Falkus inner circle were the opposite. A Lakeland-born teacher and a talented and sensitive poet, Rawling took fishing, and life, rather more seriously than many of Hugh's friends, so they tended not to mind too much when he chose the riverbank in preference to a poker-and-whisky session.

But Rawling was both a dedicated angler and a competent writer on the subject and he was in thrall to Falkus and his teachings, having learned about them from the first edition of *Sea Trout Fishing* and practised them successfully on the Cumbrian rivers. Rawling's devotion to Falkus and his methods bordered on adoration. 'He has complete mastery of his tackle - it does exactly what his brain tells it to do' he wrote. 'He moves like a great tiger, intent on his prey, observing and assessing its behaviour.' Rawling's reports of the success the Falkus approach had brought him were a valuable boost for the book, and earned Falkus' lasting appreciation and gratitude.

Hugh was very comfortable in the company of those true disciples, like Rawling, whose adherence to his teachings was total. He could be equally at ease with those who did not challenge them simply because they did not fish. Into this category came Tim Rickett, one of the three men to whom he dedicated the second edition of *The Stolen Years* (the others were Antony Witherby and David Burnett).

Rickett was for many years Secretary of the Flyfishers' Club, and, like most holders of that esteemed post, he was a non-angler. In the company of Hugh's friends, he made up for that by the strength of his personality. Fred Buller describes him as 'a wonderful raconteur with a great sense of humour - an expressive and witty man, whose laughter was contagious'. Rickett was also a great favourite of Kathleen.

On visits to London in the 1970s, Falkus would stay with Tim Rickett in his flat at the Flyfishers' Club. But in the summer of 1980 Rickett collapsed as he was stepping from a taxi outside the club, and died on the spot of a heart attack. Falkus, deeply upset at the loss of his friend, resigned, saying that there was no point in continuing his membership. David Burnett followed suit. 'I did so like that man' Falkus wrote to Jo Rippier that September. 'He was a true friend and a very *kind* man. I have felt utterly depressed since hearing the news. Whatever shall we do without him?'

Falkus and Buller by the tarn at Knott End.

Buller felt that Falkus was glad to have an excuse to resign from the Flyfishers', because by the time Tim Rickett died he was finally ready to break off relations with the city which had once been his headquarters.

'He would stand outside the cottage, swing an outstretched arm around the skyline and say "that's where civilisation ends"' says Fred Buller. 'After his broadcasting career finished he had no reason to leave the valley except for fishing and shooting expeditions, and in his last few years he hardly did so.'

No one was a more valued Trusty than Fred himself, dubbed by Falkus the finest angler he had ever known.

We had a hunger for each other's company. We never went more than four or five weeks without meeting, but after the first few years I never went to Cragg for the fishing. It was always to see Hugh. When I got there we couldn't wait to get into the study to discuss the news and go over the latest developments. I would feel drunk with pleasure during those encounters, they were so stimulating, so uplifting.

Hugh had a terrific brain, as well as a great talent for communication and a knack of getting to the core of a problem. His great skill lay in recognising good ideas, analysing them to see how they could be improved, and then promoting them to other anglers.

Just once Buller remembers a serious row, over the rules of poker. Falkus brought everyone's suitcases down and ordered him and two other friends, Russell and Valerie Bancroft, out of the cottage at two in the morning, something he was apt to do when he lost his temper and was the worse for whisky - particularly if he had been mixing it with wine or brandy. Fred had to join Frank Plum and his partner Mary Smallbone at their hotel (Frank had seen the storm coming, and he and Mary had quietly slipped out to avoid it).

But both men knew that their friendship - and their work together - were too important for such squabbles to be allowed to get in the way. When Fred needed to ring his co-author a week later to discuss the manuscript of *Freshwater Fishing*, the incident was not mentioned.

Fred learned early on that to remain in Falkus' company for too long at a time was a great mistake. No matter who you were and how you behaved, Hugh's patience would run out after two or three days; it was then only a matter of time before the demons would appear. Fred, like Frank, learned to spot the signs, and to find an excuse for leaving while harmony still reigned.

This understanding with Fred Buller was undoubtedly the driving force behind Falkus' greatest publishing success. The help he had given Buller with the manuscript of his second book, *Pike* (1971), had kicked off a successful writing partnership, and one that was beginning to win recognition; the pair were invited to write a series of articles for *Creel* magazine. The publishing world had just discovered partworks (no publisher recognised their possibilities earlier than Hugh's own son, Christopher) and in the early 1970s the pair were asked to contribute to one on angling.

Falkus liked to be able to see a profit from any writing venture - it was, after all, a vital part of his income - and he and Buller could see an opportunity to earn money from three sources for essentially the same work. Having developed the material for the articles and the partwork, they could use it as the starting point for something much more substantial and lasting - an authoritative volume on freshwater fish and fishing.

Buller researched most of the material for the book and wrote all the chapters, except that on the sea trout, which Falkus wrote alone, and those on the salmon, trout and eel, to which both men contributed. Buller tackled each of his chapters by researching the natural history of the fish and the history of angling for it, in the UK and abroad. Every few weeks he would drive up to Cragg so that they could work together on the text.

Buller may have done most of the work on *Freshwater Fishing*, but he is emphatic that it could not have been produced without Falkus. 'Hugh was a fine writer and a wonderful critic' he says. 'The book simply would not have worked without his input.'

In their introduction, the authors call *Freshwater Fishing* 'a book of simple purpose'. Simple its purpose may have been, but at five hundred and twenty-two closely-researched pages it is arguably the most impressive general guide to its subject ever published, thanks to the sheer weight of experience and depth of knowledge of its two authors and their determination to build solidly on the centuries of piscatorial learning that had gone before.

The book gave modern angling its proper hinterland of historical lore and technological development. Modern techniques were compared with older ones; experts across five hundred years of angling literature were quoted in context. Every fish an angler might conceivably encounter was visited, from the shads, loaches and lampreys to the vendace and the gwyniad. Cocking a snook at modern attitudes, there were even recipes for cooking most of them, though it is unlikely that any of Falkus and Buller's readers would have had, or taken advantage of, the opportunity to kill, cook and devour such rarities. Even the sturgeon and the burbot (the latter may already have been extinct in British rivers - it certainly is now) were included.

Freshwater Fishing came as a refreshing contrast to the superficial get-fish-quick angling guides which crowd the shelves of tackle shops and sporting bookshops. The reviews ranged from the excellent to the ecstatic. The film director Sir David Puttnam, writing in the *Sunday Telegraph*, dubbed it 'the most authoritative book on fishing ever written', while the angling writer Peter Stone asserted that 'no reviewer could possibly do justice to this mighty work'. Stephen Vaughan in the *Times Literary Supplement* called it 'a work of catholic collaboration as felicitous as it is knowledgeable, barbed with wit, ground-baited with arcane facts and judicious quotations, to be relished for its charm and consulted for its authority'.

Falkus was enormously proud of the recognition his writing and broadcasting achievements earned for him, and assiduously filed his reviews. One of his proudest possessions was a letter in longhand from Phoebe Somers of the Queen's English Society, which still hangs on the wall of his study. It is undated, but was probably sent in the late 1970s:

May I congratulate you on your pleasant, measured broadcasting - especially on not using popular current phrases - and even more especially on not using words to the detriment of the language, as do so many broadcasters on radio and television today. The content and the delivery of your broadcasts are a pleasure to listen to.

The year 1975 was something of an *annus mirabilis* for Falkus, thanks to the publication of his two most successful angling books; the much-expanded second edition of *Sea Trout Fishing* appeared later the same year. The friendship with Fred Buller which was cemented with the collaboration on *Sea Trout Fishing* and *Freshwater Fishing* would continue unbroken until Falkus' death.

Fred's introduction to Hugh came through the man who, in Buller's view, has been the most successful modern British angling writer of them all - Fred J. Taylor. Taylor's first visit to Cragg was in the summer of 1968, on the return leg of a trip to Scotland with his wife Carrie. Falkus escorted him up to Hazel Dub. Here Fred looked into the pellucid deeps and found himself gazing upon a shoal of sea trout which he estimated to number the best part of three hundred. "They're a harvest to be reaped!" urged Hugh, and Fred, whose skill with the worm has long been legendary, fished that night and took a good bag.

Falkus urged them to stay on for a few days, but Carrie was adamant that an appointment with her family in Fleetwood could not be broken, so Fred went back alone a week or two later. For the rest of Hugh's life, and after, he remained a regular visitor to Cragg. At first his brother Ken would accompany him; when Ken's ill health intervened, Fred's angling companion Alec Martin took his place.

Fred's favourite pool was one he called Shingle Dub - actually Knott End Dub, opposite Bill Fowler's farm. 'In the early days, those summer nights just weren't long enough' says Fred. 'I would fish all night on my own and pray the dawn would never come. It was the friendliest little river I've ever known - there was never any question of feeling scared of the dark. I would usually fish a freelined worm, with no float or lead to put the fish off. I never had a monster, but there were plenty of fish to six pounds or so.'

Falkus had a rule that the captor of any fish over five pounds must buy a bottle of champagne - and it had to be the real stuff. But Fred found later on that with advancing age (he was only one year younger than Hugh) and shrinking stocks of sea trout, fishing the night through became less pleasurable.

Not that Falkus made any distinction. His propensity for playing the bully at times is well demonstrated by this story of Fred's:

One night Ken and I were on the river and it was chucking it down. We were getting colder and colder and wetter and wetter and catching absolutely bugger all, and the water had started to rise - it was in full spate by the morning. Hugh wasn't fishing, of course - he was warm and dry in his study, putting the world to rights over a bottle of Scotch with his mates.

We were using walkie-talkies to keep in touch with 'base' and we had to keep calling in to report. Each time we spoke we told him we thought it was time to pack it in and come back and join them. But Hugh was having none of that. "Persist!" he kept saying. He always took the view that fish in the river were there to be caught and that it would be a crime to waste them.

In the end we were so miserable and so cold and wet that we began to wish we'd never come. He could be a swine like that. But he always got away with it - we still thought the world of him.

'Fat Fred', as Falkus liked to call him when he was in bantering mood, was one of the very few who got away with challenging Falkus on his teachings. Having caught sizeable fish from southern rivers which had been stuffed to the gills with coarse fishermen's maggots, he was not happy with Falkus' assertions that sea trout almost never feed in fresh water, so he wrote to raise the point with Falkus. Hugh, who had enormous respect for Fred and his writings, suggested that the fish must have been immature - a defence which cut little ice with Fred, as the maggot-scoffers had included fish of three pounds and more.

Taylor had first been encouraged to write about fishing by Richard Walker, as inspirational a figure on the coarse fishing scene as Falkus became in the game fishing world. In the 1970s, Walker asked Buller if he could arrange a visit to Cragg. Fred was glad to facilitate a first meeting between two such remarkable anglers. Buller drove Walker up for an overnight stay. The pair got on well, but the contrast in their natures - Walker was a much gentler and more diplomatic man than Falkus - would have made a close friendship unlikely even if they had not represented different regions of the angling spectrum. Falkus and Walker did however collaborate, along with Buller and Fred J. Taylor, on a book. *Successful Angling*, published in 1977 to satisfy an agreement with Hardys, was a book about coarse fishing, largely written by Fred Buller. Falkus lent his name and his blessing to it, but little else.

Falkus could be wary of anglers - and particularly angling writers - whose experience and reputation might pose a challenge to his own status. David Burnett tells a story of a game fair at which Falkus was a celebrity guest.

Fred J. Taylor and Hugh with Kathleen and Fred's friend Alec Martin.
Inset: Hugh and Richard Walker on their one encounter, at Cragg in 1977.

He found himself sharing a marquee with the American angling writer Dave Whitlock, a fly-tyer of exceptional skill. Falkus, having expected to have the stage to himself, refused to acknowledge Whitlock's presence, and the American responded in kind. When the anglers crowded round Whitlock to watch him tying a grasshopper imitation it was too much for Falkus, who coolly urinated on the grass a few feet away, Burnett holding his coat up as a screen.

He had a rather better relationship with Eric Horsfall Turner, the all-round angling expert, writer and casting champion (he once held the British trout fly distance record). Like Falkus, Horsfall Turner was one of those men who tend to excel at everything they do. He had been a top-class rugby player, an amateur heavyweight boxer and a near-scratch golfer, while his skill with the pen qualified him to edit *Anglers' Annual* for many years (while he was Editor, Falkus, with his approval, wrote a spoof article for the magazine entitled 'The development of the philosophy of dry-fly fishing for eels', under the pseudonym Oliver String).

Horsfall Turner made something of a name for himself in the years after

Morning after - Bill Bruxby and HF with the night's catch.

the war in the big-game angling world; he landed a string of giant tunny, those gigantic members of the mackerel family which were then still numerous in the North Sea. He also helped to found both the British Casting Association and the Anglers' Co-operative Association. Despite all the fishing, he somehow found time to serve for thirty-two years (1939-71) as Town Clerk of Scarborough.

Horsfall Turner ('Horsey Turnips', as Hugh liked to call him) is one of the quintet of anglers portrayed in the frontispiece of the second edition of *Sea Trout Fishing*, tackling up on the lawn at Cragg for a night-fishing session on an August evening in 1966. Alas, strangeness crept into Eric's syntax in his elder years and mental deterioration eventually took him out of circulation.

Bill Bruxby, the man on the left in that picture, fell out of favour with Falkus with great suddenness. Bruxby, an architect from Southport, lived close enough to Eskdale to be able to visit the valley regularly, and in the late 1970s he took the opportunity to buy the fishing on the Linbeck water, immediately above Knott End, from Bill and Sheila Barron. Falkus had long liked to regard the whole lower river as his for the disposing, and counted on being able to send guests up to Linbeck. But Bruxby did not wish to turn up for a night on his own fishery to find the pools occupied or recently disturbed by Falkus' guests, so he asked him to stop.

There was a further provocation. Bruxby had begun a relationship with his secretary (they later married), and had already greatly irritated Falkus, who disliked her 'townie' dress and attitudes, by bringing her with him on his visits to Cragg. The takeover of Linbeck was perceived by Falkus as one insult upon another, and the two men never spoke again. Bruxby was even cropped out of the picture for later editions of *Sea Trout Fishing*.

Arthur Oglesby, a close friend of Eric Horsfall Turner, is also in that frontispiece. Oglesby first met Hugh Falkus on Speyside in the 1950s.

Arthur Oglesby on a shoot with Falkus in Eskdale.

A retired Army officer - he was wounded leading his men into battle at Dunkirk - Oglesby spent the post-war years building up the family business (its flagship brand was Nurse Harvey's Gripe Water, the first on the market) and by the 1960s he had done a good enough job to be able to hand the business over to his brother. Still in his forties, Arthur settled in Harrogate and retired to devote the rest of his life to fishing - along with writing about it, filming it and teaching people to do it. He also wrote about shooting and photography; so prolific was his pen that he had to adopt a *nom de plume* for some titles to avoid over-exposure. In 1967 he became European Editor of the American magazine *Field and Stream,* following it up with the editorship of *Angler's Annual* and a long-lasting weekly column for *Shooting Times.* Arthur's name was scarcely out of the angling press in the 1970s and 1980s, when he took a number of enormous salmon from Norway's river Vosso, one just a few ounces shy of fifty pounds.

In 1979 the rod-making firm of Bruce and Walker, seeking exposure for its new range of carbon-fibre rods, commissioned Oglesby to make an angling film for them. Knowing Falkus' expertise in this field, Arthur approached him for help. *Game Fishing* was directed and narrated by Hugh and shot by Arthur, skilled with both moving pictures and still. They called in a professional film editor, Roger Cawood.

The film was an enjoyable, if somewhat superficial, conspectus of game angling through the seasons in England and Scotland, with a bonus visit to the Vosso in Norway. The sponsor's rods were shown being flexed by the likes of casting champion Jack Martin, Reg Righyni and Bob Church, the stillwater expert and tackle designer. Arthur and his wife Grace, an elegant caster herself, were shown fishing the Spey and Loch Voshimid in the Hebrides, and of course there was an appearance by Hugh on his beloved Esk.

The following spring Oglesby followed the film up with a second, *Fly Casting.* Hugh directed this one too, but it was Arthur, as the casting expert, who did the commentary. He took us through the correct cast to use for each occasion, from the simple overhead cast and the double haul to the steeple cast (Hugh on the Esk again) and the spey cast. This was demonstrated not by Oglesby but by Eric Robb, one of the finest spey casters in Scotland.

Oglesby was a friend of the writer, angler and conservationist Jack Hemingway, son of the novelist Ernest Hemingway, who had been a hero to Falkus since youth. Hugh himself never met Jack, but he wrote to him in the late 1980s after being put in touch by his friend Anthony Desbruslais, who met the author on a fishing trip to Labrador. Hemingway sent him a copy of his 1986 bestseller *Misadventures of a Fly Fisherman: My Life With and Without Papa*, with a note thanking Falkus 'for the pleasure his writing has given me over the years'.

Equally high on Hugh's list of influences was Henry Williamson, author of *Salar the Salmon* and *Tarka the Otter*. Williamson - Falkus told friends he had met him before the war - visited Cragg and corresponded with Hugh. In 1972 he sent him a copy of his book *Tales of a Devon Village*, apparently in return for *The Stolen Years*, which he praised in an accompanying note:

You appear to have had a marvellous childhood and youth . . . the illustrations appeal to me - clear, simple and KNOWLEDGEABLE (I write with some unhappiness over an unpublished book which took from 1955-1972 to finish - after 18 versions . . .) I had no idea you were so famous a writer and broadcaster.

(Williamson's publishers would nod at that reference - he was notorious for his inability to sign off a manuscript.)

Many of Hugh's friends were prominent figures in the angling world, and one or two were well-known in the world outside it as well. The late actor Sir Michael Hordern was one of these. Falkus had met Hordern in his days on the London stage, when the pair had enjoyed wildfowling together on the Essex marshes. In 1964 the actor tracked his old friend down through his publisher, and wrote to ask if he gave shooting instruction. He also mentioned his passion for fly fishing, and expressed a desire to pursue Hugh's sea trout with him.

'I'm ashamed to say I haven't bought your book (I will do so) but I read the articles as they come out in the *FG*' he wrote. 'The stage and various sizes of screen keep me pretty busy, but I wish I could win the pools and retire to the country.'

Hordern became a regular visitor to Cragg, and their friendship culminated in a cameo appearance by the actor in Falkus' 1977 film *Salmo the Leaper*.

Hordern was a gentle and self-effacing man. The wildlife cameraman Hugh Maynard, who filmed *Salmo*, remembers him coming down to breakfast one morning with a large Medicine Fly buried in his scalp. He had not wanted to interrupt anyone's fishing the previous night by asking for help.

But even the mild-mannered Hordern fell out with Hugh in the end, over an assertion by Falkus late one night in 1980 or 1981 that the job of an actor was simply to deliver lines written by someone else, and was thus inferior to that of a writer. It was the whisky talking as usual of course, but Hordern packed his bags on the spot and called for a cab to take him back to London. They never met again, and neither Falkus nor the Esk are referred to in Hordern's autobiography.

Sir Michael Hordern.

Patrick Allen, a household name in the 1970s for his film and television work and for being the the 'voice' of Barratt Homes, along with several other big brands, was another actor with a passion for fishing. After Mike Daunt introduced him to Falkus, the trio pursued the salmon of the Scottish rivers several times together. Patrick had promised to contribute anecdotes to this book, but sadly he died in July 2006, before it could be arranged.

For a time, Antony Witherby was a regular visitor. He was not quite as skilled at night fishing as he was at publishing, and tripped over a particular rock so many times that Hugh named it Witherby's Rock.

Falkus was a great admirer of the revered Irish game fisherman T. C. Kingsmill Moore, quoting extensively from *A Man May Fish* (which he put at the top of his list of favourite books) in *Sea Trout Fishing*, and the two men wrote to each other regularly. He visited Kingsmill Moore, a distinguished judge of the Irish High Court and Supreme Court, in Dublin during his research for that book. A new edition of *A Man May Fish* published in 1979 includes a two-paragraph foreword by Falkus in which he calls it 'by far the best book on Irish sea-trout fishing I have ever read', perhaps not quite so generous a comment as it sounds, given that such titles are not exactly numerous.

Kingsmill Moore seems to have thought very highly of Hugh and his writing. In a 1976 letter to him about *Sea Trout Fishing* he said he felt 'filled with mingled feelings of admiration for you and shame for myself'.

Conrad Voss Bark was another guest at Cragg who had achieved prominence in both the professional and the piscatorial spheres. Voss Bark, for many years the BBC's political correspondent, appeared briefly with Hugh in a scene in *Salmo the Leaper*. He died in 2001. Anne Voss Bark, who still runs the Arundel Arms Hotel in Devon, remembers fishing the Esk with her husband one summer's night.

'Hugh showed us where to fish and left us to it' she says. 'I have never seen so many sea trout - they were jumping constantly. He insisted that we fish through till dawn. We caught quite a few, but by the end of the night I could hardly lift the rod.'

Hugh's friend Maurice Wiggin, who had given him so much encouragement with his writing before the publication of *The Stolen Years*, was prepared to share his high opinion of Hugh with the world, as this passage from *A Cottage Idyll* (Thomas Nelson, 1969) shows:

Hugh is a great character, a large person, larger than life as it is lived in these emaciated times of too much mass communication and too little private communication. He has had a strange, chequered life, full of drama and not without tragedy: he is a brave man. He is very big and handsome and a great fighter, but as gentle as need be.

It is worth mentioning that, according to Fred Buller, the idea of a book along the lines of *A Cottage Idyll* had first been mooted by Falkus. When Wiggin ran with this idea and published the book without further recourse to his friend, he caused some indignation back at Cragg. Possibly his adulatory comments about Hugh were intended as an olive branch.

While most of Falkus' regular fishing and shooting companions travelled from other parts of the country to visit Cragg, there were some local men among them, not least the Woodall brothers of Waberthwaite referred to in Chapter IX. Bar, Eddie and Joe Woodall had been fishing the lower Esk since their father's days before the war, and still own the rights from Cropple How down to Cragg.

In his early years at Cragg, Falkus, never too happy about having to share what he saw as 'his' river with his neighbours, sought access to these beats to add to the fishing he already had at Cragg and Knott End. A day as the Woodalls' guest on Eddie Woodall's shoot at Langley Park, near Waberthwaite, revealed to Falkus how much he could gain by co-operating

Bar Woodall fishing on Crummock Water

Falkus shooting by the river, 1970s.

with them, and from that time on the Woodalls were regularly invited to shooting parties at Cragg. In return Hugh was made welcome on the Woodalls' shoot days and on the sections of the river they controlled.

'Once he'd seen how much sport we could give him access to he started laying some butter on us, as we say up here' says Joe Woodall. 'We didn't mind - he was such great company. Once he joined forces with us, we were friends until he died. He looked after us well at Cragg. The Christmas parties were the best - Kath's cooking was superb and there was always plenty to drink. There were wonderful presents for everyone. Eddie used to dress up as Santa Claus and hand them out.'

The Woodalls have many tales to tell of their shooting adventures with Falkus. There was the time he called in a lone mallard from an extraordinary height over the estuary, bringing it spiralling down until it was within range. Another day, when they were shooting from an islet in the estuary, they watched him shoot a wigeon, strip off, swim out and bring the bird back in his mouth (he had no dog with him). The larder was empty, and he had promised Kathleen that he would bring back a duck.

Falkus still shot with the 12-bore 3-inch BSA magnum that had belonged to his father, and some time after the war - very likely when he was married to Lady Margaret - he had acquired a pair of Stephen Grant sidelocks which had been made (according to an interview he gave to Mike Yardley of *Shooting Times*) for the honourable Henry Brougham and still bore that gentleman's name on the trigger-guards. Since no one remembers Falkus having two Grants (he would scarcely have needed them in Eskdale), it seems likely that he sold one of them to raise cash not long after the couple split up.

The 4-bore was rarely if ever used in anger after Hugh settled at Cragg, but all his friends knew how proud he was of it. Its home for decades was the wall over the door that led from the sitting-room into the kitchen. Fred Buller was a gunmaker, and could see it was in need of attention. One day in the mid 1970s he found an excuse to remove it for a while. A few weeks later he returned it to the wall stripped, cleaned and newly engraved. Falkus was delighted. Shortly after this Fred found Hugh a gun that would become his favourite for the rest of his life, a 12-bore boxlock ejector by William Armstrong.

Falkus had a penchant for giving the Esk pools new names, a source of mild irritation to those who had known the river from childhood. Hazel Dub, his favourite, was one of those he rechristened; its original name, Pool Above, was not poetic enough for him. The spot he called Willow Pool, below Cragg, was originally Kitling Pool.

This proprietorial attitude to the valley extended to doing what he could to keep out strangers and unwanted sightseers. Fans who found him in a good mood might be entertained to whisky, a lecture and a book-signing, but cold callers who caught him at the wrong moment could find themselves wishing they had never tried to make the acquaintance of the Master. On one occasion when a brace of uninvited visitors appeared at the door, Mike Daunt remembers Falkus loudly urging him to tell them to 'f*** off', knowing full well that they would hear.

Falkus' BBC friend Mike Kendall says he habitually turned round the sign at the Birkby turn-off to confuse would-be visitors. The council complained loudly through the local press, but never discovered who was behind it.

Yet Falkus could be kindness personified to those whom he saw as converts or disciples. One of these, David Pilling, met Falkus in June 1975 as a result of his decision to purchase a day-ticket for the Knott End water.

'I hadn't been fishing for more than a few minutes when Hugh Falkus himself strode up and challenged me' he says. 'He gave me quite a telling off - not for fishing where I shouldn't be, but for using a rod that was too

Falkus pours the whisky in the kitchen at Cragg.

Falkus in his familiar striped cricketing cap in a 1966 team picture for Eskdale Cricket Club.

The little blue Peugeot (the identities of the two men with Falkus are unknown).

short. But he was very kind. He put me down on Donald's, and I caught two sea trout and a grilse. He didn't ask for a penny for this, but he did make me promise to buy his book, which of course I did.'

Falkus became increasingly xenophobic in his later years. A letter to Jo Rippier dating from the early 1980s reads: 'Sellafield has done wonders for our life up here by frightening off the hordes of happy holidaymakers who would otherwise have destroyed the valley. "Hooray! Hooray!" I shout. "Keep the buggers out!"' (Following a string of accidents, the nuclear plant at Windscale had just been renamed in a not-very-successful attempt to give the place a better image.)

Rippier, then a lecturer in the English Department at Frankfurt University, had got to know Falkus in the early 1970s as the result of his admiration for the first edition of *Sea Trout Fishing*. He suggested to two friends who were going into publishing that they might ask Falkus if he would allow them to produce a new edition. One was of course already under way, but Falkus invited Rippier to Cragg and the two wrote to each other regularly from then on.

Hugh was a wonderful correspondent, whatever he was writing about. Once he decided you were a friend, every word revealed the man to the bottom of his soul. This openness, this total frankness in all things, took one by surprise. It was a privilege, and demanded an equally honest response.

Many of our letters were taken up with the subject of writing. Nobody should be fooled into thinking that Hugh's magical lucidity fell from heaven. He spoke frequently of the struggle and said how 'damnably difficult' it was - and, astonishingly, that he had failed every time, a claim with which few of his readers would agree.

Falkus' old passion for cricket had continued to burn since the post-war years. In the mid 1960s he managed to rekindle enough local interest to get a cricket club going in Eskdale. He persuaded some of the best players in Cumbria to join him in the venture, and would press-gang any visitor with cricketing experience into joining the team, however out of practice they might be. 'The club plays cricket far superior to the village-green variety we might expect' wrote 'Skiddaw' in the local paper.

Falkus lectured occasionally at the Outward Bound Mountain School at Eskdale Green, where he would show his films. After Roger Putnam, the principal there for twenty years, left to take on the Muncaster Country Guest House, Falkus would send casting-school pupils to him for bed and breakfast.

Now that Falkus' reputation extended the length and breadth of Britain, his hospitality was spread more thinly. Though there is nothing to suggest that he fell out with his old friend Bill Fowler, the pair were certainly seeing much less of each other by the 1970s. Remembering what Fowler knew about Falkus' past, and in particular his war, it is hard to resist the suspicion that Falkus may have had his reasons for keeping him away from his new circle of friends.

Bill's marriage was cooling too. One day in 1972, as he and Toni were driving back from Whitehaven after seeing *Butch Cassidy and the Sundance Kid*, she found herself telling Bill she wanted a divorce. Bill agreed without a murmur, suggesting that the decision was a relief for them both; it was not the attitude that Toni, who still loved him despite his indiscretions, had hoped for.

It was not in Falkus' nature to get close to a beautiful woman without making a pass at some point, usually successfully. After the collapse of her marriage, Toni saw no need to resist. An unoccupied bedroom at the Bower House provided a convenient setting for a discreet afternoon liaison.

Bill's drinking got the better of him in the end. He took to brewing his own 'moonshine' and his health, both physical and mental, declined rapidly. He died at Knott End in November 1977, at the age of sixty-three, of a ruptured aorta; on the day of his death Toni was devastated to discover that three months earlier he had secretly married his housekeeper.

XII

The World About Hugh

I believe in an à la carte approach to film making,
as I believe in an à la carte approach to life.

1976 TALK TO THE BRITISH KINEMATOGRAPH SOUND AND TELEVISION SOCIETY

NIKO TINBERGEN was one of the great naturalists of the twentieth century. A charismatic teacher, he showed the world the value of looking beyond an animal's appearance to reach an understanding of what it was doing and why. In 1973 his work in laying the foundations of ethology - the science of animal behaviour - won a Nobel Prize.

In the late 1950s, not long after Tinbergen had left his native Holland to join the Department of Zoology at Oxford University, he discovered Ravenglass. The windswept dunes to the north of the estuary were untouched by humanity. A walk among them would yield traces of all manner of interesting creatures, from hedgehogs and foxes to wading birds and rare beetles. Of particular value to Tinbergen and his studies, the dunes were home to the largest colony of black-headed gulls in Europe.

Tinbergen was fascinated by the sands of Ravenglass. According to his biographer, Tinbergen's compatriot, student and fellow zoologist Hans Kruuk[11], he liked nothing better than to roam them at dawn, when the low morning sun would reveal the previous night's comings and goings as a welter of tracks and trails through the sand. Kruuk wrote: 'They formed a magnificent scenery, one of the most beautiful dune landscapes in Britain, with high tops and huge, bare sands in sensuous curves, with rich little valleys and small lakes inhabited by natterjacks and lapwings, all part of a long, uninhabited peninsula between a wide, rich river estuary and the sea.'

Hugh and Niko on the Ravenglass dunes (picture by Lary Shaffer).

Tinbergen made the dunes the focus of his studies, and each year through the late 1950s and 1960s a party of his zoology students would converge on Ravenglass and camp on the dunes for the summer while they carried out their experiments. At intervals Tinbergen would drive up from Oxford to join them.

The students' work was ground-breaking. One series of experiments examined how the birds combat nest predation. By painting eggs different colours and planting broken shells, dummy eggs and other objects, the students were able to show how the gulls' behaviour had evolved to maximise their breeding success; for example, they proved that parents which remove broken eggshells give a better chance of survival to eggs which have not yet hatched.

Hugh Falkus heard about Professor Tinbergen and his students over a pint in the Pennington Arms, and waded across the estuary to see what they were up to. He hit it off immediately with Tinbergen, and as the zoologist was all for a little publicity for the work they were doing he was more than happy to go along with Falkus' suggestion that he should feature their work on television. Falkus was at this time presenting an evening diary slot on Border Television called *Five Minutes with Falkus*, and he felt the work of the students would make ideal subject matter.

'Niko was very taken by Hugh' wrote Kruuk. 'He did four of his little programmes on our research, and we all loved them.'

Falkus felt that the work Tinbergen and his students were doing on the dunes of Ravenglass merited something more substantial than a few minutes on a regional news magazine, so he started to look further afield. At that time the BBC Natural History Unit's regular wildlife vehicle was *Look*, a series of half-hour films about the natural world. The first *Look*, featuring the pioneering cameraman Heinz Sielmann talking to Peter Scott about foxes, had gone out in June 1955.

The series producer for *Look* was Jeffery Boswall. Falkus wrote to Boswall about Tinbergen's work, and Boswall invited him down to the Natural History Unit HQ in Bristol to discuss the possibilities. The upshot was three films for *Look* which went out around 1964. They were, in order, *The Gull Watchers*, *The Sign Readers* and *The Beachcombers*. Tinbergen enjoyed the practical side of film-making as much as the zoology, and contributed some footage of his own.

An unidentified newspaper cutting found among Falkus' papers gave one of several excellent reviews of *The Gull Watchers* before going on: 'Hugh Falkus directed it, but never appeared. This is modesty gone mad. Hugh Falkus, fighter pilot and fisherman extraordinary, is one of the originals: a character out of his age, larger than life and twice as handsome, a Viking who should be appearing before us regularly to reassure the populace that England still breeds such men.' Small wonder he saved it.

John Sparks, a zoologist who joined the Natural History Unit in the 1960s and went on to become its head, was a great admirer of the *Look* films. Nearly thirty years later he told Hans Kruuk: 'They were lessons in clear, popular scientific exposition, and full of simple revelation - a breath of fresh air. The intellectual level of natural history programmes has now sadly dropped well below the standards of those shows.' Decades later, they were still being used in lectures on animal behaviour. Kruuk wrote: 'What especially impressed Niko was what he learned from Hugh, who was a superb communicator and knew how to use the medium of film on television like nobody else.'

Sparks was one of the first BBC men to meet Hugh on his home ground, travelling up to Cragg several times in the mid 1960s to make radio programmes with him. He found working with Falkus highly stimulating. 'To observe Hugh working on his scripts, soft pencil and rubber always with him, searching for the precise combination of words that would clinch a story, was inspirational' he wrote thirty years later in his obituary of Falkus for the *Guardian*. 'My dear Johnny' he would say. 'There are three rules to script-writing: use simple words, write with rhythm and add a touch of alliteration.'

Falkus had already earned his colours with Border Television by helping them to create a studio programme format which would prove extremely popular in later years. In the early 1960s he discovered a treasure trove on his doorstep - an eclectic assemblage of antiques, rustic curios and sporting paraphernalia amassed by a wealthy local man, Jos Milbourn of Carlisle. Having won Milbourn's trust, Falkus would borrow a selection of the more arcane items each week and carry them off to the studio, where he would challenge a 'panel' of his friends, usually including his 'court jester', Frank Plum, to examine them and pronounce on their identities and provenance. Many of the items had links with countrymen and country sports - there were traps, eel spears, line winders, bait cans and bait horns. The programme was a big hit for Border.

In 1968, television showed us the glories of the submarine world for the first time. *The Underwater World of Jacques Cousteau* was a huge hit with British audiences, but the BBC could not use the somewhat patronising American commentary recorded by the owners of the series, so they called in Falkus to provide a new one. It was at this time that Mike Kendall, the Natural History Unit's researcher and librarian, got to know him.

'Hugh had to adapt a translation of the French commentary, building in more information about the creatures that appeared on the screen and turning the whole thing into a compelling narrative' says Kendall. 'He was superbly good at it. He had an instinctive appreciation of what the animals were doing and why. Particularly of course, he understood fish - very useful for an underwater series.'

Hugh would raid the BBC library for information, and Mike's wife Val, a classics scholar, answered his queries about the roots of the French words.

'The commentaries were a triumph' says Kendall. 'Hugh brought to life for the English-speaking viewer everything that was happening on the screen.'

The compliment was not always repaid when English-made films were broadcast on the other side of the Atlantic. Lary Shaffer, a Tinbergen student who worked with both men, remembers Falkus' reaction when he first saw one of the *Look* films dubbed over with a sentimental, Disney-style commentary, not just revoiced for the American audience but completely rewritten and dripping with anthropomorphic saccharine. 'Hugh was furious at what they had done' says Shaffer. 'He was banging the cottage wall. Even as an American, I entirely agreed - his voice-overs were superb, there was no need to change them.'

Forty Cousteau films were broadcast by the BBC, and Falkus wrote and narrated them all. He flew to the South of France to meet Cousteau and his team on board *Calypso*, the Frenchman's famous yacht, though he never tried his hand at diving. John Sparks ended the arrangement with the French studio in the early 1980s, when the quality of the films began to fall - both Cousteau and the ocean were increasingly being reduced to walk-on parts.

Mike Kendall, an ornithologist who can identify any bird in the Western Palaearctic by its call, became firm friends with Falkus; a diplomatic and gentle man, he was one of the few members of the team who did not clash with him. Kendall's home in a leafy corner of the Somerset Levels was Hugh's lodging on nearly all his visits to Bristol in the Sixties and Seventies. There were dozens of these, typically lasting a few days to a week. Falkus would drive down from Cumbria in his old Peugeot estate, bringing the Kendalls bottles of wine and whisky or buying punnets of strawberries for them from the Cheddar Valley growers. At night he would sit out in the garden watching migrating waders or listening for the hooting of owls and the scuffles of badgers and foxes, a glass of Scotch in one hand and a Player's Navy Cut in the other.

There was fishing here too, occasionally; days on the graceful waters of Blagdon Lake, a few miles north of the Kendalls' home, which Hugh had fished with Dr Bell in the years after the war. According to an account he gave a later friend, Chris Falshaw, he circumvented the no-chest-waders rule at Blagdon by striding out into the depths in his plimsolls.

Lary Shaffer remembers that someone at the BBC, in recognition either of his egocentric personality or his appetite for philandering, dubbed him Huge Phallus. It was not a name anyone would have ventured to use in his hearing.

Successful as the *Look* films were, Tinbergen and Falkus were soon planning a more ambitious idea; a film which would do justice to Tinbergen's research into animal sign language. In early 1966 they teamed up to make a fifty-minute documentary about Niko's gulls. Tinbergen would provide the science and do the filming on his hand-wound Bolex, while Falkus wrote the script and directed. The aim was to explain the language of birds to a lay audience.

The black-headed gulls of Ravenglass were not cast in the lead this time, partly because of increasing restrictions on what the team was allowed to do on the reserve. Instead Falkus and Tinbergen decided to film a large colony of lesser black-backed gulls on Walney Island, that windswept eight-mile crescent of land that lies off the south Cumbrian coast by Barrow-in-Furness.

A decade later in Bristol, Falkus told a gathering of luminaries from the wildlife film-making world that he had spent the whole of one breeding season sitting in a hide in the middle of the colony observing the gulls and learning their language. Only when he had done so did he feel ready to start filming.

Shooting of the new film, provisionally entitled *Bird City*, began in the spring of 1966 and continued through the following year. 'For two full breeding seasons Niko filmed while Hugh hectored and admonished and honed the script' wrote Kruuk. According to Lary Shaffer, quoted in Kruuk's book, Niko 'trooped out to the hides with Hugh's lists of specific shots that would be needed: close-up head-and-shoulders of gulls facing left, medium shot of mated pair with grass background, and so on . . . Hugh really treated him like a schoolboy.'

Shaffer became a trusted friend of Tinbergen's - he was later one of a handful selected by the zoologist to receive a share of the Nobel prize money to buy equipment for their studies. He proved not just an apt pupil but a dab hand with a ciné camera. Tinbergen told him what it had been like to work with Hugh.

'They were approaching the filming with different requirements' says Shaffer, who now lives in Maine in his native USA and devotes his energies to building fine furniture. 'Niko was concerned with showing the gulls' typical behaviour and wanted every frame to be authentic and representative. Hugh was much more concerned with pictorial quality. And Hugh always got his way. If he didn't like the footage, he would order Niko off to shoot it again the way he wanted it.'

A 1968 letter from Tinbergen to Falkus gives an insight into their working relationship and the difficulties that Tinbergen, at least, knew they had to overcome. 'For this type of film you and I just sink or swim together' he wrote. 'These occasional brushes are the inevitable consequence of us being made the way we are, and it is because we both work under such tension that we clash now and then.'

Shaffer is in no doubt that Tinbergen thought the world of Falkus, despite this repeated humiliation. 'For years he had been making these little films to support his teaching, and then Hugh came along and showed him how to do it properly. Hugh really understood film, he knew exactly how to tell a story with pictures, and Niko admired that.

'Niko used to say quite cheerfully that Hugh had parasitised his research. He was happy to let him do it because of the publicity Hugh had got him for his work, and what he had learned from him about filming. I'm sure Niko loved and respected him to the end, despite the bullying.'

Although he could be arrogant and overbearing when at work in the field, Falkus knew better than to carry this behaviour into the studio. He was capable of putting on a display of disarming modesty on air, or to a live audience. 'I am a pretty poor naturalist, I just bumble about the country-side - I am probably one of the least observant naturalists you will find' he told BBC Radio Bristol in 1976. 'I'm simply not in the class of Professor Tinbergen.'

Contemporary correspondence indicates that *Bird City* was still the chosen title for the film as late as September 1968, but by the time it was broadcast that December it had been renamed *Signals for Survival*. Consisting as it does almost entirely of scenes of grey-and-white seabirds hopping about and squawking, *Signals* is not the visual feast we expect from wildlife documentaries today. But its appeal was on another level. It did not simply show us a group of animals and invite us to marvel at their beauty; it instructed us to watch their behaviour, and translated it for us as we did so.

'This is a great bird city, extremely well organised' began Falkus, over footage of thousands of screeching gulls. 'But it's by no means a city of friends - far from it. This is a city of thieves and murderers.' Skilfully-shot film and a wonderfully clear script showed us exactly what he meant. *Signals* laid bare an animal communication system so effectively that it was like watching an avian version of *East Enders,* complete with courtship, rivalry, conflict, deceit and robbery with violence. For the 1960s, it was revolutionary.

In an interview with Frank Bough for the BBC's *Nationwide* when the film was repeated in the mid 1970s, Falkus explained that he had wanted to make it because he was not satisfied with the way wildlife was being por-trayed on television. 'We'd be shown some pictures and the commentator would say, here's a lovely little animal, look it's green or red or blue, and look at the way it's hopping about' he told Bough. 'And I said no, to hell with that, I want to know *why* it's coloured that way. I want to know what it *means* when it's hopping about like that.'

John Sparks thinks this criticism was typical of Falkus, and quite unfair. 'Hugh tended to rubbish every film that was not his own' he says. 'His comments were not justified - there were many excellent films coming out of the Natural History Unit and Anglia at the time.'

But he has always been full of praise for *Signals*. 'Hugh's script was first class, slowly unravelling the language of this gull' he told Kruuk. 'There was some doubt about whether the audience would sit through such a long film, but they did (they might not today - or so we are led to believe), and the programme was considered a triumph.'

The film met with widespread acclaim. The BBC was sufficiently impressed to select it as its entry for the documentary category of the Italia Prize at the 1969 Montreux Film Festival. It won first prize, an achievement which the corporation, nearly forty years on, has still never repeated, even with blockbusters of the breadth and quality of *Life on Earth* and its successors (according to Sparks, *Life on Earth* would have won a decade later had the judges' French chairwoman not taken an irrational dislike to it). *Signals* even beat a documentary on the Apollo 11 moon landing. In the USA, it won the Blue Ribbon Award at the New York Film Festival. Falkus himself did not attend either ceremony, grumbling to his friends how much he hated 'all that bullshit', but he was delighted with these triumphs.

The film led to a pictorial book of the same name, co-written by Falkus and Tinbergen, which made a far bigger splash in the press than either of Falkus' previous works. Under the headline 'Sex and the single gull', *The Times'* Philip Howard commented on the depressing resemblance between existence in a gull colony and life in a big city, with 'everybody herded together, preying upon, competing with and occasionally killing their neighbours'.

In 1970 Falkus made a single film with Ronald and Rosemary Easton, produced by Christopher Parsons, Head of the BBC Natural History Unit. Broadcast on BBC2 in May, it was called *The Way of a River*, and concerned a year in the life of Hampshire's river Test. Hugh's friend Maurice Wiggin, in his *Sunday Times* TV column, praised Falkus' 'impeccably lucid' commentary.

After *Signals* Tinbergen worked with Falkus on another BBC TV series, though Tinbergen no longer held the camera - his role was a less hands-on one, as series supervisor. This was a set of thirteen programmes jointly commissioned by the BBC and Time Life, under the title *Their World*, rechristened *Behaviour and Survival* for American audiences. Three of them were made by the Natural History Unit. Again, the aim was to show how and why animals behave as they do.

Falkus wrote and narrated the series and produced one of the BBC films,

The film-makers' 'camp' below Cragg Cottage.
Right: HF with a tame crow.

The Riddle of the Rook, which was entered at the 1972 Venice Film Festival. Chris Parsons produced the other two; they were a film about animal tracks and signs called *Tracks, Trods and Traces* and one about oystercatchers, for which the team went back to Walney Island. We were shown how individual birds could be classed into two groups, the 'prizers' and the 'stabbers', according to which food-gathering strategy they adopted.

Shaffer was closely involved with this series, and he saw how uncomfortable Tinbergen was with the way Falkus treated him. 'He bullied us both, but that was OK by me, because as a young student I could accept it. Niko really couldn't take it, you could see how it chewed at his guts. But Hugh was oblivious. As soon as the filming was over, he would pour out the whisky and laugh and joke with Niko as if nothing had happened.'

The first time Shaffer went over to stay with Falkus, Tinbergen left a note for him on the Land Rover seat that said 'Do NOT ride with Hugh. Ever'. Not that the zoologist was much better. 'Niko preferred to straighten out the curves on the back roads by just cutting them off' says Shaffer.

Niko could play the prima donna as well as Hugh. John Sparks had been lined up for the job of series producer of *Their World,* but he had incurred Niko's displeasure by criticising the lack of variety in his camera work (Niko

Falkus directs a shoot.

tended to shoot everything at eye level). When Sparks was late for a meeting in Oxford because he had been held up in traffic, it was the cue for Tinbergen to insist that Parsons remove him from the series.

Niko could not forget the humiliation Falkus had inflicted on him during the making of *Signals* and *Their World*, and their relationship never recovered. He gave up making films to return full-time to academic work. His place in zoological history was secured when in 1973, with Konrad Lorenz and Karl von Frisch, he was awarded the Nobel Prize for Physiology or Medicine for discoveries in the field of animal behaviour.

In 1976, Tinbergen, presumably writing in response to a new proposal from Falkus, formally broke off relations with him. 'We reached the peak of what we as a team could do, then decided to each follow our own lives' he wrote. 'Let's keep it like that. We rub each other up the wrong way, or at least you upset me. Let's not try and start anything together again, for that would lead to disaster.'[12]

Although Tinbergen never again used a ciné camera professionally, it is for the film he made with Hugh Falkus, alongside his Nobel Prize, that he is most remembered.

The partnership with Tinbergen was over, but Falkus' film-making career was just getting into its stride. *The Tender Trap* (September 1974) was the result of a collaboration with the wildlife-filming technology pioneers Oxford Scientific Films. It was a production about carnivorous plants, an idea which had been suggested to OSF by Niko Tinbergen. Hugh wrote, narrated and produced it with Chris Parsons. The epithets flew - 'breathtaking', 'spellbinding', 'incredible' - and it received first-class TV reviews. The BBC reported an abnormally high audience reaction index. In 1975 *The Tender Trap* won a Certificate of Merit from the British Association for the Advancement of Science.

Falkus wrote the script for a later OSF film which covered some of the same ground but with the inclusion of animal trap-makers - this was *Death Trap*, broadcast on Channel 4 in 1977.

Eventually *Look* ran its course, to be succeeded by *Wildlife on One*. Meanwhile the Natural History Unit had introduced a new heavyweight wildlife vehicle, *The World About Us*. It was devised for BBC2 by David Attenborough, then head of BBC2, in discussion with the NHU and Travel and Features in London. These films were not pure wildlife-watching programmes like *Look* but took in wider issues from the natural world, such as cultural and environmental topics, adventure and exploration.

John Sparks was the series producer, and he invited Falkus to do the commentary for a *World About Us* film he produced and directed about the rich wildlife of the Waddenzee off the Dutch coast. A BBC-WDT co-production, it went out in 1974.

'The project was suggested to us by Niko' says Sparks. 'I invited Hugh to write the commentary and narrate it. We both loved mud and shorebirds.'

Another successful film, *The Day of the Zebra*, also directed by John Sparks, followed. But it was Mick Rhodes, the energetic new head of the BBC Natural History Unit, who suggested on a visit to Cragg in 1974 that an excellent subject for *The World About Us* lay much closer to home. Why not make a film about Hugh's beloved Eskdale, suggested Rhodes, with the producer and writer at the centre?

Falkus did not need much persuasion, although he did insist on directing it himself. Drawn out by the *Lancashire Evening Post*'s reporter, he said: 'I get fed up with all the bad news and people mumbling and grumbling. I thought it was time someone did something different. It is a form of protest, if you like.'

Self Portrait of a Happy Man was not strictly an accurate title - the ostensible subject is Eskdale rather than Falkus himself - though in giving us his impressions and feelings about his beloved valley, Falkus revealed

Hugh and Kathleen dining in the kitchen at Cragg, 1978.

Hugh Falkus in his element - by the river with
his dogs in the early 1970s

something of his passions and what he stood for to his audience. 'Somewhere out there is the world about you' he began. 'This little valley, with its people, its wildlife and its river, is the world about me.'

Self Portrait painted a countryman's picture of the valley which had been a spiritual headquarters to Falkus for three decades and his permanent home for two, showing us its scenery, its wildlife and its rural pursuits. There was a taste of local history - we were treated to a seventeenth century murder and ghost story from Muncaster Castle before being whisked off to the Roman fort up at Hard Knott, where Falkus struck an imperial pose on a rocky pinnacle as he evoked life for a Roman soldier in the second century AD. Bar and Joe Woodall appear in long shot in one sequence, trout fishing from a boat on Devoke Water, and Falkus himself is briefly glimpsed in his striped cricketing cap, going into bat for his beloved Eskdale Cricket Club. There is a sequence filmed at sea on Paul Pedersen's boat ('I come in exhausted, mentally refreshed and extremely happy') and at summer's end we see the hunter at work with dog and gun, bringing down ducks and woodpigeon for the larder.

What we discovered about Falkus from the film we learned by implication: his passion for the river and all that swam in it and flew over it; his feelings about the fisherman's life at sea, 'as valid as any in this extraordinary life that nobody understands'; and his life at Cragg Cottage, where he felt 'a feeling of security that I get nowhere else'.

Filming *Self Portrait* took a year. The job went to Hugh Maynard, a BBC staff cameraman whose recent trials with one of the first image intensifiers had attracted Falkus' interest because it provided a means of capturing night fishing for sea trout on film (there is an enthralling nocturnal sequence of the capture of one). Maynard would drive up to Cragg to stay for weeks at a time while they shot the necessary footage. The two Hughs hit it off from the first.

'His approach to filming was orthodox, but he understood the cameraman's job very well indeed, better than most broadcasters' says Maynard, who is still filming wildlife thirty years on. 'To Hugh planning and attention to detail were critical, and he put a great deal into the construction of a film. He was always thinking about the light, and wouldn't hesitate to get up at dawn day after day to capture the best possible moment.

'He never tried to persuade me to film when conditions weren't suitable. We spent a great deal of time putting the world to rights over a bottle of Scotch, but we got the job done.'

John Sparks also praises Hugh's skill as a presenter. 'He was superb working to camera. In particular, he knew better than to keep looking at it, as so many presenters insist on doing. In conversation people don't look at each other the whole time - we let our eyes wander, then look back to emphasise a point. Hugh understood that, and used it.'

Jonathan Stedall was scheduled as producer, but on the first day of filming he was delayed. Characteristically, Falkus could not wait to get started, so he commandeered the producer's job for himself and Stedall wound up with a credit only as associate producer.

Hugh Maynard is one of the few men who managed to work with Falkus for any length of time without having a serious disagreement with him. Only occasionally were there professional differences. There is a scene in *Self Portrait* where Falkus stands by the river at Meadow Dub and, speaking to camera, tells the story of how, twenty years before, he had brought his ailing labrador, Dog, to this spot to give him a merciful end. Falkus is shown in wide shot, with the dog's grave beside him and the river flowing behind.

The sequence in the film is the first take. Falkus wanted Maynard to shoot it again in close up, but Maynard disagreed, feeling that it had worked perfectly the first time and would only be spoiled by trying to reprise the performance. For once, Falkus gave way.

Watching *Self Portrait of a Happy Man* reminds us that thirty years is a long time in broadcasting. Falkus' avuncular, proprietorial presentation is very different from the breathless, down-and-dirty style beloved of today's presenters. Scarcely a voice is heard other than Falkus' own, and there are no interviews. The farmworker, the huntsman and the village cricketer, even Kathleen herself, are specimens, to be observed with the same scripted affection as the sundew, the heron and the roosting rook.

In one sequence Falkus shows us Kathleen baking on the red-formica-topped kitchen table which became so familiar to so many over the years. The line 'If you haven't tasted Kathleen's home-made bread you haven't tasted anything' would have fitted the scene precisely, but in fact, in an odd resonance, it is from *Shark Island*, filmed twenty-five years earlier; that Kathleen, of course, had been a fictitious character, played by Claire Mullen.

BBC Radio Bristol interviewed Falkus about *Self Portrait* in January 1976, just before it was first shown. Asked what it had been like to make a film about himself, Falkus replied: 'It isn't easy at all, I can assure you. It's rather like indecent exposure. I don't think anyone's really set out to do it before and I wouldn't have done it had the BBC not asked me. The difficulty comes in making your mind up that you are really going to do it. I'm a professional, I can take a dispassionate view - when I see myself on the screen I'm merely a figure moving about and I think "what's this chap doing, what's he trying to tell us, is it coming across?"'

Self Portrait of a Happy Man received wide press approval, and a unanimously positive reaction from viewers. *Shooting Times* called it 'a wonderful uplift . . . the most enjoyable 50 minutes it has been my good fortune to see for a long time'. Conrad Voss Bark wrote to Hugh to tell him: 'They will show it a hundred years from now and people will say, this is it, this is England, here are the English, and this is their love for the land.'

Richard Walker told him that the film had given him and his wife more pleasure than any other TV broadcast they had seen. 'You accomplished more in an hour than the British Field Sports Association [*sic*] have done since their inception' he wrote. 'What you said about having to shoot your old dog had a tremendous impact on the kind of animal lover who, through ignorance, is opposed to field sports . . . people of that kind who saw the broadcast will now see shooting and fishing in a different light.'

Niko Tinbergen wrote to praise his old partner for 'documenting something very precious'. T. C. Kingsmill Moore enjoyed the film too, but his attention was on less abstract matters. 'Tell your wife from me that she moves beautifully, so balanced, so lissom' he wrote to Hugh after watching it.

In February 1976, a week after the film's first showing, Falkus gave a talk to the British Kinematograph Sound and Television Society, at Jeffery

Boswall's invitation, on the subject of 'writing for wildlife films'. Among the senior film makers present was Sir Peter Scott. Introducing Falkus, Boswall called Falkus 'the most professional man I have ever worked with'.

Something of Falkus' way with an audience comes through on the transcript of his talk published in the BKSTS Journal later that year:

There is in the English language a very beautiful word, serendipity, which means the faculty of making happy discoveries by accident. One day I was sitting in my little study writing a film commentary. I hadn't seen the film, but was slogging steadily away with a stopwatch and a shot-list. I was working happily down the list until suddenly I came to a sequence headed 'Elephant Seals' - and I stopped.

Even today, I know very little about elephant seals. Then, I knew nothing - I didn't really believe in elephant seals. I had, I admit, once seen a drawing of an elephant seal, but fancied it was by Edward Lear. None of my friends could help me. Even my wife Kathleen, who knows everything, knew nothing about elephant seals.

Then, quite by chance, I turned over the piece of paper I was writing on and there on the back I found Sir Peter Scott talking about elephant seals! I shall for ever, sir, call you Saint Peter, because everything I needed to know about elephant seals was written on the other side of that sheet of paper.

Falkus went on to argue that the standard way of making wildlife films - to film first and then work up a script to explain the pictures - was putting the cart before the horse.

Every film I make starts with a blank sheet of paper and an idea. I capture this one flash of inspiration and work on it until I have a storyline. Then I go away and write a film-length story - and I won't start filming until I have finished it, because it's the story that really matters. If I start with a good story and if I can film that story, I know I can't finish up with a bad film. I know, before I start, that the film will hold an audience.

He suggested that the end of the film should be written first, followed by the beginning, which would then define the story. Everything else should then follow. The full support of the cameraman, said Hugh, was essential:

It is of the utmost importance that the cameraman should have confidence in the story. He's my great crutch. It's his skill and expertise in the field that I'm going to rely on. If all goes well and he likes it, we can start to film. After that it is a process of evolution - the writing and the camerawork develop together. Sometimes I find a delightful phrase which I capture and write in, or the story is modified to include an entirely new sequence

- hitherto unthought of - or we get some unexpected and valuable shots, and again adjust the story accordingly. The whole thing is evolving and improving all the time. Because we are working to a carefully-written story, we are saving time and money on footage and location expenses.

Falkus described how this emphasis on preparation and planning had helped to make two key sequences in his films possible - a scene in *The Riddle of the Rook* where the older birds were seen driving out yearlings, and one in *Self Portrait* where a heron is filmed flapping into a clump of pine trees before being driven off by a crow. In both cases the cameraman had known that the sequence would be needed because it had been written into the script, and had recognised the opportunity in time to capture the vital footage.

John Sparks feels this polemic is typical of Hugh's habit of assuming he knew more than anyone else about making wildlife films. 'To Hugh, his way was the only way' says Sparks. 'His assertion that we were all putting the cart before the horse was unfair. Anglia's *Survival* had a tendency to shoot everything in sight and then work out a story from the material, but at the BBC we always researched our films, wrote storylines and tried to achieve them. Wildlife filming being so unpredictable, we usually managed to film only three-quarters of what we wanted, but usually we got unexpected sequences which enabled us to make up the shortfall. The same is true today. Hugh was a wonderful man - the sort of person who enriches one's life - but he could also be maddening, obstinate and unreasonable.'

The success of *Self-Portrait of a Happy Man* opened the stage to Falkus for a follow-up, and he decided to make a film about the lives of the migratory fish he loved so much, the salmon and the sea trout. Again, Hugh Maynard was behind the camera.

Salmo the Leaper was a tribute to the family of fish many regard, with Falkus, as the most beautiful and desirable creatures that swim. It was a wildlife film, but it was also about the paradoxical love a hunter feels for his quarry. It had huge appeal to Falkus' fellow anglers, in the days when such things were not marginalised to the satellite channels. Salmon and sea trout were shown leaping, migrating, mating and hatching. They were also cast for, played, hooked, landed and despatched, with no concessions to those who might feel squeamish about field sports or uneasy about their ethics. As far as anyone involved with the programme can recall, there were no complaints from viewers. It would have been hard to challenge the obvious respect and dedication Falkus showed for his quarry.

The film is beautifully constructed. 'They come in from the dark sway of the sea, from lonely reefs and wrecked ships hairy with weed' began Falkus, over film of white water and leaping salmon (he had used almost the same words fifteen years earlier to open an article on 'The Mysterious Sea Trout' for *Animals* magazine, and would return to them again for his book *Salmon Fishing* - Falkus frequently recycled turns of phrase that pleased him.)

After watching intimate footage of the salmon's spawning ritual, we follow the development of the young fish and their journey downriver to the hazard-laden ocean. Very soon we are embarking on the great adventure of fishing for them, but without didacticism - this is not truly an angling film, though for three decades anglers around the world have been watching it enthralled. He muses on the salmon's mysterious preference for a large spinning lure early in the season and a small fly in high summer, and reminds us that it is something of a miracle that migratory fish will take a lure at all. He goes on to marvel at the remarkable number of big salmon taken by women, a topic to which he would return.

The most memorable sequence in *Salmo the Leaper* is that in which Falkus casts himself off the high bank at Black Dub, fully clothed, to prove that falling in is nothing to worry about provided you keep your head and remember the correct procedure (turn on to your back, extend arms sideways, let the current carry you feet first until you reach shallow water). It was shot on a cold winter's day, and for obvious reasons it had to be done in one take. When the film went out in September 1977, this little stunt, based on the picture sequence enacted by Frank Plum for *Freshwater Fishing*, made Falkus somewhat notorious and earned tabloid news coverage ('Man who survived a tragedy sets out to prove a point' headlined the *Daily Mail*). It also made a big impression on the BBC, and John Sparks selected the sequence for a later compilation of highlights which went into a 'best of' programme about *The World About Us* and *The Natural World*. Falkus claimed in the 1988 second edition of *Freshwater Fishing* that the advice given in *Salmo* had so far, to his knowledge, saved forty-one lives. Later he revised this to one hundred.

Sir Michael Hordern, who once said he preferred fishing to acting, was a natural choice for a walk-on part in the film. In one scene where he and Hugh are packing up empty-handed, Kathleen appears from upriver, proudly carrying a salmon newly landed from Meadow Dub, her favourite pool. The episode was contrived of course, every frame of it (the salmon was from the Cragg freezer), but having a professional actor (and a very well-known one) on the team must have helped. 'He was a lovely man to work with' says Maynard of Hordern. 'There was barely a trace of the great actor about him.'

Falkus took no prisoners when it came to getting the shots he wanted. David Burnett wrote in his obituary for the *Independent*:

During the making of Salmo the Leaper, *I happened to be on the riverbank with the camera crew when Falkus was setting up a short sequence showing the passage of a spinning lure through the water. The cameraman was submerged, filming the lure as it was cast in front of him. After an hour I got bored and wandered away upstream. Returning two hours later, I found the team in the same position and the unfortunate sunken cameraman still at his task. That scene lasts a few seconds in the finished film, but Falkus had to get it just right.*

The film impressed many far beyond the angling world. In the *Daily Mail*, TV critic Shaun Usher, despite confessing himself sceptical about angling, called Falkus a 'spellbinder' and praised *Salmo* as the most individualistic documentary of the season.

It was David Burnett who drew Falkus into one of his most successful publishing ventures. The writer's success with *Signals for Survival*, coupled with the skill as a naturalist he had displayed in the second edition of *Sea Trout Fishing*, had given Burnett - who had not then met Falkus - an idea for a new book. One spring day in 1976 he took the train north to Eskdale. On the platform he soon spotted Falkus waiting to collect him, 'a powerful-looking man in dilapidated clothes, dishevelled white hair, a keen eye'. After a 'crunching handshake' they got into Falkus' old blue Peugeot and lurched off towards Ravenglass and the lane to Cragg.

'It was obvious that Hugh was more accustomed to planes than cars' recalls Burnett. 'By the time we reached the cottage I was sick from swerving up mountains and down into valleys.

'Kathleen appeared with their two black labradors, and I loved her at once, as everyone did. She was warm, welcoming and fabulous, with shiny brown hair and smiling eyes.'

Falkus took Burnett into the study and bade him deliver his proposal. Burnett, somewhat intimidated by the writer's baleful blue eyes and fearsome reputation, explained that he felt there was an opportunity for the author to do a book about nature detection. Falkus did not give his answer immediately. Instead he dug out a clipboard and some sheets of paper and sat Burnett down at a table with a jar full of immaculately-sharpened pencils.

David Burnett with Kathleen and Hugh in 1978.

"I'm going to sea," he said. "Why don't you sit down and write out your ideas for this book? Tell Kathleen to make you some tea. I'll be back in a few hours."

Burnett applied himself to the creation of an outline. Some time later Falkus returned, pronounced it good and set to work, drawing on his experiences with Tinbergen on the dunes and raiding the BBC library for caption information.

Burnett found working with Falkus hugely stimulating, and was enormously impressed by his dedication, professionalism and painstaking attention to detail. Many years later, in his obituary of Falkus for the *Independent*, he wrote: 'He worked harder, longer, more intensively, than any angling writer I have known, and took great pains over every page. He would sit up half the night to make one perfect sentence. Between huge draughts of whisky he applied the most formidable concentration.'

The result of the collaboration with David Burnett was *Nature Detective*, first published in 1978. It set out to open the eyes of the ordinary visitor to the coast and countryside by showing how much can be discovered from the tracks, trails and signs animals and birds leave behind them. The book was enriched by more than two hundred superb black-and-white and colour photographs by Niko Tinbergen, Arthur Oglesby, Tom Rawling and Fred Buller, as well as Hans Kruuk and others - there was even one by Fred J. Taylor, of an eel travelling across wet grass.

Nature Detective was a huge hit, much acclaimed by the critics. Falkus was particularly pleased by a review in the *Flyfishers' Journal* which said that the introduction was such an exemplary piece of English that it deserved to be examined by every student of prose.

He was even more delighted by the sales. It went on to be published in the USA and Germany as well as the UK, and there was a book club edition and a Penguin paperback. A second hardback edition appeared in 1987. By Burnett's reckoning *Nature Detective* made Falkus more than £25,000, his first real profit from writing. The money enabled him to have a garage built alongside the cottage.

Nature Detective cemented Falkus' reputation as an expert on watching wildlife, and after its publication he was much in demand for talks and broadcast appearances. Burnett wrote of his skill with an audience in his obituary for the *Independent*.

I took him to the studios at Pebble Mill in Birmingham for a live television appearance. In the course of his interview, with the timing of a born showman, he suddenly brought from his pocket the wing of a tawny owl and explained how the feathers were constructed to allow the bird to glide silently upon its prey. Then he produced the foot of a peregrine falcon and showed its killer thumb talon to the camera. After he had overrun by several minutes, the producer managed to switch to the next item, but no, there burst out all round the studio loud and prolonged applause from the audience as Falkus strode to the anteroom. In there, the telephones started ringing. Who was the man with the owl's wing, and where could one get his book?

Falkus' last film for *The World About Us* was *Highland Story*, a history of Scotland's rugged landscape. Falkus strode about the Cairngorms, stick in hand, pointing out the evidence for the way the Highlands had formed and how they had looked in the past, and introducing us to its characteristic animals, birds and plants.

This time things did not go quite so smoothly. Bad weather halted filming on several occasions, the money began to run out, and there were one or two differences of opinion between the two Hughs. Falkus insisted on setting fire to a ruined bothy to recreate a scene from the Clearances. Maynard was sceptical, feeling the flames would be all but invisible in the bright sunshine. The shot came off, but only just.

Typically, Falkus cast diplomacy to the wind in describing the damage the custodians of the Highlands had done to the landscape over the years. 'The true tale of the Highlands is one of relentless devastation' he opened. 'This wilderness is very largely man-made. Our forefathers destroyed it. It was the great natural Caledonian forest, and most of it was burned down . . . they took what heart there was out of this land, because by destroying the tree cover they let in the force of the weather, which added to the formation of the sour, infertile blanket peat which lies down here, the stuff that's choking the life out of so much of the Highland soil.'

When it was broadcast in 1979 *Highland Story* provoked several complaints from landowners who felt Falkus' criticisms had been too sweeping and that his account was oversimplified - perhaps not surprising, given the need to compress several centuries into fifty minutes. The Scottish Film was written out of film-making history and never broadcast again, a decision which Falkus bitterly resented.

Falkus made another film for *The World About Us*, now largely forgotten. Filmed and broadcast shortly after *Salmo the Leaper* and entitled *The Killing Trade*, it was an examination of animal and human aggression, exploring the connections and contrasts between killing for food, committing murder and waging war. Audience reaction was in the main extremely positive, though some viewers took exception to the more gruesome sequences. According to the BBC's audience reaction report, 'Hugh Falkus was widely commended as a lucid, informed and interesting presenter, whose unobtrusive yet authoritative style was particularly liked'.

'The viewing figure was enormously high, but we had a huge outcry from the intelligentsia' Falkus told Brian Martin of *Shooting Times* in 1989. The intelligentsia won the day - Aubrey Singer, Controller of BBC2, was so dismayed by the programme that Sparks received a telex instructing him to wipe the tape so that it could never be shown again. Although Falkus was unhappy with this decision, Sparks says he was amused at having provoked such outrage among the BBC establishment.

By the time *Highland Story* and *The Killing Trade* were done and dusted, Falkus had a strong notion that his days with the BBC were numbered. He repeatedly expressed his fears in letters to his friend Jo Rippier. 'I am terrified!' he wrote in July 1980. 'I go to the BBC on Monday to discuss the possibility of further programmes - and dread the result. I have a sneaky feeling they want to put me out to grass! Which hurts. Not least because, after all, they may be right. I can't get good new ideas. It doesn't seem to work any longer - whatever it is that produces them, that is!'

A letter from the BBC dated 3rd July, 1980, indicates which programmes must have been under discussion, though there is nothing in it to indicate any uncertainty about Falkus' involvement. The first was *Giants of the Vermilion Sea*, produced by Krov Menuhin (Krov and Anna Menuhin had worked with Falkus before and had visited Cragg), for which Falkus was to write and record the commentary. The other was *Strathspey*, to be produced by Peter Jones, but not due for completion for two years. The fee for this was to amount to £2,400, nearly ten times the fee for *Giants of the Vermilion Sea*, presumably to reflect Falkus' greater involvement in the programme; he was to research, write and deliver the script to camera.

It is not clear whether someone at the Natural History Unit had indeed let Falkus know that he and his style of filming were no longer in favour, or if this was simply foreboding; either way, he was proved right. Falkus made no more films for the BBC.

John Sparks believes Hugh's assessment of his position was not far from the truth. 'Everything he came up with around this time was a combination of his valley, the river and its fish, and Hugh tramping the countryside with his faithful dog' he says. 'His style had simply had its day. Hugh would never take advice. Being stuck in his own ways, he would not have the sense to recognise a good idea when one was presented. He would say, "OK my dear chap, we'll do it your way and we'll do it my way, and your way will end up on the cutting-room floor." But I still regard him as one of the greatest influences on my writing, although I could never aspire to his standard of prose. And he did have a wonderful voice.'

Friends supplied moral support as always. 'I have been missing you of late on TV' wrote T. C. Kingsmill Moore in 1979, possibly rubbing a little careless salt into Falkus' wounded pride. 'When may I look forward to another programme? They are quite the best things that TV produces. Greetings to your wife, with her beautiful easy walk.'

Though the BBC sent no more film-making work Falkus' way after *Highland Story*, another letter to Rippier, written in September 1980, reveals that Falkus offered at least one proposal of his own. He did not record the subject matter; very likely it was a film based on *Nature Detective*, a project for which he is known to have made plans. 'To heighten my terrible feelings of utter uselessness, the BBC played me very dirty over a proposed new film, on which I had already done a lot of work' he wrote. 'I won't bore you with the details, but the result is, no film! So I am waiting for something to turn up.'

What turned up was not a film, but another award. In 1982 Falkus

Falkus in classic pose near Cragg, the flooded estuary behind him.

received the Royal Geographical Society's Cherry Kearton Medal and Award, made for artistic portrayal of the world's wilderness areas, for his wildlife films. Though it was not meant as such, Falkus must have felt that he had received his valedictory gold watch from the industry he had loved so dearly.

Only one short chapter in Falkus' wildlife film-making career remained to be written. In 1986 the BBC relented enough to ask Falkus to supply the script and (for the English edition) the voice-over for *Miracle of the Scarlet Salmon*, a documentary about the life cycle of the Alaskan sockeye. The film was shot in British Columbia, but the executive producer was the Natural History Unit's Richard Brock. John Sparks remembers Falkus recording the narration in his usual rich tones at the Bristol studios 'despite downing a quantity of whisky that would have turned anyone else into an imbecilic wreck'.

The film, much of which was shot underwater, was visually stunning, and met with widespread critical acclaim. But *Miracle of the Scarlet Salmon* was Falkus' last film for a general audience, and his last for the BBC.

Falkus had made a very considerable mark in the worlds of film-making and angling literature, and his sixty-fifth birthday was on the horizon; those who knew him only by his works might have expected him to begin easing gracefully into retirement and old age.

No one who knew Hugh personally would have made that mistake. The image of bucolic contentment conveyed by his broadcasts was increasingly being undermined by his own hunger for romance of a different kind. Kathleen and the life she made possible for him at Cragg had suited Falkus, his lifestyle, his image and his career well enough for twenty years, but their friends agree that it was never a match of true love.

Falkus was well known for his sexual indiscretions, but not all his relationships with women were based on physical lust, and not all were requited. There was a powerful romantic streak in his nature which time and experience never quenched.

It seems that as late as 1979 he experienced the pain of an unsuccessful love affair. He said little or nothing about this adventure to anyone in his circle, but to Jo Rippier, several hundred miles away in Germany, he must have felt he could afford to be less discreet. He wrote to Rippier in September 1979.

I have just returned exhausted and emotionally drained after a journey to the North. Your letters lay on my desk where I had left them after writing my miserable replies, and I have just re-read them. Clearly, I owe you some sort of explanation of why I wrote such depressing drivel.

The reason for my utter depression was the closing stages of what has been the deepest and most harrowing love affair of my life. I can hear the snigger, 'No fool like an old fool'. And of course it is true. But you see, this girl, so much younger, so very very attractive, a fellow professional in radio and television, vivacious, talented . . . (you can write the script yourself!) had seemed the most wonderful person I had ever known in the whole of my life.

We met by chance when I was in the death throes of Highland Story *- a film I despaired of ever finishing owing to continuous bad weather and a depleted budget - a time when my professional reputation hung by the slightest thread - when I was, really was, on the verge of a nervous breakdown (me, the professional toughie, the strong man whose shoulder has been cried on by all his friends - who has never cracked up - who was huddled in the corner, crying with his thumb in his mouth - who quite simply <u>did not know what to do</u>.) Well, she picked me up and brushed me down and gave me the love and affection that I thought I had forgotten years ago, when that girl of mine was drowned. And I fell absolutely, completely, hopelessly in love with her. (And before you smile sadly and shrug your shoulders remember that I am fitter than most men half my* *age, physically, I mean; I am no heavier than I was thirty years ago, and sexually with no hang-ups whatever. Indeed, our love-making exceeded anything I have ever known.)*

It seemed an idyllic relationship. We seemed made for each other. I had already planned a new film that we could make together, researched it, started to write it . . . And then, without warning, as though plunging a dagger into my back at the very moment of ecstasy, she stood off and cut me into little pieces . . .

I have staggered away home to lick my wounds. Here, Kathleen - who has suspected much, but has stood by me - met me with sympathy and kindness. Now, I am on my feet again. I feel as though a huge weight has been lifted from my mind. Already, I am planning another film based on my life here in the valley - a sort of Nature Detective *thing. But emotionally I feel drained dry as dust. I suppose you will say it's all hurt pride. Well, there's probably a lot of that. But most of all, I think, it's the absurdity of it. As though some law of nature had been suddenly turned topsy-turvy; as though gravity had stood on its head and the apples were flying up into the sky.*

It has stripped away my last feeling of confidence. How could I have been such an idiot? How did I ever let it happen? What should I have done? What could I have done?

Of course, I realise that I must help myself. That I and I alone can settle this matter once and for all. Already I think I have begun the fight back. But, by God! I took a hammering . . .

Let's just say that I have been the bloodiest of bloody fools and leave it at that. But I am still puzzled. Hopelessly puzzled. Why? I keep asking myself. Why?

My publisher has been at me to write some more about my life. So far I haven't had the courage to start. Where do I start? How far do I go? It all seems so artificial, and God how boring! And what is an idiot like me doing, writing about himself?

And yet while it lasted it was so wonderful. It was like a gorgeous, glorious, uplifting dream . . . and I thought it could go on for ever. But it was wonderful. And she really was such a wonderful girl . . . There was so much love - and so much laughter. This is why I cannot understand . . . I shall never see her again.

A typically extravagant account of a particularly passionate adventure. He seems, however, to have made a full recovery from it. By November 1979 he was able to write to Jo that he was once again 'in pretty good nick'.

The ravens have been dispersed - if not destroyed - and life is returning to something like normal. If there ever was anything 'normal' about my life. At any rate I have got that wretched girl out of my system (although not entirely out of my mind) and can view the whole effort with a now dispassionate eye. Still can't make up my mind quite what to work at next, have spent a fortune on some new camera equipment and have started an illustrated book version of my film [Self Portrait of a Happy Man].

That romance was over, but within two years Falkus was lost hopelessly in the pursuit of a new one; one which would inflict much deeper and more lasting damage to the security of his life at Cragg.

XIII

Autumn Run

You will laugh at what I am scribbling, but I can't find the words to describe what
had happened to me. Nothing remotely like it had ever happened before, nor had
I imagined anything like it. After all, how could it possibly happen to me?
At my age. A drunken, bloody <u>wreck</u>.

LETTER TO TIM THOMAS

T HE PUBLICATION of the second edition of *Sea Trout Fishing* in 1975 was
the trigger for a nationwide upsurge in recognition for the sea trout
and the angling possibilities it offered. But for its author, it marked an end
rather than a beginning. Falkus already knew that the carefree years when
the Esk had run silver with fish and summer nights were loud with the song
of the reel had gone for ever.

The fishery had met with disaster in September 1966, when UDN (ulcer-
ative dermal necrosis) had hit the Cumbrian rivers like the Black Death,
slaughtering fish by the thousand. The Esk slowly recovered through the
rest of the 1960s and into the Seventies, but Falkus' hunger for night fishing did not. By the time he became nationally recognised as an authority
on sea-trout fishing, he had already abandoned the role of the solitary,
deadly night hunter his writings had exhorted us all to become. Instead his
energies were focused on helping others to experience the thrill he had discovered - in so far as it was still possible.

By the 1970s the Esk's runs of fish were back at a healthy level, though
they never again became as plentiful as they had been in the post-war years.
But then, at the beginning of the following decade, the little river was
struck another devastating blow, and one from which it has still not entirely
recovered; the curse of acid rain.

It started in June 1980, with a spell of heavy rainfall. An early summer spate on the Esk would normally be an occasion for rejoicing, and the signal for a dusting-off of tackle ready for the first salmon and sea trout of the year. Not this time; there was something badly wrong with the brown water that poured down from the granite slopes below Scafell. It produced not leaping silver salmon and sea trout but the pale flanks of dead ones, and all along the river farmers and fishery owners scratched their heads over the slaughter.

At the end of 1982 Knott End changed hands again; Bill Fowler's son Tim had outlived him by only a few years. On Tim's death, his widow Georgina put the property up for sale. The buyer was Bill Arnold, a Lancashire man who had set up a tiling business with his father after the war. Through hard work and a good business brain, Bill had built Lionel Arnold Ltd into a national company employing more than two hundred people. At its peak the firm was winning tiling contracts across Britain, from Runcorn town centre to the London Underground.

Bill Arnold was a keen shot and a passionate game fisherman, and Knott End was just what he was looking for. With the house, cottage and fifty-five acres of land came a quarter of a mile of fishing on the Esk and shooting rights over three hundred and eighty acres of woodland and fell, plus the rights to further ground which Bill went on to rent from the Armstrongs. On top of all that he would have Hugh Falkus for a neighbour, and Bill already knew Hugh well.

It was the Spey that had brought him into Falkus' circle. It started in the late 1950s when Teddy Bentley, one of the Spey regulars and a friend of Bill's, invited him to fish the prized Tulchan beat as his guest. In 1959 the invitation was extended to two days, to include a night in the Palace Hotel at Grantown-on-Spey, the headquarters of Speyside salmon fishing. On the first day Bill took three salmon, the biggest a mighty fish of 32lb. When he came downstairs for dinner, he found the front hall gleaming with silver trays laden with fish. On the tray next to Bill's salmon was another, taken by Bentley; it was heavier by two ounces.

'Teddy dragged me to the bar and introduced me to the rest of the company' says Arnold. 'Gathered around were George Mortimer, the tackle dealer, Tommy Edwards and Arthur Oglesby, and with them was Hugh Falkus. There I was downing a glass with the angling élite of Speyside, and me just a young tiler. I soon found out what serious whisky drinking was about.'

Arnold made a favourable impression on these gods of the double-hander and became an annual visitor to Grantown, though he was not invited to join them at the dinner table - the class divisions of the time ruled out any such familiarity (it seems unlikely that Falkus brought up his job at Windscale over the port and cigars). There were also encounters on the Lune, Arnold's home river, where Falkus and Oglesby fished the Newton beat.

Bill had discovered the Esk for himself back in September 1947, when he was still in his teens. Taking a break from a tiling contract (at Windscale, as it happens) he parked at the foot of Birkby Lane and walked up past Cragg and on to Cropple How, the next farm up the valley. He found his way down to the river and peered into Hazel Dub;

Marie Arnold with Paddy.

it was black with fish. From that moment it was not a matter of if he would return, but when.

So Bill had scarcely waved away the removal van when he phoned Cragg to tell the Falkuses that he and his wife Marie were their new neighbours. Hugh and Kathleen were delighted. The Falkuses came over to inspect, and the two women quickly struck up a friendship. Egged on by Hugh, Bill set to work making the most of his new playground.

But Bill's first season in Eskdale had yet to run its course when he found himself dealing with the river's second major fish kill in three years. He counted one hundred and twenty-five fresh-run fish, including a twenty-pound salmon, dead on his own few hundred yards of water. He was shocked at the devastation, and made up his mind to get to the bottom of it.

The Institute of Terrestrial Ecology investigated. Bill took responsibility for collecting samples of rainfall or dry deposition every day for the next three years, along with two-hourly water samples whenever the river was above a certain height. Eventually they pieced together enough evidence to work out what had happened and what might be done to stop it happening again - not just in Eskdale, but in upland river catchments across Britain, and indeed in northern Europe.

Today the problem is well understood and well publicised, but in the early 1980s it was a novelty - and for the game angling world, a bitter shock.

It emerged that the source of the pollution was the acid-rich gases emitted by manufacturing and processing plants in industrialised regions of Europe, including the UK. These noxious vapours were drifting up into the atmosphere to be carried to earth again in rainfall, often hundreds of miles downwind from the source. Such rainfall can be acidic enough to kill fish on its own, but in granite areas like Eskdale the problem is much more serious, because the acid liberates the aluminium compounds associated with the granite - and aluminium is highly poisonous to fish.

The problem had been building up in the background for years, but its effects had been masked by agricultural liming. After the war, the Government introduced a subsidy to enable farmers in the less fertile upland areas of Britain to increase productivity by liming their land. In 1976, against a background of growing prosperity, it was withdrawn. After that it was just a matter of time before weather and ground conditions combined to create the conditions for a major fish kill. Unfortunately, no one saw it coming.

In Eskdale, the problem was exacerbated by an unlucky quirk of the terrain. A pool of stagnant water would collect in an old back-eddy of the river below Brantrake Crag, above Bill and Sheila Barron's home at Linbeck. Sulphuric acid from the rain combined with humic acid created by the boggy environment to turn this pool into a toxic sump. Evaporation would increase the concentration week by week - until the rains came.

In the third week of September 1983, they came with a vengeance. The lethal liquor was scooped up by the flood and washed straight into the river. The fish had no hope of surviving the combination of low pH and high aluminium.

Since that year acid rain has been monitored rigorously, and the governments of most of the offending countries have reluctantly recognised the need to impose laws for the control of industrial emissions (none dragged its heels more than the UK, which in 1984 led the European league table with an annual emission of 5.1 million tonnes of sulphuric acid). There have been no more major kills, but nor have the great runs of the mid twentieth century reappeared. The Esk remains clear and unpolluted for the most part (although there is always the insidious threat, as with most rivers in these upland sheep-farming areas, from the run-off from sheep-dips), but few would claim that it is the river it once was.

Local anglers like the Woodall brothers, who have seen the Esk through rich years and lean over more than half a century, point out that the huge success of *Sea Trout Fishing* must itself be partly to blame for some of the river's decline. Falkus made it famous, and small rivers cannot afford to be famous. Angling and poaching pressure becomes too great.

Falkus' friends continued to pursue the Esk's sea trout, but their host now left his old quarry well alone. Instead his attention was focused almost entirely on the salmon. He fished the Spey, the Tweed and several other Scottish rivers, according to the invitations that moderate fame sent his way. As early as the 1960s he had taken a rod on the Dunthwaite Beat of the Cumbrian Derwent, where he would fish with his great friend and mentor Briggy Wilson. The Derwent, which flows from Derwentwater north through Bassenthwaite before striking out west to join the sea at Workington, flows through some of the most glorious upland scenery in England. It is as productive as it is beautiful, consistently producing among the best catches in the country.

The salmon became Falkus' new passion, and as usual with a new passion, it was not long before he turned evangelist. The time had come to follow up the success of *Sea Trout Fishing* with a companion volume about the king of fishes. There were (and are) many more salmon fishermen than sea-trout fishermen, and the potential audience for the book was large and lucrative. Falkus felt that he was in a strong bargaining position following the success of *Sea Trout Fishing*, and his approach to Tony Witherby was a good deal more forthright than it had been for his first book.

He demanded a large advance. When Witherby baulked, he offered the book to David Burnett, who was now with Gollancz. Burnett insisted that the book should stay with Witherby's to make a companion volume to *Sea Trout Fishing*, and told Tony Witherby that in his view, he had no choice but to take it on. Reluctantly, Witherby agreed to pay an advance in the region of £3000 and royalties at 12.5%; then, worried that the author might expire before the manuscript was delivered, he took the precaution of quietly taking out insurance on Falkus' life.

The book had been promised, the readers were waiting, the publisher was poised; but for once, Falkus' muse deserted him. The words did not come.

Instead Falkus busied himself with work which was somewhat peripheral to his normal territory. In 1982, David Burnett at Gollancz published two volumes involving Falkus which had nothing to do with fishing. *Master of Cape Horn* was the story of Captain William Nelson, a Victorian sea-captain who had spent forty-seven years at sea in square-rigged sailing ships out of the Cumbrian town of Maryport, then a thriving sea port. Nelson's grandson, Dr Thomas Nelson Marsham, was a sailing friend of Hugh's who had spent many hours with him afloat off the Cumbrian coast.

Master of Cape Horn was followed later that year by *From Sydney Cove to Duntroon*, 'a family album of early life in Australia' written by Falkus with Joan Kerr, an Australian historian. This book arose from Falkus' friendship with Peter Curtis, who had put Hugh up in his home at Rothiemurchus in the Cairngorms during the filming of *Highland Story*. Curtis' wife was a member of the Campbell family, which had set up an early trading centre in Sydney back in the nineteenth century. The book told the story of two Australian women pioneers who had married into the family.

When he had embarked on *Sea Trout Fishing*, Falkus knew he had discovered a great deal that was genuinely new (at least to the vast majority of the country's game fishermen) and writing a book was just a matter of transferring the storm of ideas and learning from his head to the page. The salmon was a very different quarry for his pen. Falkus knew how to catch them, but so did many other clever and articulate men - and a remarkable number of them had already recorded their wisdom in print. Updating the 'knowledge', and adding to what his predecessors had to say on the scale that would be needed for a 450-page book, was quite a challenge.

To add to the problem, Falkus was suffering repeated fits of depression and self-doubt. He was well into his sixties, and the drinking was getting worse; always controlled, but always leading him on to the same downhill slope into black depression. Repeatedly he put the project to one side. It is quite possible that it would have remained on ice for years, if not indefinitely, had it not been for a new force in his life.

Turn to page 7 of *Salmon Fishing* and thumb your way down the long list of acknowledgements in the preface. A few lines from the bottom of the page you will see that Falkus wishes to applaud two 'accomplished fly-fishers' for lending him their 'keen eyes' at the proofreading stage. The first is his friend Jo Rippier. The second name, R. N. Booth, is a woman - Romille Booth.

Romille seems to have entered Falkus' world in the spring of 1982. She enrolled that year in his casting course at Boat of Garten on Speyside, and Falkus' friends noted that instructor and pupil were paying great attention to each other. In the first week of May the following year Falkus started his own speycasting school at Boat of Garten, and Bill Arnold believes Romille was helping him to market and run it.

Romille, then in her mid thirties, was a good-looking woman with an eye-catching figure, and Falkus, though he was about to qualify for his pension, was pathologically incapable of overlooking an attractive female form. For her part Romille made little secret of her interest in this ageing but charismatic angling star with his commanding charm and unshakeable confidence.

In the early months of 1983 Falkus was taking a keen interest in a project his new neighbour was undertaking at Knott End. Bill Fowler's late son Tim had made an attempt to dig a pond in the boggy ground between the farmhouse and the river on the spot where, thirty years before, the rows of mink cages had stood. Bill Arnold was a practical man, and had the resources to get the job done properly. In early 1983, he hired diggers and set to work on the construction of a $3^1/_2$-acre tarn.

In the early weeks of this project, Hugh spent a good deal of his time at Knott End aiding and abetting Bill with it. It was therefore all the more obvious to Bill when his friend began disappearing from the valley for days at a time.

Kathleen confessed her suspicions to the Arnolds. She guessed that a woman might be involved, but did not know who. Bill and Marie had a good idea, but were still hoping it would all blow over; a vain hope.

Since 1979 Falkus had been running week-long sea-trout fishing courses on the Border Esk at Canonbie. The business side was looked after by Keith Allan, a BBC producer who had worked with Falkus. Allan took the bookings, looked after the guests and saw to the financial side. He also shared a room with Falkus at the Riverside Inn.

In the early summer of 1983 Keith Allan took a call from Romille; she wanted to know if there was any objection to a woman joining one of the sea-trout courses. Allan (who did not know Romille), checked with Falkus, who gave the green light. He did not tell Allan that he already knew her.

'Romille joined one of our courses in early July, and it was immediately obvious that something was going on between her and Hugh' says Allan. 'He was paying so much attention to her that he more or less abandoned his other clients. Within a couple of nights he had moved out of our room to be with her. By the end of the week Hugh was asking me to help him look for a place they could rent together.

'I refused. I also pointed out that he was neglecting his other pupils, and told him that some of them were threatening to ask for their money back. Hugh barely spoke to me after that. It was the end of our courses at Canonbie.'

Allan says Falkus drove back to Cragg halfway through the week to tell Kathleen that he was leaving her. She rang the Oglesbys to tell them what

Hugh in the early 1980s, around the time he met Romille Booth.

had happened, as a result of which Arthur turned up at Canonbie to try to persuade his friend that he was making a mistake.

'They had a blazing argument' says Allan. 'Hugh told Arthur that no one was ever going to tell him what to do. Arthur got absolutely nowhere.'

Falkus, for all his magnetism, was in dubious shape medically and free of any suspicion of wealth. He was not much of a trophy for a woman thirty years his junior who had been living a life of security and comfort; Romille was married to a wealthy businessman. But it seems such considerations were swept aside by the depth of the couple's passion for each other.

Matters moved with remarkable speed. When the course ended, Hugh and Romille stayed on at the Riverside Inn while they continued house-hunting. Briefly they rented a temporary hideout, a cottage in Sutherland on the remote west coast of Scotland. Within a matter of days they had moved from there into a two-bedroom property of their own: Watcarrick Cottage, in the valley of the White Esk south of the village of Eskdalemuir in Dumfries and Galloway, on the Scottish side of the Solway Firth. Surrounded by high moorland and forestry, remote and largely unspoilt, Eskdalemuir holds the British record for the highest rainfall in a thirty-minute period.

The move took place on 25th July. A few days before, Bar Woodall had a surprise visit from his friend.

'Hugh came to the door' says Bar. 'I could see that he had Romille in the car behind him. He wanted to bring her in to meet me, but I refused, out of respect for Kath. He came in on his own to say his piece. I made it clear that I didn't approve of what he was doing.'

A few days later, Falkus wrote to Jo Rippier from their temporary address.

I am writing this in pencil because it so much easier than scratching about with a thin-tipped Biro - and the time is 3.30am and I can't sleep! At present I am in the wilds of Sutherland. It is blowing a gale from the Pentland Firth and bloody cold. Life has been rather traumatic recently - one reason why I've not written in reply to your last long and interesting letter.

As you know, I found the completion of my book Salmon Fishing *almost impossible. This was because unhappiness came into my life at Cragg. Advancing age and a general sense of frustration and failure, exacerbated by heavier and heavier drinking, had brought not only a feeling of utter depression but the rapidly increasing desire to blow my brains out.*

So why didn't I? Because some time ago I met a girl and fell instantly in love with her. For over a year I couldn't believe it possible that she *could be in love with* me*. To start with she was (seemingly) happily married to a very rich man, extremely attractive, both physically and intellectually, and thirty years younger. To stop myself behaving like a lovesick idiot, the butt of every dirty joke ever coined about 'silly old men', I did everything I could to keep her at arm's length. I was unkind, rude, contemptuous - especially when she was fishing with me on various 'courses' I ran when I was doing some instruction. No good. Everywhere I went, that girl would materialise. And then one night, at Grantown-on-Spey when I was literally at the end of everything - drinking like a fish, couldn't write, every vestige of confidence and self-respect gone, I suddenly discovered that she really did love me. It was a revelation. Never had anything quite so astonishing and dramatic happened to me before. The result was even more fantastic. It was as though I had suddenly woken from a terrible dream; that in some incredible twist of time I had seen the dawn; had died and somehow been given another chance of life.*

You will laugh at what I am scribbling, but I can't find the words to describe what had happened to me. Nothing remotely like it had ever happened before, nor had I imagined anything like it. After all, how could it possibly happen to me? At my age. A drunken, bloody wreck*. How could a young and attractive girl possibly be in love with* me*! And yet, it had happened. A millions upon millions to one chance, one that over the years I had sometimes dreamed about, but never seriously thought possible. It was as though two lost and lonely people had by some incredible chance collided in the vastness of outer space.*

The upshot? Well, we have both left our respective homes, and are now living together. In a year or two, if a divorce can be obtained, we shall marry. We are utterly devoted to each other.

With the little money I had saved, I have bought a tiny cottage in the wilds of Eskdalemuir (very lovely peaceful valley) and we move in next Monday (25th July). We have no money, very little furniture and no immediate prospects - except my pen, and a fantastic new-found confidence. What a challenge! But, my God, it makes me feel fifteen or twenty years younger. Just when I thought life was all washed up for me, it starts all over again. Now I will find out whether I am really any bloody good as a writer!

Well enough of that. Please drop me a line some time - and if you are in the North, do come and pay us a visit. I long to see you. Not least because nearly every so-called friend I thought I had has deserted me. Even the most intimate friends of friends of twenty or thirty years have suddenly cut me dead. It has shocked and saddened me, but I am getting over it now (human nature has never ceased to astonish). So, if you feel you can still bear to know me, please write.

Of course I know what I have done. I am still very fond of Kathleen and always have been. But life at Cragg has been very difficult - at times almost impossible. This is what so few people have ever suspected. On many occasions over the years I had contemplated starting a new life - but I had neither the place to go nor anyone to go with. Kathleen has never really loved me. And I was so sick of being shouted at. But nobody knew that I was secretly so unhappy - or why. So now, I suppose, they can't understand my doing what I have done. If this had not happened, I would be a dead man now. In a sense, Romille (my love) saved my life. I have not touched one drop of whisky since we came together. The only alcohol I drink now is a glass of wine and a tiny brandy at night-time. I have lost a stone and a half in weight and feel fitter than I have for many years. Even so, my so-called 'friends' think me callous and insane. Well now I know who my real friends are. They are very few!

There is a wild and windy sunrise spreading over the barren Sutherland hills and the sea is creaming in across the sands below the cottage. You would like it here. The little river is dead low, but yesterday I caught a salmon on a tiny dry fly. Saw him rise, put on a 3/8' no 16. He came up and took it like a big trout! Tremendously satisfying. The book is finished (thanks entirely to Romille) but I still have all the drawings to do. Must get straight on with them as soon as we have moved into Watcarrick (means Roman fortress on the rock!). Rather apposite. Shall need to keep the bums at bay for a time!

Bless you for reading all this! Yours ever, Hugh.

In Eskdalemuir Hugh and Romille began a life which in practical terms was not very different from the one he and Kathleen had led for the previous twenty-five years at Cragg. They ran a kitchen garden, the produce from which supplemented the quarry that fell to Hugh's rod and gun, as it had there.

Romille was happy to join Hugh's fishing and shooting expeditions to the domains of his various contacts. On Mondays they would drive across country to Norham on the lower Tweed, where Falkus had taken a rod; it was not much more than an hour's drive across the Cheviots. Hugh's friend David Drake had a Tuesday rod, so they would team up with Drake and share two days of sport. There was also fishing on the Annan, the Tay, the North Esk and the Border Esk, where Hugh had run his sea-trout courses, and occasional trips further afield, to Loch Maree and the Isle of Lewis in the Hebrides.

At home, Romille looked after him with great devotion. He was not an easy charge, not least because his health was now distinctly shaky. Though he would complain that he was suffering from colitis, his friends suspected that it must be something more. His digestive system was in a perilous state, and he needed daily medication to enable him to control his bodily functions. This made it difficult for him to manage his little Citroen, so he abandoned driving almost entirely, calling upon others to chauffeur him whenever possible.

Romille added the roles of nurse and driver to those of lover and muse. She even managed to wean Falkus off whisky and on to wine.

It seems to have been Romille's suggestion that Falkus should market his fly patterns. He compiled a set of of his favourites, and came to an arrangement with Riding Brothers of Preston to supply them in a presentation fly box, one each of salmon and sea-trout flies, the boxes labelled personally by Hugh in silver script. They were advertised in the angling press and sold well. Romille would handle the orders and despatch them.

Friends and acquaintances visited from time to time. Jo Rippier flew over from Germany, and found his friend a good deal less well than he had expected. 'They seemed happy enough as a couple, but Hugh was coughing repeatedly and looked pale and drawn' he says.

In May 1984 a Welsh deputation dropped in, by helicopter. The pilot was Scruff Oliver, a keen angler and a former RAF officer. On board was the Welsh sea-trout maestro Moc Morgan, a rally driver, Phil Llewellyn, and his co-driver. The fifth man was Tim Thomas, a Welsh sportsman who had met Hugh at a game fair and invited him back home to enjoy some fishing and shooting, an invitation which was readily accepted. Thomas was a psychologist (he was then Educational Psychologist for Pembrokeshire County Council), and had earned Falkus' gratitude for rallying to his side at a time

Tim Thomas at Cragg, a goose in one hand and Kathleen in the other.

when most of his established friends were berating him for his treatment of Kathleen. 'You showed me great kindness and understanding when everyone else was kicking me in the face with great ferocity - I shall never forget that. During the past two years I have learned who my friends really are!' Hugh wrote to him.

In fact Thomas was repaying a compliment. At the end of the 1970s he had become embroiled in a case which had led to his putting his head above the battlements, and very nearly getting it shot off. It concerned June and Jennifer Gibbons, the highly-intelligent twin daughters of a West Indian family living in Haverfordwest, who had refused to talk to anyone apart from each other since early childhood. At nineteen, after creating a trail of attention-seeking havoc in the town, the 'Silent Twins'[13], as they became known to the news media, were found guilty of arson and theft and sentenced to life in Broadmoor. Jennifer eventually died there.

Thomas, having assessed the twins, felt they needed constructive help rather than punishment. Dismayed by the authorities' insistence that they be treated as criminals, he blew the whistle by reporting the case to the *Sunday Times*. The resulting avalanche of disapproval nearly buried him.

Falkus did not hesitate to jump to Thomas' side. He wrote several rousing letters of support which greatly lifted the Welshman's sagging spirits. Reading them gives an insight into the power and warmth of his friendship. It also reveals how little this man who had once read stories on *Children's Hour* thought of children.

I urge you to keep your head well out of sight; and, especially, your name out of the press. From all the signs, social work of whatever type is becoming very unpopular, whatever the truth behind the allegations. Most children are wholly untrustworthy and are natural bullies, thieves, arsonists, devil-worshippers, sexual fiddlers and potential rapists. They need little adult encouragement to indulge their sense of lust and violence. It is _innate_. _It is of course, politically incorrect to mention this at present but the climate of thought is changing, I believe. So dear Tim, remember your pension and your glittering OBE. Don't get caught in the child-care abuse trap!_

I have the impression that you are taking things rather too seriously. It simply isn't worth it. There is a mad, bad world out there and you must play your part in it until the curtain drops and you can claim your pension with its concomitant freedom. Surely you are not concerned about an appearance in court? What a wonderful opportunity to show off. Just relax and let it all flow over you and around you. Think of the publicity you will get - which will irritate all your colleagues who have still some years to serve and will envy you your 'notoriety' (there is no such thing as bad publicity, provided, of course, they get your name right). Enjoy the limelight. Who knows, with a bit of luck it might lead to further promotion and an even better pension, not to say a more golden handshake . . . Perhaps it is the armour of all my wartime experience, but when faced with the unbelievable I just roar with laughter.

The year 1984 was the year Chris and Vivien Falshaw bought a holiday cottage in Eskdalemuir. Falshaw, an angler and an ornithologist, had met Hugh three years earlier on the Border Esk, so when he heard that he was living nearby he made contact.

We got to know them and exchanged dinners. They seemed a happy enough couple, and Hugh seemed to be in good health still.

The first time they visited us, Hugh enquired about the availability of brandy. We had none but we did have some raki, recently brought from Crete. I poured him a measure. He told us it was just the brew he and his fellow prisoners had distilled in the POW camp. He had several more.

At New Year we were invited down to join them. Before the meal he kept topping up his sherry glass, but when Romille was out of the room he told us it was really brandy. I'm sure she knew what he was up to.

We had been to the Edinburgh Festival that year, and Vivien sported a jumper with a logo announcing that she was a Guardian reader. 'Guardian readers - I'd bomb the lot of them!" he exclaimed. He went on to say that he had been in the war to keep the country free, and not to be taken over by a lot of 'lefty pacificists'. We nearly upped and went at this point. I said in fairly strong terms that we had also been in the war, and had bombs dropped on us. He softened then, and was very generous for the rest of the evening. So much so that he gave me a casting lesson the next morning - free.

We did enjoy his company. Just listening to his tales was magical.

The late angling expert and tackle designer Peter Mackenzie-Philps once told Falshaw of a party he had attended at which Falkus had heard Romille refer to him as her 'kept man' - it was meant as a joke, but Hugh had failed to see it (it was too near the truth, of course) and insisted on leaving immediately.

While cordial relations continued for many of Falkus' outer circle, it was a different matter for those who were close to Hugh, particularly his Eskdale friends, because they were also close to Kathleen and had benefited from her innumerable kindnesses over the years. They found it difficult or impossible to forgive what he had done to his bemused and blameless wife.

The patient Fred Buller was one of those who felt, and said, that Falkus' abandonment of Kathleen was beyond the pale. The loss of Fred's friendship was not something Hugh could countenance lightly. In January 1984, he wrote to Fred to explain that his relationship with Kath was over and to urge him to travel up to meet Romille.

It is a long time since we met - too long. You do not approve of my change of life, I know. But then you do not, I think, know all the facts. Anyway, leaving that aside, life is getting steadily shorter (shorter indeed for me than for you!) and it is time we met and talked together as we did years ago. There is much to discuss, if only my new book Salmon Fishing, *which I am sure is going to make you a lot of money.[14] It will, I feel certain, cause much interest, for it contains much new thought.*

Buller was having none of it. 'It was the only serious disagreement we ever had' he says. 'Hugh lost quite a few of his friends over it, and some of those he kept never quite thought the same of him again - though they would never be indiscreet enough to tell him so.'

Arthur and Grace Oglesby, whose friendship with Hugh had already been undermined by his tendency to run Arthur down, sometimes in public, were not impressed by his treatment of Kathleen. Frank Plum, a staunch Catholic, weighed in by pleading with him to end the relationship for Kath's sake; Hugh dismissed his plea out of hand.

Conrad Voss Bark's political skills did not save him from falling out with Hugh. Conrad wrote to Kathleen to express his support for her and his indignation at the way Hugh had treated her. Falkus was furious at this perceived meddling in his affairs. 'Who does he think he is?' he stormed to Fred Buller. He refused to have anything to do with Conrad after that.

But Romille gets full credit from his friends for her pivotal role in the eventual successful publication of *Salmon Fishing*. Initially a distraction, she now became, as Kathleen had before, his amanuensis. Demonstrating both resolute determination and an unexpected literary talent, she worked with him, and on him, until he finished it. When Bill Arnold called he would find them sitting facing one another, either side of a double desk with a type-writer each. As Falkus typed and scribbled away, Romille assembled the fair copy.

'No creature on earth treats the dogmatist more sternly than *Salmo salar*, the Atlantic salmon' began Falkus in his preface. 'Anyone writing about this extraordinary fish enters a literary minefield.' Into the minefield he swept, though he wisely paid more attention to the landscape than he had when he had embarked on *Sea Trout Fishing*; he was no longer on his personal territory. And he took care not to go alone. Earlier writers and experts of Falkus' acquaintance were quoted extensively. Respectful credit was accorded to the likes of A. H. Chaytor, John Ashley Cooper, Esmond Drury, Eric Taverner and his personal mentors Richard Waddington, Briggy Wilson and Arthur Oglesby.

The book is nevertheless Falkus' own take on salmon fishing; neither revolutionary nor (for the most part) iconoclastic, but full of shrewd observation and enlightenment, and as comprehensive and entertaining as his sea-trout book had been. Stressing, as with the sea trout, what he had learned from experience, he suggested that much of what had hitherto been written about the salmon was fallacy, and set out to suggest a practical approach.

There was plenty of theorising mixed in, however. Among Falkus' angling friends was Dr David Goldsborough, a keen salmon fisherman who happened also to be a lecturer in physiology. Egged on by Falkus, Goldsborough had developed an analytical approach to the age-old enigma of the salmon's willingness to take a lure at times (without which the sport of salmon fishing would of course be impossible) despite its well-known abjurement of feeding in fresh water. Put very simply, the 'Goldsborough Hypothesis' pointed out that natural variation should be expected between one salmon and another and between one moment and another in the degree of appetite suppression the fish experiences, as well as in its hormonal state and the operation of overriding instincts such as fear and aggression. The variable interaction of these three aspects of salmon biology (carefully explained with bell-curve diagrams), said Falkus and Goldsborough, offers an explanation as to why some fish, sometimes, are prepared to take a lure, and why the manner of their taking it varies so much. But Falkus admitted that the conjecture does not enable the angler to predict which salmon will take and when. Like chaos theory, the

Goldsborough Hypothesis is not a lot of use for predicting specific events.

There are few genuinely new ideas in *Salmon Fishing* - in fact there is much that was not new even to Falkus' own pen (serial digressions about sea-trout fishing, badgers, canoeists and early angling literature among them) - although his discussion of the value of fishing at dusk and even into the night was a departure from convention, as was his insistence on a stealthy approach to a fish which many had considered indifferent to human presence.

By the spring of 1984 the crafting of the book was in its climactic stages. For the final checking of the manuscript, Falkus needed expert help. Jo Rippier helped by studying and marking proofs sent over to his home in Germany.

Considerable help came from Malcolm Greenhalgh. Greenhalgh, a game fishing writer with a PhD in biology, had met Falkus the previous year when the author had visited his club, Bowland Game Fishing Association. He wrote about the visit in *Salmon, Trout and Sea Trout*.

He looked very much the country gent - red stockings, tweed breeches and a battered old tweed jacket of a different pattern. The sloppy off-white shoes didn't match at all.

He divided the evening into three sections. In the first he stood up and, without notes or visual aids, talked sea-trout fishing, quoting vast chunks of his book. As he did so he looked piercingly at every member of the audience as through trying to spot any dissenter. He spoke as an evangelist and considered that anyone who disagreed with him on any angling issue was an infidel! After an hour he explained that there would be a break for refreshment and that during the break we should write any questions on slips of paper and he would answer them at the end.

The gathering then adjourned to watch *Salmo the Leaper*, after which Falkus resumed, holding a sheaf of questions.

'Now, question time! Would I always use a sinking line in the second half of a night's sea trouting? Well, the answer to that is in my book. I have some for sale here, if you still haven't got one.

'The second question is quite stupid! Are not size 10 and 12 flies sometimes more effective? Whoever asked that question is a ninny! Of course they are not. As I said in my book, if you double the size of the fly you will go a long way towards doubling the size of the bag.'

And so question time proceeded, every question being greeted by 'Buy my book!' or 'This is quite stupid!' It was noticeable that at the end of the evening there was a long queue of folk handing over cash (Christian money, HF called it) for copies of his book.

Salmon Fishing was published in the autumn of 1984. It achieved all the impact Antony Witherby had hoped for. The former Conservative Prime Minister Lord Home, a keen sportsman, asserted in *The Field*: 'Any reviewer of this book who fishes will be lost in admiration at the accuracy of his observation and at the patience with which he has assembled so much knowledge about the Atlantic salmon . . . If the reader acts on the advice given, he can say it is the fish's fault when he loses a salmon.' Moc Morgan was equally enthusiastic: '*Sea Trout Fishing* was the best angling book ever, until I read *Salmon Fishing*, which is even better.'

By angling book standards, sales of *Salmon Fishing* were a sensation. The first run of five thousand copies sold out within months, and the book soon settled down to steady annual sales of well into four figures, which it has maintained year after year ever since. The book and its author were even singled out for tribute by Paul Torday in a postscript to his recent best-selling novel *Salmon Fishing in the Yemen*.

While the slow-burn success of *Sea Trout Fishing* had been earned entirely on its merits, anglers bought *Salmon Fishing* largely on the reputation of its author.

'It was enormously successful, but it was not as good as *Sea Trout Fishing*' says David Burnett. 'Hugh had to pad it out a little to get it to the same length, as he was determined to do - he was very proud of what he called his "matched pair".

'Unlike Arthur, Hugh was never one of the salmon fishing aristocracy. He lacked hard experience on the big East Coast rivers where most of the serious salmon fishing is done. He was a subversive angler who was quite happy to use a worm, if that was the way to get a fish.'

Falkus' income from his writing was now becoming substantial, with half a dozen books in print and selling well at the same time. A January 1984 letter from Watcarrick to David Burnett mentions his reaction to the new arrangements whereby authors were paid each time a book was borrowed from a public library. The rate mentioned is 0.9p per borrowing. He was surprised to learn that as a lending library title *The Stolen Years* was the most successful of his books, having been borrowed more than six thousand times in a year, which was earning him more than the book was bringing in in royalties. *Nature Detective* was in second place, with just over four thousand borrowings.

Falkus' friends had been defecting on all sides, but as if in compensation a new Trusty-elect now appeared on the scene. In 1984 Professor Peter Behan, Professor of Clinical Neurology at the University of Glasgow, wrote to Falkus at Eskdalemuir to ask for his help with research into the salmon's brain, and in particular the mechanism by which its appetite becomes suppressed in fresh water. Behan's letters were at first intercepted by Romille, who insisted that Hugh was too ill to see him. But he persisted, and eventually managed to speak to Falkus on the phone and to secure an invitation to Watcarrick Cottage. A few days (and a case of fine claret from Behan) later, the two were firm friends.

'At first Hugh was deeply suspicious, but he was fascinated by what I had to tell him about the salmon's brain and how a study of it could explain its feeding behaviour' says Behan. 'He would listen intently, take it all in, and then go away and think about it. He would come into my room in the small hours with a mug of tea to raise some point he was struggling with. The next day he would go over it all again to make sure he had understood.

'I wouldn't say his was an exceptional intellect, but he was certainly a great one for learning. And once he had understood a concept, there was no stopping him.'

Behan even managed to secure a small grant for Falkus from a pharmaceutical company in respect of his contribution to the project. Their collaboration led to a lasting friendship; it also gave Behan a deep insight into Falkus and the nature of his relationships with women.

One night Hugh told me that Romille's response to him varied unpredictably from night to night, and that this worried him a great deal. He asked me if I would have a chat with her, as a medical man and a friend, to try to find out what was going on. When I thought he'd gone up to bed I got into conversation with her in the sitting room. But then she said something critical about Hugh, and he jumped out from behind a curtain - he had been listening in all along. There was a huge row. I went to bed and left them to it.

He was an extremely insecure man - there were situations he could not cope with at all. When Romille was fishing one day with some Army officers and there was some flirting going on, Hugh was so threatened by it that I would have described him as clinically suicidal.

But physically he was wonderfully fearless, even in his late sixties. We were fishing the North Esk once and the gillie told him he wouldn't be able to fish a particular pool because it was in a rocky gorge. Hugh wasn't going to let anyone tell him where he could fish and where he couldn't. He let himself down on a rope and waded out through the torrent to a rock in midstream, then ripped line off the reel and started covering the water from that rock as no one else had dared. It was Hugh at his best - the way I'll always remember him.

Falkus never had much time for gillies - on rivers where their assistance is customary, he would insist on fishing alone. Undoubtedly, one reason for this was his disdain for fishery rules. If he could not get a salmon on the bank using the approved methods, he would not hesitate to resort to the worm or the prawn. It once got him banned from the Junction Beat on Tweed.

Back in Eskdale, Kathleen was trying to make the best of things, as she always did. She found it hard to believe that her husband had left for good, and lived in hope that he would change his mind. Both Bill Arnold and Fred J. Taylor observed that each morning she would take the dogs down the lane in the forlorn hope that she would see Hugh, turning in unannounced from the A595 to tell her he had thought better of his adventure and had decided to come home at last.

Kath had been entirely dependent on Hugh for money, and although she had been left a small sum by her father on his death in 1982, she now found herself in some financial difficulty. Fred J. Taylor tried to help by arranging for the letting of the short section of fishing she had also inherited, the few hundred yards down from Donald's, opposite the cottage. He promoted it in the London paper he wrote for, the *Evening Standard*.

It was the Arnolds who kept Kath going. She and Marie became close friends, and most days during Falkus' absence she would dine at Knott End. It was now that Bill and Marie realised that she was drinking heavily, and seemed, unlike her husband, unable to control it. It did not help that Kathleen suffered from porphyria, a disease which is very variable in its effects but which is widely agreed to be incompatible with alcohol. In Kathleen's case it exaggerated the effect alcohol had on her brain, making her garrulous, disinhibited and repetitive.

Sometimes anger would get the better of her. Shortly after Falkus had left Cragg, Bill Arnold looked down the valley to see a column of smoke and paper ash rising from the cottage garden. He drove down on smoking tyres to find Kathleen hurling armfuls of her husband's belongings through his study window and out on to the lawn, where she had lit a bonfire. Bill managed to calm her down and bring the destruction to a halt, but hundreds of letters, film scripts and photographs were lost, along with Hugh's fishing and shooting diaries and many of his clothes.

Falkus reacted with fury when Bill told him. Yet within moments, his anger turned to regret. 'What have I done?' he groaned, head in hands.

Hugh and Romille remained at Eskdalemuir for two years. Though there was little or no direct contact with Kathleen, Hugh kept himself constantly abreast of events in Eskdale through Bill and Marie.

'We would speak on the phone most days' says Arnold. 'He kept needing books or papers sent up for his work on *Salmon Fishing*. But he would always ask about Kath. I'm sure that right from the beginning he was having regrets. He was missing Eskdale, and missing her.'

Falkus supplied some evidence for this in a letter he wrote to Tim Thomas in November 1984:

Alas, after a great deal of thought, I think it best that we do not come to Wales at Christmas. I feel I ought to go and spend some time with Kathleen over the holiday period - perhaps the Boxing Day or whatever, and take her some goodies. So please forgive me for treating your very kind invitation in such cavalier fashion. It is so difficult trying to please everyone all the time! . . . kind regards to dear Moc M.

Hugh's direct contact with Kathleen started to become more regular, and by 1985 he was telephoning her frequently. She welcomed his calls, though she would find the conversations distressing and usually wound up afterwards at Knott End, being consoled by Marie Arnold.

Hugh kept a supply of stationery and writing implements at Knott End, which he had begun to use as his new Eskdale base. A September 1984 letter written there on Cragg notepaper reads:

*Please excuse scribble. Writing this as I drink the early morning cup of coffee and b. Off to Meelee's after breakfast . . . then we shall be going on the Tay with Ross Munro and David Drake. I do feel much fitter . . . that week of your great kindness in Wales really set me up. I cannot remember having a week of such loafing in my life. It came at just the right time . . . I have decided to retire! The book (*Salmon Fishing*) is selling well, so I should get enough to keep me, plus my OAP. And then there will be time to do lovely things - fish with Meelee and come to Wales and so on. I feel great.*

By 1985 Hugh had had some postcards printed with a Watcarrick Cottage letterhead, but they would soon become obsolete. Encouraged by Tim Thomas, the couple had already made several visits to his stamping ground of West Wales, where sea trout and salmon, pheasants and wildfowl were as plentiful as they were in Cumbria. Thomas was well connected in the Welsh fishing and shooting world and could promise a plentiful supply both of comradeship and sport.

Now he suggested to Falkus that Wales would be the ideal place for a long-term home, not least because Kathleen and her allies would be a safe distance away. Hugh and Romille put Watcarrick on the market and, with

Tim Thomas' help, started looking for a new home. In April 1985, Falkus wrote to Thomas:

Great news about the sale of Watcarrick. But at present we have nowhere to move to!
. . . Romille will be with you all on Saturday afternoon some time. Bless you for giving
her sanctuary. Please, very tactfully, try to guide her final choice - she is, as you know(!)
very impetuous. But she is a great girl with many redeeming features! I long to see you
again and feel the wind on my face. It has been so long since I went to sea. Too long.
Make sure the outboard is reliable (I know little about them).

For a time the couple rented a place at Felinwynt, on the Pembrokeshire coast north of Cardigan, before moving to a house in the village of Moylegrove in the Pembrokeshire Coast National Park. The house, Glanawen, had four and a half acres of gardens bordered by a little trout stream.

The big Welsh sewin (the Welsh term for mature sea trout) had begun their early summer run, and Falkus had the Principality's game-fishing

Glanawen, Moylegrove, as it is today.

251

crachach to effect an introduction to them. Tim's circle included Moc Morgan (shortly to publish *Successful Sea Trout Angling* with Graeme Harris), the fishery scientist Lynn Hughes and Sir Edward Dashwood, who owned and managed some of the finest fishing and shooting in West Wales (he still does). There was shooting with Sir Edward and on Lord Lisburn's Monachty Shoot, near Aberaeron, and nights on Colonel G. H. F. Chaldicott's prime water on the Towy below the Junction Pool with the Cothi at Nantgaredig. Thomas wrote in his diary that he had taken a five pound sewin which Falkus netted for him, but had been broken by another. He noted that the temperature was 62° Fahrenheit and that Falkus told him that fish could be expected to stop running above 63° or below 42.

Sir Edward, who had taken care to consult *Sea Trout Fishing* before tackling the sewin of his own water on the Eastern Cleddau, much admired Falkus' writings. He also found him fascinating as a personality. The pair got on so well that although they spent many days and nights together on the river, very little actual fishing took place.

'We fished the West Wales rivers and my beat on the Wye as well as Hugh's Esk' he remembers. 'We never seemed to find time to do any fishing as there was always so much to talk about. Hugh loved to recite poetry - Milton, Dylan Thomas, Kipling - and he had a wonderfully natural way with verse.'

Falkus was already planning to replicate at Glanawen what Bill Arnold had done at Knott End. He wrote to Bill in August 1985 to tell him that he had received approval for the construction of a 'trout/casting pond' on their land, and that the 'pondmaster' was expected in October. Tim Thomas says that in fact Romille was furious about this plan; Hugh, typically, was treating her property as his own domain to run as he wished, and she was not the kind of woman to hand over control.

Undoubtedly he was now missing Eskdale. In August 1985 he wrote to David Burnett:

We have a small boat (the 'Tub') which is splendid for the mackerel and pollack fishing. I got 11 at once (feathering) the other day, though such profitable strikes are rather rare. I spend every moment of good weather out at sea. This is keeping me very fit . . . I have just sold one of my guns and with the money am going to make a proper lake where people can fish for trout and I can teach my casting and make some money.

But I miss Cragg very much. Fancy your fishing Hazel (it was once a fabulous sea-trout pool, years ago - oh, how I miss that little river). But I remember it all as it <u>was</u>. It isn't like that any more - don't suppose it ever will be again. Sometimes I feel almost *suicidal with regret. But I __had__ to go away when I did - or I'd have drunk myself to death by now, and would __never__ have finished writing* Salmon Fishing. *But oh, how I miss it all as it used to be. I never fish for sea trout any more, and very rarely for salmon. Don't want to catch (or kill) them.*

To Bill Arnold a little later he wrote: 'Half of me is still living at Cragg and I suppose always will be. I shall never forget all the wonderful times I had at Knott End in the old days, with rod and gun.' The regrets were becoming clear, and very soon so were the cracks.

The final months of the relationship were increasingly stormy. Eventually, Tim Thomas brokered a resolution. In April 1986, accepting that he could continue the relationship with Romille no longer and knowing Kathleen was ready to have him back, Falkus left Glanawen, and Romille, for good.

But he was not yet ready to make a fresh, and permanent, commitment to Cragg and Kathleen. Instead he needed a safe haven on neutral territory. He headed east, towards Buckinghamshire and the home of his senior Trusty, Fred Buller.

Falkus spent three weeks with Fred and Pauline Buller. There were long phone calls to both Cragg and Glanawen. He even explored a third way; still believing that he had something to offer a suitable representative of the fair sex - preferably, a rich one - he went so far as to compose an advertisement for the personal column of a newspaper. According to Buller:

He was feeling quite lost, and asked me what he should do. I felt I had to be honest, and used the language of one of his own wildlife films. I told Hugh that he was an alpha male without a territory. I pointed out that he didn't own anything - had never owned anything - and reminded him that he was nearly seventy and that his health was not good. He had very little to offer a woman. Cragg and Eskdale were the nearest thing he had ever had to a domain he could call his own, and going back to Kathleen was his only way out. He nodded his head in agreement. He knew I was right. From that point on it was just a matter of when, and how.

On top of this, Falkus was in poor shape and getting worse. Domestic conflict and the stress of living in exile had taken their toll of his health; he was underweight and in frequent pain, his digestive system shot to ribbons. In May, he finally pointed the car north towards Eskdale, Kathleen and home.

For her part Romille has kept her counsel about her years with Hugh, although she once told Fred Buller that she felt privileged to have been a part of his life. She is now married to Tim Thomas.

XIV

Beating Maggie

Teach them to cast. Flog them a rod and reel. It's so easy, it almost hurts.
<small>LETTER TO JO RIPPIER</small>

IN *Sea Trout Fishing*, Falkus had written: 'Since overhead, double-haul, Spey, roll and switch-casting methods have been dealt with in detail in a host of publications, I will not waste space by covering such well-beaten ground.' By the 1980s he was beating it himself, and harder than anyone else.

It started two hundred miles to the north east, on that finest and wildest of the big Scottish East Coast salmon rivers, the Spey. Arthur Oglesby had been teaching on Speyside since the late 1950s, working, at first unpaid, as second-in-command to the great Tommy Edwards, the leading casting instructor of his day. When Tommy retired in 1968 at the age of eighty-three - he died before the season was out - Arthur took over as chief instructor. The following year, with a group of enthusiasts including Esmond Drury and Jack Martin, he set up the Association of Professional Game Angling Instructors.

Oglesby now enjoyed a secure position at the head of the Speyside salmon fishing plutocracy, with the Grantown tackle dealer and angling expert George Mortimer as his second-in-command. When Mortimer stepped down, Oglesby began to call on other prominent men in angling, including his friend Hugh Falkus, for assistance. Falkus had no background or training in casting instruction; his value to Oglesby lay in his personality and reputation, rather than in his expertise as a caster.

In those days, most fly fishing for salmon was still done with the overhead cast. The 'tick tock' style, as it was sometimes rather derisively referred to, was easy and quick to master and quite good enough for most purposes. It enabled new recruits whose time on the river was brief and precious to get a fly working and a fish on the bank with minimal waste of time.

The courses would generally run from mid-April until the end of May, preparing pupils to do battle with their quarry during the peak months of the season. This arrangement also gave the instructors the opportunity to steer their (often well-heeled) charges straight from the casting clinic on to a nice bit of prime fishing - good for the pupil, who could look forward to some quick results, good for the instructor, who would gain the credit, and good for the local angling economy.

Although speycasting's history stretches well back into the nineteenth century, it remained, until the 1970s, largely the Spey gillies' property. The added complication of trying to teach it to newcomers to the sport was considered unnecessary, given that most pools on most rivers could be covered quite satisfactorily by overhead casting. So Edwards, Oglesby and their counterparts on the other big Scottish rivers had rarely bothered.

Falkus was quick to cotton on to the advantages of speycasting - the opportunity it gave to fish with trees or a high bank behind you, the reduced muscular effort and the sheer elegance of the cast. But it seemed to him that it had failed to move with the times. Developed in the days of heavy wooden and cane rods, it needed to be rethought for the carbon-fibre era.

He proceeded to rethink it. He studied it as practised by Oglesby and his fellow instructors, then applied himself to the literature on the subject.

When it came to the practical research, the new home he shared with Romille at Eskdalemuir on the banks of the White Esk proved very convenient. Falkus told Fred Buller that during his time at Watcarrick Cottage he would go down to the river almost every day, regardless of the season, constantly trying new variations of the spey cast and reconstructing the anatomy of each variant in minute detail. Whatever might later have been said about the approach he developed, he could not be accused of skimping the testing phase.

'Hugh broke it all down into elements' says Bill Arnold. 'He was constantly coming back to me with requests for this book or that article. He was fascinated by the spey cast and wanted to understand it better than anyone had before. I believe he succeeded.'

Conventionally, speycasting is done from either shoulder and in two modes, single and double, making four distinct casts to be mastered. Which one you choose depends on which bank of the river you are fishing from and whether the wind is blowing upstream or down.

Swapping shoulders also, conventionally, means swapping hands. If you were fishing from the left bank in a downstream wind (double spey) or from the right bank in an upstream one (single spey), you would place your left hand at the top of the butt, instead of your right, as is more natural if you are right-handed.

Falkus looked at all this from the point of view of the beginner, and set out to develop an approach to speycasting which he could teach successfully. He decided that switching hands added an unnecessary difficulty, and set out to persuade the world of this. He felt that a better solution for the average angler faced with the need to cast off the 'wrong' shoulder was simply to swing the dominant hand across the body, so you never had to lead with your weak hand. It might look less elegant, but it was easier to learn and just as effective. There was another advantage - fishing with the 'wrong' hand made it awkward to get at your wading staff. Falkus told a story (almost certainly apocryphal) about how he had rescued a friend who had been swept away by the current because he had lost his balance while fumbling for his stick.

Crucial to the success of any spey cast is the final manoeuvre, the roll cast, so simple yet so dependent on correct positioning and timing. Falkus was always merciless in his insistence that pupils should not attempt the earlier stages of the spey cast until they could roll-cast properly.

He made up his mind that it was impossible for him or anyone else to teach the traditional technique for the single spey cast successfully, because it depended on developing a feel for the correct pressure on the line. Instead he developed a variation that involved bringing the line round in a figure-of-eight manoeuvre; the shape of the eight was the guide to the correct execution of the cast.

Falkus was so convinced that his technique for speycasting and his approach to teaching it were head-and-shoulders above everything else in the business that he spent a large part of his remaining active years promoting it as if his life depended on it. In 1983, apparently with Romille at his side, he set up the Hugh Falkus School of Casting. His base was the Boat Hotel at Boat of Garten, eight miles upriver from Grantown, where the Speyside casting industry had its headquarters. He was not a man to get involved with the responsibility and tedium of running a business, so he reached an agreement with Bruce Wilson, the manager of the Boat. Wilson would run the operation and take the money, leaving Falkus free to concentrate on promoting and running the courses.

A letter of terms from Wilson to Falkus written in 1986 reveals that the charge per head that year, for instruction, fishing and seven nights' dinner, bed and breakfast, was £295 a week, of which Falkus received £95. With a dozen or more anglers on a course, that was a killing of well over a thousand pounds for the week. He also enjoyed free fishing on the hotel's water.

An early promotional letter, headed 'Hugh Falkus on Speyside', runs:

How much can you learn about salmon and sea trout fishing in a week? The answer: a great deal, if you concentrate on <u>learning</u> rather than fishing. Many people who join angling courses spend most of their time trying to catch fish. Almost invariably they end their week in frustration, having caught nothing and learned very little. This course is designed to pay you handsome dividends - <u>in the future</u>. To get the most out of game fishing you must learn the roll, single Spey and double Spey casts. I have devised my own methods of teaching these casts. If you are prepared to practise them hard you will find a week ample time in which to become a proficient Spey caster.

This remained Falkus' thesis, and few anglers who took one of his courses would challenge its wisdom.

Falkus' reputation ensured great interest in the venture. The courses were advertised in the angling press, and anglers across the UK eagerly signed up to be commanded, corrected, and occasionally humiliated by the man with the flowing white mane who had revolutionised night fishing for sea trout and now promised to do the same for speycasting. Though he was too nice a man to complain openly, there is no doubt that Arthur Oglesby lost a great deal of business to Falkus.

The relationship between the two men had been creaking for some time. Never a man to accept second place, Falkus deeply resented Oglesby's greater fame and status, and could not resist doing what he could to undermine it. He would cheerfully insult Arthur behind his back, and sometimes in his presence.

One night on Speyside, probably in 1982, Oglesby was entertaining a group of American anglers in the hotel. Falkus, as his assistant, gave a talk. Repeatedly he made little digs at Arthur, belittling what he had said. Arthur could not have enjoyed the experience, but he was not one for a confrontation.

Grace Oglesby was made of different stuff. She left the room in disgust. When Falkus had finished, she confronted him.

'I told him that he owed a great deal to Arthur, who had always treated him so kindly' she says. 'Hugh assured me that he loved him like a brother. That was nonsense - he was desperately jealous of him. I told him, "Yes - like Cain and Abel!" I don't think we ever spoke again.'

The conventional approach to casting instruction followed the military model. It involved lining up your pupils on the bank, giving them an introductory chat and then drilling them step by step in the required manoeuvres. Falkus' approach was more entertaining, and much more colourful. At Boat of Garten the week would begin on the Sunday evening with introductions and a champagne reception, then five days of instruction would follow. The mornings were devoted to casting, while the afternoons were used to examine various angling-related topics such as how to read a river, salmon fly presentation or night fishing for sea trout (though Falkus had long since given up stalking the riverbank by night, he still carried a metaphorical torch for the game). Each evening he would hold forth about a particular angling issue, such as fly presentation or why salmon take, and then conclude with a showing of one of his films, starting on the Monday with *Self Portrait of a Happy Man* and finishing on the Friday with *Salmo the Leaper*.

Saturday was declared an anglers' 'fun day'. The pupils were let loose on the river to see who could catch the most fish, with Falkus on hand to provide individual instruction. On the last evening there was a farewell banquet, when Falkus would present prizes.

Mark Bowler, now Editor of *Fly Fishing and Fly Tying*, joined Falkus for a course at Boat of Garten in 1987.

We knew we were in for an experience as soon as we arrived. At the front of the hotel he had chalked out a parking space with the words 'reserved for Hugh Falkus' scrawled across it in big white letters.

Hugh shot up in his little blue Citroen and reviewed our equipment. "So who's taped up his rod?" he asked. Of course, none of us had. So before we could go any further, we were all ordered off to the local shop to buy a roll of insulating tape each.

The first challenge was to learn roll casting. He lined us up along the river, six on one bank and six on the other. Then he walked on to the bridge and looked down on us as we practised, like a Roman general inspecting his troops.

We all started flogging away like mad, hoping we were doing it right, not daring to look up in case we attracted his attention. It was just like being back in the classroom with a particularly ruthless schoolmaster.

Then we heard a great roar - "No no no no NO!" and we all looked up in fear to see who had incurred his wrath. He lumbered down from the bridge towards our bank - he couldn't move very fast - and we could see the six chaps on the far bank all breathing sighs of relief because they knew that, this time at least, they were safe.

He stomped along behind the line of anglers, all of us concentrating furiously to try to avoid humiliation. Then he stopped behind the man who had offended him and you could practically see the poor chap's knees shaking. "It's an S, not a bloody Z!" Falkus shouted. He started throwing his arms up and down in a theatrical gesture of despair and we heard him groan, "Why oh why did I ever decide to teach f . . . ing speycasting?"

He didn't care who you were or what you thought, you were his pupil and you were there to learn. He even had us beating a molehill with a stick to try to get the roll-casting action right.

The class would gather each evening at the bar for a debate, which tended to turn into a monologue from Hugh about a pet subject such as sportsmanship or the evil of acid rain. He would dine alone at his own table, and was always first down to breakfast the next morning.

Gregor Murray from Midlothian met Falkus in 1988 when he went into Mortimers in Grantown to buy a salmon net. 'I told Grant Mortimer I wanted the one pictured in Hugh's book, and asked if they had a copy so that we could look it up. Grant replied "Why bother with the book, why not ask the man himself? He's standing behind you." It was a little like asking to consult a Bible and being told "Why not ask God? He's standing behind you."'

Falkus identified the net in question, waited until one was found and then showed Gregor how to use it in various situations. He still treasures that net.

Gregor signed up for the following year's course.

Hugh's first questions were about what we all did. He seemed to like to begin by categorising people either by job or geography - perhaps it was easier to remember than a name. At first I was 'Money Man'. One pupil said he was from Norfolk, and became 'Norfolk' for the rest of the course.

We would meet in the bar before dinner, and Hugh would sit at the far end with his back to the wall and tell marvellous anecdotes, often against himself. Much later he told me how tiring he found it having to entertain everyone, but at the time he seemed to be in his element, laughing and joking with the best of them. Afterwards we all sat at a large table while Hugh ate on his own.

When dinner was over we would go upstairs for an evening session. On the first night Hugh told us to concentrate on learning for that week; we would have the rest of our lives for fishing. At one point he was interrupted and lost his thread. He snapped, "Never, never, never interrupt me when I'm in mid-flow." There was an uneasy moment before we moved

Left, top to bottom:

A casting class at Boat of Garten.

Falkus and Mike Daunt (next to him) with pupils.

A rare chance to rest. Mike Daunt in centre of picture.

'Daunty' and HF.

Old Falk.

on. Later, Hugh pointed out of the window and said, "Remember this light, gentlemen. This is the light that will give you the best chance of catching a summer salmon." We all sat for a moment or two looking at the dropping light, the sky to the west and a few clouds, and I went to bed anticipating the morning.

There was the real pleasure on the first day of watching a practised master at work. Hugh had had a little wooden platform built by the river and he stood there and gave us a demonstration, throwing out a very long line in all directions apparently effortlessly. He started us casting ourselves, with the roll cast and then the double spey. Suddenly it did not seem so easy.

At night Hugh gave us a talk on the angler's approach. 'Treat every day as the day you will catch the biggest fish of your life. Attention to detail is essential. It is no accident that big fish are often lost; they are the strongest. _Always_ change your leader before fishing. _Never_ use nylon that has been exposed to sunlight, nor hoard nylon from previous seasons. _Always_ strip line to the backing, check the join and rewind evenly. _Always_ test the hook.' Hugh demonstrated this last piece of advice by putting the points of a large double hook on to his thumb nail and pulling till it straightened. "D'you see?" he said. "You might have fished with that."

The following day Hugh gave us a demonstration of the single spey cast. He distinguished his method from the traditional way, which he said he could not teach because it involved developing a feel for how hard to pull the line past you. In the evening he talked about rivers, pools and where fish lie: the shapes of rivers source to sea, shapes of pools, changing lies at different water heights, fish behaviour (resident v. running), taking lies, tactics in different conditions and covering salmon in different ways.

On the third morning we had a demonstration of the reverse single and double Spey casts. We also had more practice. Hugh would sit on a bench with a large flask of coffee, shouting corrections and encouragements to everyone with mumbled asides to himself or whoever was sitting with him. "One, two, three, u-u-up. That's better. Well a bit better. You could always try a hand line." One senior Edinburgh lawyer was having trouble getting the line out with a beautiful split-cane rod that had been his father's. "No, no. Make the forward stroke harder, as if you are trying to break the rod." Spurred on, he gave the forward cast a heave with all his might. The rod broke. Hugh thought this was one of the funniest things he had seen in years. They must have heard him laughing up in the village.

It was Hugh's birthday while we were there and he was on top form. At dinner we presented a member of the group with a salmon, it being his birthday too. Hugh came across to our table to see. Stroking the fish, he gave an address that had the packed dining room of the Boat Hotel - American tourists, blue-rinsed Morningside ladies, businessmen and courting couples - hushed and mesmerised. This was no ordinary fish. This was a Spey spring salmon fresh in from 'the dark sway of the sea'. A female, its shape distinguished *it from those of other rivers like the Tay and Tweed. Its journey and life story had been extraordinary.*

*"Take a good look at this fish, gentlemen," he said. "The way you all cast, you have f***-all chance of catching one yourselves." The manager scurried round placating people and Hugh walked calmly back to his seat. We laughed our socks off.*

Wing Commander Andrew Moir, who led 43 Fighter Squadron during the 1991 Gulf War, had got to know Falkus through taking casting lessons. When Moir wrote to Falkus from the Gulf, Falkus replied: 'I envy you. Dear God, how I would love to be with you all . . . Tell them [Moir's squadron] to feel very proud. They will never experience anything like it again. The memory of those days has lived with me (and in a strange way sustained me) all my life. When you've knocked the shit out of Saddam, come and crack a bottle with me.'

Peter Mason was one of the few anglers who ever managed to challenge him successfully. When Falkus demonstrated the tying of a four-turn water knot and advised that the end pointing up the line should be used for the dropper, Mason pointed out that his own tests had shown that the downward-pointing end was stronger (few who have tried it would disagree). The next morning at breakfast, Falkus told Mason that he was right, and that the text of *Salmon Fishing* would be changed accordingly, which it was.

In 1985, on the eve of the move from Eskdalemuir to South Wales, Falkus decided to commit his doctrine to film. Though still strong, he knew his health was on a downward slope and that his active teaching years must be numbered. Even he could not direct, produce, narrate and perform all at once, so he called in a production company, Intervideo, and in May 1985 made *Falkus on Flycasting*.

The location for the filming was not the Spey, but Bill's tarn. Even before Arnold had finished excavating it, Falkus had recognised the opportunities it offered for tackle trials and casting instruction on his doorstep. He had even directed the construction of a series of peninsulas to provide vantage points.

The filming was done in a day. According to Arnold, Falkus sold all his future rights to Intervideo in return for a one-off cash payment of £1500, a modest sum in the light of the subsequent success of the film, which is still selling well today as a fifteen-quid DVD (despite becoming outdated within a few years by Falkus' own refinements to his technique).

Falkus was delighted with the tarn, but he was much less happy with *Falkus on Flycasting*. In fairness, it must have been quite a challenge to make

HF and Bill Arnold at Knott End in around 1990.

HF by the tarn.

an interesting fifty-minute film in a day about an old man casting into a lake. Nevertheless Falkus, dressed as if called away from mixing the dogs' breakfasts in check shirt tails, shooting stockings and Hush Puppies, put on a powerful demonstration for a man of sixty-eight. The mane was thinning and the shoulders were now severely hunched, but the voice was as melliflu-ous as ever. 'It's like drawing beautiful curves on cartridge paper with charcoal' he told us, flicking out yet another effortless figure-of-eight.

Bill had stocked the tarn with trout, which made it useful for fishing as well as for casting. Among those who enjoyed the sport there in the 1980s was Cardinal Basil Hume, head of the Roman Catholic Church in Britain; he would visit Knott End at the invitation of his colleague Jack Brewer, the RC Bishop of Lancaster, who was both a keen fisherman and a friend (and pupil) of Bill Arnold (Arnold is an active Catholic and a Papal Knight of St Gregory). Falkus was delighted by the visit. He behaved with great courtesy towards Bill's guests and did not let a single four-letter word pass his lips. Bill says the four of them spent as much time in the hut drinking red wine as fishing.

By now Falkus had begun an informal professional partnership with Michael Daunt, son of his wartime flying chum of the same name. Daunt had just sold his London wet-fish business and was open to the right offer; in 1984, he got it from Falkus.

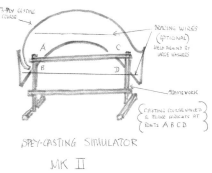

Falkus' sketch for the Speycasting Simulator Mark II and demonstrating the Mark I simulator (Bill Arnold).

Their paths had crossed several times over the years, but the pair did not get to know each other properly until 1983, when Daunt was commissioned by *The Mail on Sunday* to interview Falkus for a feature. Falkus saw something of himself in Daunt, an outgoing, supremely confident personality who shared his contempt for pomp and pretentiousness, as well as his passion for salmon fishing. At the first opportunity Falkus gave 'Daunty', as he quickly dubbed him, a crash course in speycasting. Daunt already had a talent for instruction which had been well developed during his Army service.

'He told me that if I did one overhead cast I'd be sent home' he says. 'I managed it, just. From then on he called on me to help him every season.'

Falkus' interest in Daunt was partly motivated by his desire to ensure that his teachings and his name should live on after he had gone. Bill Arnold arranged for a contract to be drawn up to allow Mike to teach after his death under the Falkus name. Daunt still runs the Hugh Falkus School of Speycasting, though he has transferred it three hundred miles south to the river Test, within reach of his home in Berkshire.

'Hugh was very concerned that the angling world should remember him after his death and that there would be someone left to teach his style of casting' says Daunt. 'He had a great fear of being forgotten.'

After Falkus' return from his years of self-imposed exile, the annual weeks on Speyside began to degenerate from a joy and an escape into something

David Profumo with Falkus.

of a chore. Faced with having two instructors to put up instead of one, the hotel began to drive a harder bargain, which made it less profitable. Falkus was no longer well enough to drive and came to rely entirely on Daunt. By the end of the 1980s his digestive system was in such a poor state that he was obliged to leave the river several times an hour, which was both embarrassing and inconvenient.

The Scottish courses ran for only four further years after his return to Cragg before Falkus motored to Speyside for the last time. After that, he scarcely left Cumbria; all teaching took place on the tarn, and Bill shared the instruction with Hugh.

The format at Knott End was very different. It was not possible to teach large groups of anglers simultaneously on the tarn - two at a time was plenty - but against that anglers did not expect fishing as well as tuition, so there was no need to confine instruction to the spring and summer months. The Knott End Academy of Speycasting and Game Fishing, as Falkus and Arnold christened their new venture, welcomed its first pupil, Mr Robert Gibson-Bevan, on 10th January, 1989, in time for even the earliest of spring salmon fishermen to prepare for the new season. The courses ran through until October, by which time more than eighty happy pupils, including visitors from Ireland, Belgium and Liechtenstein, had vouched for their satisfaction in the visitors' book.

'I didn't believe I could learn so much about speycasting. I shall never forget the man - the personality - the master' wrote Mike Newton. The writer David Profumo, who won Falkus' friendship through writing about his methods, said that he had 'learned more in three days than in the previous three decades . . . Hugh Falkus is quite simply the best'. More candidly, Profumo says he wrote in his diary that he had found him 'brilliant, rugged, delightful. Would not want to cross swords with him, however'.

No one had tried to run speycasting classes on a lake before, and Falkus' peers were sceptical. Hugh was not amused when Arthur Oglesby ran a press advertisement for his Speyside courses which urged 'Come and learn to speycast the proper way, on running water'. The schism with Oglesby became complete when Falkus heard that he had claimed while on a tour in the USA that it was he who had taught Hugh to speycast.

When Ken Walker of Bruce and Walker, the firm that had sponsored Oglesby and Falkus' angling videos (and, incidentally, supplied the rod blanks for Robert Redford's film *A River Runs Through It*), approached him to suggest that he might like to sponsor and help market their rods, he needed little persuading. At this time Bruce and Walker, whose success was founded on a pioneering approach to rod design, were developing a new range of 'Hexagraph' rods, made from carbon fibre but constructed from six V-profiled sections in the same way as a split-cane rod. This construction made for a great deal of strength and resilience but produced a slow, ponderous action by comparison with conventional tubular carbon fibre. Falkus helped the company to design several variants, including a 10-foot 6-inch Hugh Falkus Sea Trout Special, and the rods won numerous admirers. But Falkus was one of the many who felt they were too heavy for the modern caster. They were soon succeeded by a new generation of ultra-light tubular rods.

There was much experimentation during these years with tapers, profiles and configurations, and Ken Walker would drive up once a month or so with armfuls of rods for testing. Falkus and Arnold tried adding extra rings to the tip section to simulate the drag of running water, as an aid to spey-casting instruction; Arnold still has a rod with eight rings whipped on to the top joint, their legs almost touching. Walker also had a rod finished in white, to make Falkus' demonstrations easier to follow - Bill Arnold still has it.

It was all very different from Speyside. Falkus' determination to instil the correct casting action into the brains of his pupils led over these final years of instruction to a good deal of invention. Aided and abetted by Bill, he came up with a series of training devices, each more fiendish than the last.

A crayon drawing by Falkus captioned 'From the draughtsman's office, Cragg Cottage' shows the design for the first. Once made flesh by Bill Arnold, it was christened the Hugh Falkus Figure-of-Eight Speycasting Simulator Mark 1. It consisted of a bizarre-looking plywood frame, mounted on a stand by the tarn and looking more like a Henry Moore sculpture than anything to do with fishing. But it worked. The inner edges of the apertures cut into it were shaped to define precisely the movements of the rod during a correctly-executed cast.

This novel approach to teaching proved very successful. Pupils found that after a minimal amount of practice with the simulator, they could step away, do the same thing without the frame, and immediately put out a half-decent cast.

The first design proved too flimsy, so Arnold developed a more robust Mark 2 version consisting of a single carefully-curved wooden strip mounted on a frame.

The High Court judge David Steel QC, then new to salmon fishing, visited Knott End twice for lessons. Mr Justice Steel remembers Hugh with affection, helped by the fact that he went on to take two decent salmon and lose a third on his next Tweed outing. He bought a Bruce and Walker from Hugh of course, and a copy of *Salmon Fishing*.

'I can still feel that casting frame and the strange swirling manoeuvre it forced you to do' he says. 'I tried hard, and I think he appreciated that. His lessons have stood me in good stead ever since.'

There followed a series of other instruments designed by Hugh and Bill ('the great Knott End craftsman and assistant torturer' as Falkus described him) to cure bad casting habits and get the tyro on the way to success. The Emasculator and the Clapperstick were designed to punish the pupil who pulls the left hand too far back on the power stroke, while the Casting Corset and the Crucifix, a flat upright frame to which the offender's shoulders were strapped, were brutally direct ways of rendering inappropriate upper body movement impossible. 'In my early days of instructing I soon realised the impossibility of making good speycasters out of people who behave like street-corner toys' he wrote. 'At my wits' end to know how to cure them, I began to harbour a sadistic longing to nail their shoulders to a cross . . . the Crucifix is the next best thing. The pain of the cords cutting into the shoulder muscles soon convinces the most recalcitrant pupil that all the roll cast needs is the action of forearms and wrists.' When he spotted a pupil rolling his shoulders, the roar would go up 'Crucify him!'.

To demonstrate how still the upper body should remain while casting, Falkus would balance a glass of Scotch on the peak of his hat, then put out the full line without spilling a drop.

The need to get pupils roll-casting properly led to a memorable ritual called 'Beating Maggie'. The features of our first female Prime Minister, whose popularity had plummeted as a result of the infamous Poll Tax, were drawn on to a stuffed sack and visitors exhorted to beat them with Hugh's 'Thatcher stick' until their wrists were the consistency of overcooked spaghetti. 'Naturally the picture can be painted according to one's political inclinations' wrote the inventor. 'But with constant beating the Prime

Falkus demonstrates the whisky-tumbler trick.

Bill Arnold 'Beating Maggie', Hugh and Bill testing the Crucifix and Falkus strapping a young pupil in.

Minister's likeness faded and disappeared, and although in my own mind I feel certain that nothing supernatural was involved, in the light of subsequent events a belief in witchcraft became almost overwhelming.' (He was referring to her demise in 1990. In truth Falkus was a great admirer of Mrs Thatcher.)

Falkus' willingness to cast aside convention extended to tackle design, a change from the largely traditionalist approach to tackle which he taught in *Sea Trout Fishing*. 'Rod rings are obsolescent' he asserted to David Profumo, suggesting that someone should design a rod in which the line ran straight through the blank (a Midland tackle-maker had already done so for coarse fishermen in fact, but it was not a great commercial success, probably because most anglers prefer fishing tackle to look like fishing tackle). He had a white sinking line produced, on the presumption that fish generally see the line from below and that this was the least visible colour, and arranged for an outbarb hook to be made (by his preferred hookmaker, Partridge of Redditch) which he believed was a better hooker than a conventional pattern with the barb on the inside.

Perhaps his most eclectic invention was a reel belt designed to allow the angler to fish with the reel attached to his body instead of to the rod. He believed this would save weight, prevent the loss of both rod and reel in an accident and allow the angler to cast further.

Pupils were generous in their praise of Falkus' teaching skills, though some enjoyed the experience more than others. 'Leave your pride at the door and pick it up when you leave? I'm still looking for it!' wrote Oliver Leatham in the visitors' book. Ed Koch, Lee Wulff and Roman Moser were among the prominent anglers who came to the tarn from overseas. 'Truly one of England's national treasurers' commented another, the American angling author Ed Jaworowski, a casting expert himself.

The novelist Graham Swift, a keen angler, enjoyed his 1990 lesson so much that he went back again the same year. Swift had published, with David Profumo, an anthology of fishing in literature, *The Magic Wheel*, which Falkus had reviewed enthusiastically in *The Field*.

Malcolm Greenhalgh tells of the eminent surgeon who proudly presented his new salmon rod for Hugh to inspect. "You think you will be able to spey-cast with that?" bellowed Hugh. "No no no! It's not good enough! Look at the rod. No guts! And the line! You would be better off taking that down to the shore at Ravenglass and using it as a handline to catch crabs!" He then took three brand-new Bruce and Walkers, complete with reels and lines, from his store and made the surgeon write out a cheque for all three of them before the lesson could begin.

Greenhalgh also remembers a Welsh angler who called at the cottage to ask Falkus to sign his copy of *Sea Trout Fishing* and was not allowed to leave until he had bought *Salmon Fishing*, *The Stolen Years* and *Freshwater Fishing* to go with it.

The angling book expert David Beazley, who helped Hugh frequently on bibliographical matters, went for lessons in 1993. 'As a teacher he was a nightmare from one's schooldays: furious at having to say things twice, uncomprehending of one's inability to do precisely what he had just told you to do and constantly on the brink of washing his hands of you and leaving you to drown in your own pathetic incompetence' he wrote in *Waterlog* magazine. 'He would bellow a mixture of instruction and abuse across the lake like a rogue elephant.'

The television presenter Fiona Armstrong, who has written books and made films about angling, was introduced to Falkus by Malcolm Greenhalgh in 1991. In 1995 she went for instruction; she wrote about the experience in *Trout and Salmon*, saying she had found him quieter than she remembered and putting it down to his recent surgery. 'Dear Hugh, what a joy and honour to be taught by you!' she wrote in the Knott End visitors' book. 'To a truly determined pupil' responded Hugh in the book he gave her.

Falkus continued to do his best to avoid youngsters. If boys were brought to him for instruction he would generally refer them to Bill Arnold, though he made a notable exception for Mike Daunt's son Will. Daunt was called upon to help out occasionally, while the more experienced members of Millom Anglers' Association would sometimes lend a hand.

Falkus' confidence in the superiority of his casting methods and skill as an instructor did not diminish with age. 'Forget about my boasting, my conceit, my arrogance, I am far and away the finest speycasting instructor in the world; I can teach you better than anyone else how to handle a two-handed rod' he wrote to Jo Rippier in 1993, urging him to come for lessons.

In the early 1990s Falkus began work on the last book he was to publish during his lifetime. *Speycasting - a New Technique* would be his legacy to the salmon-fishing world.

It is hard to think of a more challenging subject to teach in words and pictures than speycasting, and Falkus well knew it. The book would probably never have appeared at all had it not been for a visit in the spring of 1993 by Tom Pero, a prominent American angling journalist, and a photographer, Ben Blackwell. The pair spent several days at Knott End and on the Derwent gathering material about Falkus and his casting methods for a feature for a new magazine to be called *Wild Steelhead and Atlantic Salmon*. Pero remembers that Falkus was 'at times lucid and witty, at other times in obvious pain and drifting in and out of a drug-and-alcohol haze'.

Blackwell took many photographs, and it was this wealth of illustrations (which he was able to use without payment) that enabled Falkus to get his book off the ground. Most of its 250-plus pictures are by Blackwell.

When it came to the cover design for *Speycasting*, Falkus as usual knew best. 'What the artist should go for, I feel, is beauty of line, simplicity and beautiful curves - symbolic of the cast itself. It must be *simple and beautiful*' he urged to David Burnett, whose Excellent Press published it. He accompanied the note with his own rough outline, showing the title at the top, 'a new technique' below and a picture of an angler executing the Falkus technique of two-way fishing, in which a loop of line is thrown to enable the angler to retrieve the fly in opposite directions during the same cast. The eventual cover illustration was a photographic version of this idea, using a full-page bird's-eye-view picture taken for the purpose on the Spey at Boat of Garten by the Danish photographer Orla Bertram-Nielsen.

Falkus was not a man to put diplomacy before honesty in passing judgement on his peers. 'Unhappily, the huge improvement in salmon fly rods has not been accompanied by an improvement in speycasting and instruction' he wrote in the book. 'What many teachers are lacking today is instruction in how to instruct.' No gracious exemption was accorded to Oglesby, Falkus' friend, sponsor and mentor; in fact the book did not mention Arthur at all.

The book is the largest and most lavishly-produced of all Falkus' works and went out at a princely £25. Nevertheless it sold well. It is now changing hands on the second-hand market for four or five times its original price.

The angling writer Tom Fort gave a perceptive judgement of *Speycasting* in the *Weekend FT*.

The voice is that of an elderly, opinionated, irascible prep schoolmaster addressing a gaggle of more or less ignorant boys. But the unrelieved didacticism does not matter if the lesson is sound - which, I would guess, this is. The photographs, arranged mainly in sequences like stills from a film, give as fluid and vivid an impression of the techniques as a book could possible provide. The great majority of them feature Falkus himself, white-maned, stern-faced, in an interesting selection of threadbare jerseys. I am told that he is now in poor health. If this should prove to be his last testament, it is a worthy one.

As Tom Pero had noted, Falkus was indeed in poor health, and getting worse. During the 1995 season the teaching sessions became increasingly sporadic. On 14th October David Wallace from Strathclyde wrote in the visitors' book: 'After two days receiving instruction from Mr Falkus I will now enjoy casting as much as catching.' It would be the last entry.

XV

Old Falk

'Let there be a bonfire of angling books' I said aloud. 'And a roasting of anglers.
Let their clacking voices, like their clacking reels, be silent.' And the ravens
cackled in chorus and croaked: 'Silence will come soon enough!'

LETTER TO JO RIPPIER

H UGH LIMPED home to Cragg in June 1986 resigned to making the best
of life with Kathleen. He met a warm, if subdued, welcome. As the
summer went on, with the aid of Bill's friendship and moral support and
Kathleen's care and cooking, he began to recover his energy.

The return of Hugh and his income allowed some improvements to be
made at the cottage. He paid for the windows to be double-glazed and for
the installation of a grated fire in place of the open log fire which had been
there since it was built. But these were very much his own projects - he had
grown used to living in a modernised, draught-free house - and they were
done without Kathleen's blessing.

To Kath's greater distress, the contact with Romille continued intermittently for the rest of that year. Welcoming her husband back home was one
thing; putting up with his refusal to give the relationship its *coup de grâce* was
quite another. She would eavesdrop on the calls from Wales, then go on the
attack. Kitchenware was thrown, often accurately. Even during the more
peaceful periods, the bickering and the brickbats made for an uncomfortable atmosphere for visitors - not that there were so many now.

Fred Buller remembers Hugh commenting one day that the temperature
was exactly the same as that at Watcarrick. Kath responded by walking out
of the room. Worse, when Peter Behan mentioned the double-glazing,

Falkus responded: 'Yes, I put it in for my darling Romille.' It would be hard to imagine a more disastrous slip of the tongue; it precipitated a screaming row.

A letter to Jo Rippier the following April reveals how untidy the end of the affair had been.

For some months I felt heartbroken, I missed R so much. Then, early in the New Year, she begged me to go back. I agreed. Made all arrangements. Suddenly, she changed her mind and said she never wanted to see me again! Jesus! What a mess. I nearly, so nearly, shot myself (partly haunted, I suppose, by the suicide of my old friend David Drake who shot himself exactly a year before!) But I didn't.

Once I sat down and began to think; to use what little intelligence seems to have been left to me; dispassionately for once; I realised what a lucky escape I'd had. You see, I nearly married Romille. I wanted to. I was going to. But something, some deep-down instinct of survival, kept me from going ahead with a divorce from Kathleen. So, thank God, I never did marry R . . .

For months I was shattered. It's only now that I realise that once again in my life I've survived. Although half of me still loves R I know that life with her would have been impossible. Here I have a pleasant cottage, all the fishing and shooting I could want and beautiful surroundings. I also have an alcoholic wife! Well, at least she loves me; she isn't trying to take me for an emotional ride. So, life starts again where it left off four years ago - only I'm four years older (it seems like forty) and I suppose a lot wiser. A least I have peace of mind. Do you know, I never had that all the time I lived with Romille. I could never get rid of a sense of guilt. One thing I've realised: you can run away and try to start a new life, but you're still chained. I couldn't break free of that. So, I'm happy to have said goodbye. I shall never see R again.

Frankly, I think that most women come straight from outer space!

Kathleen's drinking was indeed out of control - more so, if anything, than it had been during Hugh's absence. Early one morning Falkus realised she had disappeared from the cottage, and phoned Arnold to raise the alarm. While Hugh dialled the emergency services Bill ran up towards Raven Crag, knowing that she often went walking that way. There was no sign of Kath on the Crag, but when he headed downhill towards the river he spotted her track in the dew-laden grass. He followed it down to the river and found her sitting fully clothed in the swirling waters of the Corner Pool, drunk, drenched and sobbing.

The ambulance drew up in the lane as Bill was carrying Kath back up towards the cottage. She was put on a stretcher and rushed to the hospital at Whitehaven, where the staff began to treat her, first for exposure and then for the alcoholism. Her stay did not last long. Hating hospitals and medical supervision almost as much as her husband, she persuaded her brother Benny to let her sign herself out.

If Bill Arnold had been a valuable part of the Falkuses' lives before, he was now indispensable. 'William', as Falkus invariably addressed him - he was never content to call anyone by the name the rest of the world used - became Hugh's interface with the outside world, acting as his accountant, business manager, property manager, equerry, secretary and general factotum as well as his co-instructor. And in her own way, Kathleen came to depend as much on Marie Arnold as her husband did on Bill.

On Hugh's return to Cragg, there was some financial sorting-out to be done. Bill advised him that he could raise a useful annuity for his last years by selling some of his more valuable possessions and combining the proceeds with his share of the money from the sale of Watcarrick Cottage. The sale included leather-bound editions of Hugh's books, paintings, fishing tackle and some of his guns, the disposal of which Fred Buller arranged in London.

'We calculated that as long as Hugh lived for another seven years it would be a good investment' says Bill. 'He was determined to get his money back - he used to joke that he would make sure he lived long enough to do so.'

Relations between Hugh and Kathleen remained shaky. No longer did she talk affectionately about her Falk; no longer did he call her Pot or Totty. Yet there were good times still, and as the dust settled and the contact with Wales petered out, a degree of harmony returned. The focus of Fred J. Taylor's visits had now switched from fishing to entertainment. The summer Hugh was away in Wales, Bill suggested a barbecue at the cottage. Fred took charge of the cooking, with Kath in support, and what was left of Hugh's circle came along with bottles and food. The barbecues were repeated every year after that.

The centrepiece would usually be a spit-roast side of roe deer, accompanied by a range of other dishes cooked by Fred in his Dutch ovens. These were iron pots with flanged lids. You greased the pot, placed the food inside it, cleared a hole in the centre of the fire, laid the oven in the hole and raked the fire back over it. Fred's ovens - he would have as many as five of them on the go at once - produced delectable results with everything from cuts of beef and steaks of salmon and sea trout to potatoes, vegetables, meat pasties and bread. Fred had been a professional baker, and the loaves he produced were in a different class from anything most of the guests had

Summer barbecue at Cragg. Left to right: June Woodall, Hugh, Fred J. Taylor, Fred Buller, Bill Arnold and Dave Evans.

Fred J. Taylor prepares the barbecue   *Falkus in his study.*

tasted before. Kathleen would follow the main course up with gigantic blackcurrant pies, accompanied by jugfuls of fresh cream, while Bill Arnold, helped by his wife Marie and son Peter, laid on the wine, loaded a trailer with firewood and arranged the table.

The 15th May, 1987, was Hugh's seventieth birthday, and to mark the occasion the Woodall brothers took him for a day's trout fishing on Devoke Water, a couple of miles inland across the fells. Falkus brought with him a large and mysterious box. Once the boat was under way, he distributed menus, opened the box and began to serve a five-star feast - soup, smoked salmon, partridge and mince pies, accompanied by bottles of chilled Sauvignon Blanc, with port and whisky to follow.

That birthday, and the 25th anniversary of *Sea Trout Fishing*, were also marked by the publication by Witherby's of *The Sea Trout*, the story of the capture of his 15lb 6oz specimen from Hazel Dub which had first appeared in Maurice Wiggin's 1965 anthology. A thousand copies were printed.[15]

Falkus never stopped making high-handed demands on those around him, and on himself. Fred J. Taylor remembers a hot summer's day when Falkus was involved in a photographic shoot on the tarn. He and Alec were on standby to provide assistance. They waited to be called, but the summons never came. When the shoot had finished Hugh hunted them out and berated them for failing to come to his aid. Fred felt deeply wounded by this. But then Falkus called after him, applying the same four-letter word to both Fred and himself, and suggested a conciliatory drink.

An incident one Christmas exposed Falkus at his least charismatic. According to Peter Behan, who was there, Falkus opened the cottage door to find a party of revellers, locals from the valley, some of them dressed in festive gear. They were hoping to share a Christmas drink with Falkus, but he was not in the mood; instead they received a four-letter-word dismissal.

'They were people Falkus knew well, but he was not prepared to entertain them' says Behan. 'A little while later there was another knock at the door. It was the son of one of the men. He reminded Hugh that his father had been one of those who had showed him kindness and friendship when he was new to the valley and didn't have two pence to rub together. He told him just what he thought of him.

'Hugh went white. He filled a glass with brandy and went off up to bed. We didn't see him again until the next morning.'

In season, there was still the fishing; the annual early-summer trips to Speyside continued until 1990, and during the rest of the season there were regular days with Bill Arnold on the Derwent. Bill had been fishing the

Brockholes beat at the top of the river since the early 1980s, and after the return from Wales Hugh would join him. There followed a few seasons on the Wood Hall Beat before finally, from 1991, Arnold bought a day per week on on the Ribton Stream beat of the Castle Fishery. Here they were joined by Anthony Desbruslais, a young barrister from Nottinghamshire who had met Hugh and Kathleen through fishing the Esk in the late 1970s (he had booked a rod on the Knott End beat from Walkers of Trowell, who handled the fishing rights on behalf of Georgina Fowler, Bill Fowler's daughter-in-law). They fished with Sir Frank Barlow, then Chairman of the *Financial Times* and Managing Director of the multi-million-pound Pearson Group, and occasionally Tony Mottram, the owner of a hairdressing business in Cockermouth and the man responsible for maintaining the Falkus mane. Mottram was a keen amateur photographer, and supplied some of the pictures for *Speycasting.*

Bill drove Hugh up each Monday through the season. Falkus would buy a *Sun* and a *Daily Mirror* at the garage on the way and spend much of the day sitting reading, watching the river, and commenting on the success or otherwise of his companions. When he did fish, he was usually successful.

'Hugh had the knack of sensing when there was a taking fish nearby' says Bill. 'Very often he would wait for an hour or two, then wade out and take a fish within a few casts.'

Not everyone worshipped the Falkus legend. Bill and Hugh arrived at the hut one week to find that someone had scrawled on the wall 'Falkus is a pompous arrogant big-headed old bastard'. When they returned the following week Falkus packed a felt-tip, with which he responded 'How did you know?' There was no enmity towards the Workington lads whom they knew to be responsible, but when they were invited to Knott End a little while later and tried to match Falkus glass for glass in a whisky-drinking competition, they lost.

Having built his name on his depredations among the sea trout and salmon in his younger years, Falkus, like many an old sportsman, had developed a deep compassion for his quarry. His fishing, when he fished at all, would now be confined to a few judicious casts, in the right spot at the right moment. And when he hooked a salmon, he would usually give the rod to his companion to be played to the net. He told Mike Daunt: 'I hate the thought of that poor creature struggling for its life. If I could send an electric current down the line and kill it immediately, I would.'

He told *Fishing* magazine at about the same time: 'I feel very sorry for the fish when I see it flashing on its way to the net. I don't go along with

With Anthony Desbruslais at Cragg.

catching and releasing fish - it is wrong and unsporting. It means you are playing with the fish, using them as toys. You're getting pleasure from play-ing with these fish and in doing so you're nothing but a sadist. If that's what you want, tie your line to my labrador and I'll go across to the other side of the field with my whistle and a bone and then you'll find out what it's like to hear a reel sing.'

When David Profumo interviewed him for *Salmon, Trout and Sea Trout* in November 1991, he fulminated about the new vogue for catch and release, threatening that it would have 'a devastating effect on the sport of angling'. A couple of months later he put his views on this matter to the readership of the *Weekend Telegraph*.

In my vocabulary 'sport' is clearly defined: it means hunting - whether with horse and hounds, with dogs, gun or rod . . . Both for pleasure and for food, I strive to outwit and kill my quarry. I deplore [catch and release], *because in the interests of angling such a policy can only be self-defeating.*

The average angler, a harmless enough hunter in all truth, lives fairly contentedly in the firelight of his cave, seemingly oblivious of the dangers that threaten his sport. He probably feels he can cope with the occasional animal-rights protestor who threatens to push him into the river, but tends to ignore the millions of peaceable, non-sporting but voting citizens who lurk outside in the darkness of their ignorance . . . It is the public vote that has the power to destroy the angler, or rather to destroy his sport.

If I were an anti I would be clapping my hands and following the catch-and-release crusade with glee. I would wait until the well-meaning but short-sighted anglers pledged themselves - and strike . . . If you really believe that the salmon is an endangered species then you shouldn't be fishing for it. You should certainly not be hooking it simply for the pleasure of feeling it fight its heart out before releasing it.

Profumo was the *Telegraph*'s angling correspondent, and it was he, the following week, who hit back. Under the headline 'Don't swallow the line of the hunter-gatherer' he called Falkus' argument 'alarmist and potentially divisive', and pointed out that there was no concerted move afoot in the UK towards mandatory catch and release. Fishing for the pot, he said, was an argument 'creaking with anachronism'. Pointing out that in *Freshwater Fishing* Falkus and Fred Buller had talked about the capture, retention and release of coarse fish, he accused Falkus of a *volte-face* and concluded that it was he, not the average angler, who was 'living in the cave of the past'.

They were essentially two different ways of viewing the same situation, but Falkus reacted with fury. His reply was so vehement that the *Telegraph* refused to publish it.

It was in these last years that Hugh and Fred Buller resurrected a project which had been under way, on and off, for more than twenty years. Buller had long been fascinated by that enigmatic work *The Treatyse of Fysshynge with an Angle*, dated to 1496. Almost nothing is known with certainty about this extraordinary book, the very wellspring of English angling literature; the traditional view is that it was compiled by Dame Juliana Berners, the fifteenth century Prioress of Sopwell Priory, near St Albans, but there is not a shred of direct evidence for this and many other theories have been put forward.

In the early 1970s Fred and Hugh had made up their minds to investigate 'The Dame' more thoroughly than anyone had before. They studied the text with the aim of comparing it with the known history of angling, to see if this would throw any light. As part of this process, they (that is to say, mainly Fred) prepared a fresh translation, or rather transliteration; he drew up a crib, in which each line of the original text was reproduced with the modern interpretation below.

Work on the book languished somewhat during the 1980s, not helped by Falkus' Welsh interlude, but in the early 1990s Buller and Falkus began a revival. Part of the project involved recreating some of the tackle described in the text. Bill Arnold, ever the resourceful engineer, built a two-piece rod to the Dame's recipe, the thick butt section hollowed out with a hot iron so that the top joint could be slid down inside it when the rod was not in use. Malcolm Greenhalgh recreated ancient flies to match the Dame's drawings.

To cultivate the best-informed contacts, Fred joined Hertfordshire Archaeological Society. He even had a patch of scrub on the banks of the river Ver, near the ruins which mark the site of the old priory, cut down at his own expense. As a result of this exercise, the authors could claim to have identified the exact spot on the riverbank which was depicted by a woodcut from the *Treatyse* showing an angler landing a fish, with what appears to be a priory in the background.

The match could never be proved with certainty, but this was nevertheless an extraordinary piece of detective-work. There was even a plan to make a film about it all - Hardys agreed to build a replica rod and Grace Oglesby was all set to model as the lady angler - but it was never carried through.

Hugh and Fred both thought their book would be remembered as their most important contribution to angling literature. Yet, fascinated as he was by the *Treatyse* - which he acclaimed as the finest angling book ever written - Falkus was much more interested in what it had to tell us about the development of angling than in its historical provenance. He once astonished the angling book expert David Beazley by telling him, in response to some comments on the various theories about the book: 'I don't give a f*** if it was published on the Isle of bloody Elba.'

By now he was deeply involved with the project which had been suggested to him by Peter Behan on his visit to Eskdalemuir in 1984. Behan had studied the causes of anorexia, the 'slimmer's disease', and reasoned that there might be a connection between the mechanism that makes some people believe they are not hungry and the same condition in salmon. This led him into the whole question of why salmon take, or don't take, and in particular why they so often seem to accept lures fished by women. It appeared a promising subject for a book, and at the end of the 1980s Behan and Falkus agreed to start putting one together. Eventually Burnett arranged for Wilma Paterson, a Scottish writer and broadcaster, to research and write most of the book, with Falkus contributing only the foreword, although he helped Behan with the manuscript.

Salmon and Women: The Feminine Angle, published by Witherby's in 1990, began by recounting the tales of some fifty women and girls of all ages and

Falkus at his beloved Meadow Dub (Leon Grace).

Spring salmon in the snow, with Fred Buller.

*Hugh on the Dee in about 1988 with Anthony Royds, Mike Daunt (with a 25lb salmon),
Peter Behan and an unidentified companion*

backgrounds who had caught unusually big salmon, or many salmon, or at least more than their menfolk seemed to be able to catch in the same river at the same time. Among them were Queen Elizabeth the Queen Mother, Dame Barbara Cartland (whose ninety-eight years on this Earth encompassed the demise of several hundred salmon as well as the sale of half a billion books) and Grace Oglesby.

In a more technical second part, Behan examined the possible reasons for this, such as the recent discovery that while the scent of male human skin will drive salmon (and other fish) away, that of a woman's apparently has no effect. He then moved on to the nub of the matter by recounting circumstantial evidence for the idea that female pheromones may actually attract male salmon.

Though it was not a great commercial success, the book attracted considerable media attention. Both the BBC and Border Television turned up at the cottage to interview Falkus, who, concerned that scientific objectivity should prevail, steadfastly refused to commit himself on camera to the assertion that pheromones are the reason for female angling success.

The *Sun* was in no doubt about the matter. 'Girls make BETTER anglers because fish think they are SEXIER' it announced under the headline 'Why gals are good hookers'. Hugh was delighted with that cutting, not least because it called him 'Britain's top salmon fisherman'.

Hugh's foreword offered his own conclusion to the debate. 'Once seized with the lust to fish for salmon, [women] fish with utter determination' he wrote, and more contentiously: 'Once her claws curl around that cork grip you will never get it back . . . whisking round the house with vacuum cleaners gives women very strong wrists.'

Falkus had never had much time for popular culture or modern music, but he enjoyed listening to trad jazz and would often retire to play his collection of cassette recordings of the cornettist Bix Beiderbecke. Like many another active man grounded by age and ill health, he became a copious writer of letters and articles. There were pieces in *Salmon, Trout and Sea Trout*, including the mythopoeic tale about Antony Witherby and the birth of *Sea Trout Fishing* which later appeared in *Some of it Was Fun*, and a review of Jack Charlton's book *Salmon Run* in which he took the opportunity to jump off once again into the Goldsborough Hypothesis. In 1992 he contributed the introduction to a new limited edition from the Flyfisher's Classic Library of Chaytor's *Letters to a Salmon Fisher's Sons*.

He developed a love of 'whodunnits', entering competitions in the *Daily Telegraph* and the *Observer* to spot the murderer. There would be a race every morning for the *Daily Telegraph* crossword - Bill Arnold attests that whether Hugh or Kathleen got there first, it was always completed.

Peter Behan was deeply impressed by Falkus' love of poetry and his ability to recite Keats, in particular, by the yard. He was also struck by his obsession with one particular book; *The Riddle of the Sands*, whose origins he had investigated as a young man (see Chapter I). Behan remembers Falkus reading it repeatedly, night after night, and always having a dog-eared copy by his bedside.

In winter there was always the shooting. Falkus' love of fowling never left him, and he and Bill were still shooting on the Drigg marshes, with the aid of a hide system erected by Bill, as late as 1990. Back at Cragg, he liked to plod down to the estuary with the dogs on any winter's morning when he was feeling strong enough. On Christmas Day he would go out early to shoot a bird or two for the table, then soak in a hot bath with a bottle of champagne while Kathleen plucked them.

There were still public appearances, when he was up to it. In April 1991 at a talk in Penrith he fired a shot in the perennial high-bird debate, condemning the trend towards presenting and shooting ever-higher pheasants. He fired a second round at shooting syndicates who 'go home and leave the picking-up to the keeper' and urged shots everywhere that their behaviour must be immaculate if their sport was to survive. He followed this up with a warning about the threat to angling from the anti-blood-sports movement. According to Bill Arnold: 'The hall held two hundred and fifty people, but there must have been a good three hundred in there - the aisles were packed and people were standing at the back. It was billed to last forty-five minutes, but Falk spoke for nearly twice that and there wasn't a murmur - he held them spellbound. It finished with a standing ovation.'

Though Falkus never attended a Country Landowners' Association Game Fair - that had always been Arthur Oglesby's court - he made regular appearances at the Royal Lancs Show and the Cumberland Show. In the summer of 1992 Malcolm Greenhalgh arranged for Falkus to give a casting demonstration at Chatsworth Angling Fair.

The demonstration was fixed for 11am. At 10.59 I heard what should have been the final announcement of our event over the loudspeaker. I switched on HF's microphone, stepped forward and made my brief introduction. The crowd applauded as HF made his appearance.

"Ladies and gentlemen. Only a fool . . ." he began. The announcer interrupted: "Ladies and gentlemen, this is your last chance to see Hugh Falkus and Malcolm Greenhalgh demonstrating speycasting."

HF tried again. "Ladies and gentlemen. Only a fool would go fly fishing, whether it be for trout, salmon or sea-trout, without the ability to speycast. Now there is much . . ." Again the announcer interrupted: "Ladies and gentlemen. If you want to see Hugh Falkus and Malcolm Greenhalgh demonstrate speycasting, hurry. They have just started."

"Will someone tell that silly bugger to shut up!" bellowed HF. Mothers covered their children's ears and the anglers in the crowd chuckled with glee.

He could still show a mastery of the putdown. When he received a letter from an 'anti' complaining about the harm fishing and shooting did to nature, he wrote back:

You claim to be a 'Friend of the Earth' and that you 'tread as lightly as possible . . . thus hoping to avoid disturbing the balance of nature'. But, dear Mrs H, whatever your motives, however lightly you may tread, you cannot <u>help</u> disturbing nature. And if you are really sincere in wishing to avoid this natural disturbance, I suggest that the only logical step for you to take is to commit suicide. Yours sincerely, Hugh Falkus.

Disappointingly, the letter was never posted; perhaps Kathleen intercepted it.

Hugh's propensity for generosity towards those he cared for was never so much in evidence as in his last years. Gifts were made, not with any potential *quid pro quo* in mind but apparently from a simple desire to make his friends happy. Jo Rippier received an invitation to a weekend's speycasting instruction. On examination of the paperwork he discovered a price, carefully scratched out but decipherable as £500. No mention of the value had been made by Falkus.

There was more. 'When the lesson was over, he went over to a long wooden box attached to the wall, took out a very expensive salmon rod and gave it to me. I was speechless. This was at a time when the cancer was progressing, and I think he realised that the end was not far away.'

In 1990 Hugh and Bill went to Norway for a week, to demonstrate Hugh's casting techniques to a Norwegian audience with Bruce and Walker, who were promoting their Hexagraph rods, and Partridge, the hook manufacturer with which Falkus had had a long association. With whisky far costlier there than in the UK, Falkus decided to take his own supply - fourteen bottles, or two for every day they would be away.

'We found a four-tube rod holdall that had enough space between the tubes for all fourteen bottles' says Arnold. 'The porter at the airport wondered why it was so heavy.'

Falkus' ghosts were never likely to go away. Black depression would still hit him, often without warning. Not long after Falkus had returned to Cragg, Jo Rippier sent him the manuscript of a light-hearted, slightly sub-Beckett play he had written about three men out fishing on a lake. Hugh's answer was the most extraordinary letter Rippier had ever read.

I resolved to stop writing dreary egotistical letters, in fact to stop writing letters at all, and then your new play and a book from Coleby arrived by the same post . . . ! [Ronald Coleby was an angling book specialist, described by Falkus and Buller in the first edition of *Freshwater Fishing* as 'the most kind and knowledgeable of angling bibliophiles.']

The play is not playable. And even if it were, not 1% of your audience would understand it. I am not sure that I understand it myself. As for being what you so blithely call an 'upcheerer', I found its intimations of mortality inexpressibly sad. Those silly little men sitting like ghosts in their silly little boat, twisting and writhing and wriggling to change their silly little lives, and emphasising only that they will retain for ever their ghastly sameness . . . is that 'upcheering'? The threat of eternal darkness; the lap of water on that everlasting loch; is that 'upcheering'? The chill of loneliness; the terrors of the dark; the dreadful mixture of tears and laughter; the laughter so desperate; the tears flooding the furrows of age like rain on a sodden landscape ploughed by centuries of hands now brittle-boned and thrust back into the soil of a thousand years; ten thousand years; ten times ten thousand; is that 'upcheering'?

Or have I misread the thing? I skimmed through it quickly in the morning - and hastily pushed it into a drawer. In the afternoon, in a despairing effort to stop thinking about that bloody girl (impossible), I took it out again and furtively re-read it. Just now, at four in the morning-after, I sat in bed drinking coffee and whisky and read it again. The bedstead is of iron and very old, with ten brass knobs on railings fore and aft. And on every knob sat a raven.

Once at four in the morning there would be only one raven. It sat on my shoulder and I would shoo it away. After a time shooing wouldn't shift it, so I killed it. But it came back from the dead with one of its mates . . . then with two; then three; then four. And now there are ten of them and they huddle, preening, all along the bed rails, one on every knob. And they croak.

And this morning, just now, not an hour since, as I read your manuscript for the last time, they reminded me that on the Spey a fortnight ago I sensed suddenly that I was making my final cast; that I no longer cared whether I rose a fish; that there was no more pleasure in it for me. And as my fly swung round on its last journey and I slowly wound in the forty yards of white number 11 DTF, the clacking Hardy Marquis Salmon Number 2 seemed to echo the awful clacking emptiness of my own mind.

It was nice of you to send me Hillaby's book [Journey Through Britain]. *Very nice. It's so full of pith; so well written. But it depresses me. I no longer find its humour humorous.*

"Let there be a bonfire of angling books," I said aloud. "And a roasting of anglers. Let their clacking voices, like their clacking reels, be silent." And the ravens cackled in chorus and croaked: "Silence will come soon enough!"

Yours ever, Hugh.

Falkus had found darkness where Rippier had intended light entertainment. But the black moods always passed, and between them he felt able to claim with some conviction that he had finally found happiness. He told *Shooting Times* in March 1989: 'I suppose I'm happier now than at any other time of my life - whatever happiness is. You may have seen *Self Portrait of a Happy Man* - well I'm even happier now, without the bother of making all those bloody films.' He said his only remaining ambition was to write his autobiography. 'But at seventy-two, I'm really not old enough. All sorts of things can happen to me yet.'

In a passage written with that autobiography in mind and published in *Some of it Was Fun*, he wrote: 'My concept of immediate happiness has always hung on the reply to a simple question: whether in any given situation, at that particular time, there is any other place I would prefer to be; anything else I would rather be doing. If the answer is no, then whatever the context, I reckon to be as happy as can reasonably be expected.'

Despite the illness, despite the demise of his broadcasting career, despite the taped-up wreckage of his relationship with Kathleen, Bill Arnold has no doubt that these claims of Hugh's were honest. 'He didn't enjoy the stress teaching could give him or the pressure to get on with a book, but he was enjoying life well enough, most of the time' he says. Malcolm Greenhalgh agrees, and puts it down to two main factors; he no longer had to leave his valley, and for the first time in his life he was more or less financially secure.

There were articles occasionally, and plenty of letters. Rarely any poetry; Falkus accepted that it was not his *forte*, although he told *Shooting Times* once that his first published work had been a poem, for which the local paper had paid him two shillings. He wrote to Jo Rippier:

Why can't I write it? It seems so easy. There are no rules. It's all so simple, and yet . . . jiggle with it, start to pick it about, and wow! Suddenly it's gone! The magic has blown away. Replace it and there it is again, back in line, dancing on its toes. Here am I -

writing for my living for most of my life - films, books, articles, film commentaries, radio scripts, brochures, advertising copy, plays, adaptations, name it I've done it - anything that can be put into (I hope) good English. Almost anything, that is. Poetry? No, can't do it.

But he had not given up yet. These verses were found folded into a 1992 calendar:

FOOLISHNESS

I Corinthians III 19: 'The wisdom of this world is foolishness with God'

Does it not seem rather odd
That the wisdom of this world
Should be foolishness with God?
Indeed our erring feet may stray,
But turn it round another way
Does it then seem common sense
To seek an Earthly recompense
For such divine incompetence?

The wisdom of this world
Is spread for all to see
A catalogue of horror
Verging on catastrophe
But what makes it all so odd
Is the foolishness of God.

The ultimate inaninity
Sure sign of God's insanity
Is human inhumanity.

Falkus became increasingly concerned with his legacy, and not just because of his desire to be remembered for his achievements. Learning how well his books were selling in London, he told Tim Thomas that it gave him enormous satisfaction to think of the vicarious pleasure they were giving to city men who had little opportunity to enjoy the countryside pursuits which he had taken for granted throughout his life.

He displayed (not before time) a concern for the young. 'Everything I have written and filmed about angling has been done primarily to help younger people enjoy the freedom that I have enjoyed during my lifetime' he told the *Weekend Telegraph* in 1992. He backed up this new indulgence with a mellower attitude to the few young people who came into his life. His sister-in-law Marjorie's children Peter and Jane, long accustomed to being all but ignored by their Uncle Hugh on visits to Cragg, found that he was now prepared to sit down and talk to them at length about what they had been up to, and to explain some of the wonders of natural history to them.

In 1993 he joined Mensa, and commissioned a psychometric test on himself. The report gave him high scores for being assertive, detail-conscious, reserved, sensitive, conceptual, radical, self-sufficient, disciplined and tense/driven. The most emphatic score was, rather surprisingly, for being retiring (as opposed to outgoing). Typically, Falkus gave his own judgement on Mensa's work by 'marking' the paper throughout.

An extract from the report:

Hugh Falkus's interpersonal style is on the borderline of extroversion and introversion. He will tend to communicate with people without having a strong requirement for excessive personal contact.

His discomfort and tendency to withdraw in social situations may be interpreted as disinterest and may lead him to be considered relatively unsympathetic and aloof by colleagues and acquaintances.

On his own, engaged in solitary pastimes, he will not feel threatened. His close friends may see a different side to his character, regarding him as somewhat sensitive and understanding.

In social relationships he is quite self-assertive and self-centred, with a desire to have his own way. Confidently aggressive, Hugh is likely to have the capacity to dominate. He will have quite strong opinions which he will wish to impress on others.

He is likely to expend considerable nervous energy performing on the social stage and in situations involving a high level of interpersonal contact.

Under a section on 'thinking style', the report suggested that its subject would be naturally curious and tend to go beyond the obvious, and would tend to adopt a questioning stance which might lead him to challenge older, established points of view and 'be reticent' (*sic*) about accepting the status quo.

His inclination to be direct with people, combined with his force of character, may result in a poor trade-off between any innovations introduced and potential friction involved. He is unlikely to be highly influenced by public opinion. Hugh may be inclined to go his own way from time to time and may tend to be reclusive, finding social activities to be a waste of time . . . He is creative and somewhat introspective, being more absorbed with inner thoughts and concepts than outer realities and everyday matters. He will generally prefer to be involved in the generation of ideas, leaving routine, practical applications to others.

All these statements earned ticks from Falkus. He also agreed that he was 'somewhat sensitive emotionally and quite soft-hearted' and 'may lack sufficient toughness to deal with emotionally gruelling situations.' He did not agree that he 'would be no more easily hurt or upset than most people' or that he was 'not unduly prone to mood swings or feelings of insecurity'.

In 1993 Falkus gave his last lecture, at the Swallow Hotel in Samlesbury, near Blackburn, to members of Bowland Game Fishing Association. The club had made him its Vice President. Falkus had not lost his touch; there was standing room only. The aisles were packed and people were standing at the back.

Periodically he would revive his efforts to produce a sequel to *The Stolen Years*. According to Fred Buller, he had planned two further autobiographical volumes, one covering his career as a pilot and another dealing with his life at Cragg. But he was unable to persuade a publisher to put up the advance he needed to finance the considerable time he would have to spend working on them. Though he revisited the project at intervals over the years, he was never quite able to carry it through.

David Burnett was invited to Cragg one day in 1994 to discuss the matter. Over a post-breakfast Scotch, Falkus announced that he had begun to collect material and produced what he called 'The File'.

'The File' was a large metal-edged contraption, battered with use. Hugh had been using it for years to put together his films and books. The scripts for Self Portrait of a Happy Man *and* Salmo the Leaper, *the pages of the second edition of* Sea Trout Fishing *and* Salmon Fishing, *his material for* Nature Detective *and* Speycasting, *all had grown to completion in The File. He thrust it in my direction.*

I opened it at random and drew out a brown envelope. It bore the words: 'Chapter Seven: My Sex Life'. Inside was a single sheet with notes in pencil, barely decipherable. I read: 'War. On leave. Epping Forest. Autumn. American girl. Jill. Under tree. She on top. Very heavy. Conker up arse.'

I never saw this chapter again, nor any other parts of the proposed work. He never completed it - his heart wasn't in it. There was just too much pain and sorrow in his past to make contemplation of it possible. For him writing was part fact, part fantasy. He invented and embellished freely, like all writers. The facts, when it came to his own life, would never make a jolly story, and he knew it. Vanity might prick him on, but professional detachment held him back.

In a letter to Burnett early in 1995, Falkus fretted at his own lack of progress.

I am finding it harder and harder to shoot these days and the duck are getting very wary! I'm afraid this may be my last season. But I am hoping to do a full programme of teaching and already have several bookings. My book goes slowly on. Oh so slowly. But I think some of it is readable. So much more to do yet, though. I keep doing something and then throwing it away after repeated rewrites. I suppose this 'itis' happens to everyone? Hope you enjoy yourself in Ireland - although I strongly condemn your going there. I won't ever be going again myself.

Apart from his fishing trips, Falkus now hardly left the valley. More and more of his time was spent with Bill at Knott End. If no pupils were booked, he would walk up the lane to the farm just the same, to sit by the tarn or in the fishing hut with his friend, knocking back the High Commissioner and putting the world to rights.

The dogs, as always, were well looked after. Careful with their money in most respects, Hugh and Kathleen would spend whatever it took to restore one of their beloved animals to health if it was ill or injured, always calling the vet out rather than taking the animal to a surgery. Hugh even talked his accountant into claiming tax relief on the dog food he bought, on the grounds that they were part of the life he broadcast and wrote about.

Hugh's own poor health was now beyond denial. Increasingly weak eyesight forced him to give up driving entirely after 1990. His hands had been affected by keratosis, a thickening of the skin caused by prolonged exposure to the sun, and he would wear cotton mittens to protect them.

More seriously, there were continuing problems with his indigestion. For years he had continued to tell friends that the incontinence and the acute stomach pains were merely colitis, but by 1993 he was becoming so ill that few still believed him.

Falkus had had an early brush with cancer in 1976. Peter Lewars, one of the Trusties, noticed a dark patch on his throat which Falkus had previously dismissed as of no great significance. Lewars knew better, and immediately arranged for it to be investigated. The patch proved to be a malignant melanoma, one of the most aggressive forms of cancer, and within a week

Falkus was admitted to Workington Hospital, where it was removed. The operation left a conspicuous mark, which Falkus ever after covered with a neckerchief or scarf.

It was Peter Behan, some time in 1992, who realised that the new deterioration in Falkus' health after his return from Romille was not just colitis. Behan surmised that Falkus had developed a villous potassium-secreting adenoma. This is a type of growth which, after a year or so without treatment, develops reliably into a cancerous tumour. Behan was in charge of the neurology unit at the Southern General Hospital in Glasgow, so he pulled strings there, arranging for Falkus to be accommodated in a private room at the hospital while tests were done.

Bill Arnold drove Falkus to Glasgow. There was no possibility of persuading him to go into hospital without a supply of whisky, and equally little chance of persuading the formidable ward sister to allow such a thing. Behan and Falkus thought up a cunning plan. Behan gave Falkus a miniature of Scotch, which he put by his bed. The sister, of course, noticed it immediately, and demanded its removal. Behan pointed out that such a small quantity could do no harm, and that it was unreasonable to expect their alcohol-dependent patient to go without a modest daily tipple during his ordeal.

The sister conceded the point, and agreed to turn a blind eye both to the little bottle and to the persistent odour of whisky. Each day, Falkus meekly sipped a few more millimetres from the miniature. His main supply, two bottles of single malt, was hidden in the toilet cistern.

Ironically the tests indicated that his liver was in excellent condition, to the amazement of the medical staff and the delight of Hugh. Peter Behan had mixed feelings; effectively, the diagnosis gave Hugh a licence to drink as much as he liked.

The rest of the news was not so good. Behan's diagnosis had been correct, and Falkus was in the early stages of colonic cancer. If the growth was to be caught in time it would have to be removed anally, without delay. Behan made arrangements for it to be done by a leading specialist the following week.

Falkus insisted on returning home for the weekend, promising Peter and Bill that he would go back as arranged on the Monday. But when the time came, he changed his mind.

'I begged him to see reason' says Behan. 'I told him that if only he would consent to the operation he could look forward to a good result and many more healthy years. We had the best possible surgeon lined up for the job.

Now was the time. I pleaded with him, but there was nothing anyone could do. The great Falk had become a terrified old man.' Despite the best efforts of Behan, Bill Arnold and Kathleen to persuade Falkus to have the operation, the appointment had to be cancelled, and the cancer remained untreated.

In September 1994, Hugh received a phone call from someone he had not expected to hear from again - his son Christopher. Helen Falkus had expressed a desire to see her grandfather, and they were invited up the next Saturday. After the visit, Christopher wrote to his Aunt Daphne with a report.

SS Titanic, 13th April, 1912
My first impression was that Battersea Dog's Home had opened a new branch. An ear-splitting cacophony of barking, sudden hounds leaping at your shoulders, tackling you from behind, blotting out the sun. There seemed to be hundreds, but after the chaos subsided a careful count revealed only two. Out of the sea of canines Kathleen surfaced - very welcoming, natural, wholly nice.

We went into the kitchen. Helen had spotted Hugh, hovering just beyond the door that led to the sitting room. She told Gila he seemed not too sure when to come in, because he wanted to make a proper entrance - perceptive, that . . . no one can tell what registers and in what way with someone not only self-absorbed but also self-manufactured, in a rather eerie way.

Hugh has white hair, a big frame, rounded shoulders which have become a perceptible stoop with age, and the formidable legs of early photographs have become rather ridiculously spindly. They don't look up to the job of carrying what's on top of them.

The voice is loud, quite a slow delivery, with pauses, emphatic - very much the old RAF 'wizard prang' drawl without the slightest change in tone or inflection between, say 'won't you have a drink' and 'the war ruined the lives of everyone'.

The study was the nearest thing to an aquarium you can have on dry land. There were books about fish, pictures of fish, certificates about fish, trophies about fish. Most of the books seemed to be by Hugh Falkus, in many languages, all on the theme of fish.

The intellect is all there . . . but there are pauses, repetitions, memory struggles and a curiously complete indifference to his audience. He likes to say the same thing twice, with pause and emphasis, in marginally different ways. 'What I taught . . . was brilliant - no one else - could know. Can't be done in a book - not in a book. When I'm gone, the only people who can teach it are those I taught . . .' (that, by the way, refers to some unique method of landing a piece of string on water).

No one could have accused Christopher Falkus of being interested in fishing.

Christopher reported that Falkus was handed family photographs, but showed little interest other than to comment on how good-looking they all were; this he interpreted as his father's pride in his legacy to the human race.

The tide of reminiscences rolled on . . . Hugh explained that he was in terrible pain, all the time, and we were to forgive him if he was rude, abrupt, sharp, blunt and so on. But he didn't want to talk about it. Or refer to it, or have it referred to, etc. Not talking about it kept him quiet for about 20 minutes, punctuated by a very characteristic gesture of screwed-up brow, tightly-shut eyes, thumb and index finger pressing between the eyes.

During the Dylan Thomas story I became very aware of calls from the kitchen about tea being ready. Hugh yelled 'I'm telling an anecdote!', poured another Scotch and went on and on and on. I don't remember much about the story - fish came into it rather a lot . . . Helen sensed the talents but also the artificiality of what is a rather overwhelming personality, still.

That was just six months before Christopher died so unexpectedly. Falkus did not go to the funeral. He asked Mike Daunt to represent him, but Daunt responded that this was one duty he did not feel able to perform in Hugh's place.

Death and funerals were unquestionably a major *bête noire*. Christopher's visit took place barely a month after the death in hospital of Tony Witherby. Falkus had not visited Witherby; he had even declined a request, conveyed via David Burnett, for a picture of Cragg Cottage for his bedside. It was as if he could not tolerate the slightest contact with death, actual or implied.

Watching sport on television helped to distract Falkus from his discomfort, and in 1993 he had Sky TV installed at the cottage. Malcolm Greenhalgh pulled his leg about this, pretending to read the programme listings from the newspaper to demonstrate that most of the timetable involved minority sports. "Eight o'clock, synchronised swimming from Bratislava. Nine o'clock, world final of the netball championships. Eleven o'clock, paraplegic volleyball from Amsterdam." "That's no good," said Hugh. "Damn! And I've already paid for it."

He would watch cricket at any hour of the day or night. One night, Greenhalgh was awoken at one in the morning by the telephone. It was Hugh. "Atherton's a ninny!" came the familiar gruff voice.

'He wanted to share his disgust at the England captain's decision to put the Australians in on a good batting wicket' explains Greenhalgh. 'It never entered his head that most people go to sleep at night.'

He did the same to other friends. David Profumo got a call at midnight once - Falkus, wanting to feed his 'lonely intellect' (in Profumo's phrase) through a discussion of the difference between poetry and prose.

Falkus had long harboured the notion of a book which would appeal to the casual angling reader; something more guidebook than doctrine, an affordable, accessible reference work for the rank-and-file angler. The 'till book', as he called it - he envisaged it on display beside tackle-shop tills around the world - was the last project he hoped to see finished. David Burnett, feeling that the work would give him something positive to focus on, gave him every encouragement. But Falkus had reached the point where the physical act of writing was all but beyond him.

In September 1995 Malcolm Greenhalgh was on a fishing visit to Cragg when Falkus dragged him into his study and showed him the contents of a large cardboard box. It was the 'till book', in crude form. "I can't write any more," Falkus told his friend. "It's all in here. I'd like you to be my co-author and get it finished."

'It was with conflicting feelings of sorrow, elation and honour that I agreed' wrote Greenhalgh, who some years earlier had given up a secure career as a college lecturer in order to write, teach and lecture full-time about fishing and aquatic life. Hugh's admission that he would not be able to finish the book left Greenhalgh in no doubt that the end was near. He took the box home to Lancashire and worked on it that winter, consulting Hugh at intervals for approval.

Falkus' original plan was for a book which would summarise the teachings of his two 'bibles', *Sea Trout Fishing* and *Salmon Fishing*. Greenhalgh pointed out that it would be more useful and have greater appeal if it was widened somewhat to include techniques which Falkus had not covered, such as dry-fly fishing for both species, and new techniques from overseas. There was also scope for more detail about spinning and prawn-fishing. Falkus agreed with all this.

The Salmon & Sea Trout Fisher's Handbook was finally published in 1997 by David Burnett's Excellent Press. Falkus was able to agree the outline of the book and give his blessing to much of the content, but he was not able to play any part in its completion or publication. For all that, for Hugh, it was too late.

XVI

Last Casts

I can pass this spot without regret. I gave that dog as good a life as I could and,
when the time came, as quick a death. I only hope that one day,
if necessary, someone will do as much for me.
SELF PORTRAIT OF A HAPPY MAN

IT WAS 1990, the first Saturday in June. Mike Daunt was with Hugh Falkus on Speyside, helping him to pack up rods and tackle after the final week's tuition of the season. As they crossed the river on the homeward journey, Falkus told Daunt to stop the car. He climbed out, walked to the upstream side, leaned across the granite parapet and stared at the river for a few moments. Then he crossed the road, looked downstream and started to quote from T. S. Eliot's *The Love Song of Alfred J. Prufrock*:

I grow old . . . I grow old . . .
I shall wear the bottoms of my trousers rolled
Shall I part my hair behind? Do I dare to eat a peach?
I shall wear white flannel trousers, and walk upon the beach
I can hear the mermaids singing, each to each.
I do not think that they will sing to me.

In typically theatrical style, Falkus was saying farewell to the river he had known and loved. The performance had its effect. He turned to see tears welling up in Daunt's eyes. "For Christ's sake stop grizzling, Daunty," he said. "Come on, let's go and have a drink."

The news that Hugh had cancer trickled out gradually over those final years to the wider world outside Eskdale. In October 1994, accepting at last that hospital treatment was unavoidable, he was admitted to Whitehaven Hospital, where Christopher Metcalfe-Gibson (who had been one of his pupils) operated to remove the tumour. But the cancer had spread too far. By the end of that year everyone in his circle knew that Hugh was dying, and that he was doing it, as he had done everything else, on his own terms.

Falkus' daughter Mary found out from Kathleen; after Christopher's visit in 1994, the two women began an occasional correspondence. She had met her father only once since that meeting in Plymouth in the early 1960s. On a youth hostelling holiday in the Lakes during the 1975 Easter holidays, she had gone looking for the cottage. When she found it, she took her courage in her hands and knocked on the door, to find Hugh about to set off for the river with a party of friends. She introduced herself, fervently wishing she had not come, and was met by a stunned silence. She was offered tea, but neither she nor Hugh knew what to say and she left after a few minutes.

In 1995, knowing that time for her father was running short, Mary asked if she might come up to Cragg to see him once again. She found Kathleen eager to welcome her, though a setback in Hugh's condition at first delayed the visit. Finally that September she made arrangements to stay with a community of fellow nuns at Hyning Hall, Carnforth, within striking distance of Eskdale. 'I wanted to find out if there was anything beneath the veneer of Hugh's life, whether it had all been a show or if something might surface from the depths that would reveal who he really was - and who I really was' she says. 'I wanted to see if there would be any scrap of acknowledgement of his family.'

From Carnforth she took the train to Ravenglass; she got a quizzical look when she asked at the post office if Cragg was within walking distance. She set off to tackle the three-mile journey on foot anyway, climbing down through the grounds of Muncaster Castle and across the fields to the Birkby road before getting a lift over the final leg from a passing police car.

I walked up to the open front door, to be met by a loud welcome from two large labradors. Kathleen appeared, quieted the dogs and took me straight up to Hugh, who was in bed, propped up on some pillows. We shook hands and he said how ill he was, invited me to take a chair and offered me a Scotch. I accepted, never mind that it was half past three in the afternoon - it had been a long walk.

I poured myself one with plenty of soda and gave him one with rather less. He had had a bad night. His speech was slightly slurred, but he looked better than I had expected.

He talked about his operation. I told him about my journey and asked about his paintings, then presented a cat portrait I had done for him. This seemed to take him out of himself. He said I was more talented than he was and ought to try to make money out of it. "I sold some of my paintings years ago and so should you," he said. He admitted he was better at writing than painting and wouldn't be painting any more. I privately wondered if he would be writing any more either.

We had another Scotch and Kathleen brought up some tea. I gave Hugh a recording of our liturgical chant from the abbey. I had already sent him a copy of my book A Call to Serve, *which he said he had read with great interest. He seemed genuinely interested in my life at the abbey, but appreciated the fact that I had come in ordinary clothes instead of my nun's habit. Neither he nor I once touched on the past.*

He was very struck by the coincidence that my name was Sister Julian (properly addressed as Dame, as a Benedictine nun) and that he and his friend Fred Buller had been writing a book about a Dame Juliana. I thought it ironic that although he said he was an atheist, he used several quotations from the Bible.

When it was time for me to go he said he was glad I'd come and would like me to call again. He looked at me for a long while as he said goodbye, then kissed my hand in farewell. He called Bill and said, "My daughter is here, can you come and give her a lift to the station?" It was quite a moment when he referred to me as his daughter. I thought it was rather sporting of him to bequeath me the remaining half bottle of Scotch - I finished it in the quiet confines of Hyning Hall, without a scrap of guilt.

Before leaving I had a glimpse of Hugh's study and a sign which said 'SOD THE REST, I'M THE BEST'. There were certificates and awards for best this and best that, photos of himself and Kathleen and friends, books.

On the way to the station, Bill told me Hugh had spoken about his past to him but never mentioned Doris or my twin. It struck me that Hugh had built a life around himself so that he was at the centre of it. The act was the reality, as Christopher once explained it.

Hugh did not see his daughter again, but they stayed in touch. A letter accompanying a copy of *The Stolen Years* enclosed a £20 note, which he said he had meant to give her to pay for tea on the journey back to Carnforth. He wrote again to canvass her help with the final researches into the Dame Juliana book.

When Hugh's niece Daphne and her partner Richard Briggs visited Hugh later that autumn, they found him occupying the sofa in the sitting-room and having great difficulty in moving about. Daphne had brought some old family photographs to show him, but he waved them away.

A slow gathering of the extended Trusty clan began, one or two ex-members among them. Frank Plum had heard that Hugh was ill. Hoping to make peace with him - Hugh had not spoken to Frank since the affair with Romille - he and his partner, Mary Smallbone, drove up to Knott End.

Bill Arnold phoned Cragg and asked Falkus if he would see Frank. He was met with a point-blank refusal. Kathleen overheard the conversation and volunteered to come up to see Frank and Mary, but Falkus refused to have anything to do with them. 'The tears were streaming down Frank's face' says Bill. 'He was desperate to see Hugh one last time.' In October 1995, Hugh had a visit from Brian Clarke, angling correspondent of *The Times*. Clarke later wrote that both men knew his purpose was Hugh's obituary.

'We talked for hours, with his beloved Esk chuckling in the valley below and the sky "catching fire" to the west . . . white-maned on his mountain-side, Hugh Falkus had the stature within angling of an Old Testament prophet' wrote Clarke, years later.

Falkus' time was now almost entirely divided between Cragg and Knott End, his visits to the latter depending on how well he was feeling. As his illness developed, Bill made a series of little roadside seats and fixed them along the winding, wooded lane from Cragg up to Knott End so that he could take rests during the walk, which is markedly uphill in places. There he would sit and rest, raising his cap to passing locals in Land Rovers.

In the valley he had long since taken to dressing for comfort rather than style, resorting to sloppy deck shoes and shapeless sweaters and twill shirts (always with a neckerchief, to hide the scar on his neck left by his skin cancer operation), though he would never go fishing or shooting without dressing appropriately. He still ate well; Kathleen would serve him a good breakfast and a substantial evening meal, while he would be sustained through the afternoon at Knott End by a lunchtime sandwich, prepared to his taste by Marie Arnold and liberally garnished with Gentleman's Relish.

Cooking for Hugh and caring for the dogs was now pretty much the extent of Kathleen's day. She had by now taken to spending a good deal of it in bed. The porphyria and the alcohol together were destroying her vitality, and if there were no guests (which was usual now) she would get up only when others needed her attention.

During the salmon season Bill was still picking Hugh up every Monday to take him up to the Derwent. The actual fishing was now a very minor part of the proceedings. Hugh would spend most of the day hunched in a folding chair beside the Range Rover, reading the paper or watching the water. When he did wet a line he would use a single-hander rather than the salmon rod and fish in thigh waders, because they were easier to pull on and off.

The fisherman in autumn - HF on the Derwent.

Bill Arnold and Anthony Desbruslais.

Hugh with Bill Arnold (left) and Anthony Desbruslais on the Derwent.

Falkus fished for the last time on the final Monday of the 1995 season, a glorious autumn day with the sky deep blue over the fells and the first leaves turning gold. They parked by the river, and as usual Hugh sat in his chair taking in the scene while Bill tackled up. 'Falk sat for a while watching me and studying the river, and then I saw him pick up the rod and walk down to his favourite spot on Camerton Turn' says Bill. 'He was using his single-handed Bruce and Walker. Within three casts he was into a salmon. As usual, he handed the rod to me to land it. It was a hen fish of about nine pounds, but it was coloured, so we let it go - Hugh would never practise catch and release, but he always returned any fish that wasn't fresh run.'

The shooting season was about to begin, and though the decline in his condition was all too obvious, Falkus was not ready to abandon that passion just yet. He shot four times that season with Bill and their friends at Langley Park. The strenuous walking associated with game shooting was now well beyond him and he generally had to be put on an accessible peg, and helped to it.

Bill can still picture the last pheasant he shot. It was a day in late January, the last but one outing of the season, and the second drive after lunch.

'We were on the Oakwood Drive with Eddie Woodall. Falk poured himself a glass of whisky and sat on the tailgate of the Range Rover. We heard the beaters shouting in the distance and a hen bird appeared high over us, curling off to the side - a real cracker. Falk slid off the tailgate, raised his gun and dropped it, as neat a piece of shooting as I've ever seen.'

By New Year 1996 Falkus was getting very weak, and spending more time in bed than out of it. In February, alerted by telephone conversations with Bill and with Hugh himself that there could not be much time left, Tim Thomas made the journey to Cragg. He was shocked to see the deterioration in his friend's condition. 'It was hard to see this giant of a man reduced to a shuffle and spending so much time in bed' he recalls. 'When the time came to say goodbye, I held his hand and said 'thank you' and at that moment a spark of something quite extraordinary passed between us. It was as if we were both young again and all the world lay before us.'

In early March, with a heavy heart, Fred Buller drove up from Buckinghamshire. But for him, despite their thirty-year friendship, there was no valedictory bolt of lightning.

This was no ordinary visit. I knew he was dying and that I would probably be seeing him for the last time. We had been close friends and colleagues for nearly thirty years, so it was important to me to try to say goodbye to him properly. I was looking for something, some sort of closeness, to mark the sense of an ending, but I'm afraid that didn't happen

- there was no farewell, no signal that Hugh knew it was the end. When Richard Walker died in 1985 I sat with him and he closed his eyes and gripped my hand - we both knew that it was the end, and that we were saying goodbye. But with Hugh nothing like that happened. Perhaps he was simply still in denial.

By now Hugh was barely able to leave his bed. Never the easiest of patients, he would make up his mind that he would like to be able to see a particular hill or tree and direct the repositioning of his bed so that this could be achieved. Bill had arranged for Macmillan nurses, specialists in terminal care, to be on hand to see that he was as comfortable as possible, and they bore his demands with unfailing good humour. No one had anything but praise for them, for Hugh's GP, Rodney Gallagher, or for Falkus' stoma nurse, Annie Worth. Kath's sister Marjorie, a trained nurse, spent an increasing amount of time at the cottage.

David Profumo, still estranged from Falkus following the catch-and-release spat of 1992, came home one night to a message from Hugh on his answering machine, informing him stiffly that he would be welcome once again at Cragg (Mike Daunt had indicated to Profumo that Hugh was ready to bury the hatchet). But time had run out, and the reconciliation got no further.

On Wednesday, 20th March, warned by Bill on the phone that Hugh was deteriorating, Thomas returned to Cragg. He found him restless and confused. Thomas wrote in his diary:

He was obviously now in the last stages but was fighting the cancer and the drugs. In lucid moments he talked about his nightmares, when memories of the prison camp haunted and distressed him. By the Saturday it was getting very hard, so I did something I had long promised myself and climbed Raven Crag behind the cottage. In the afternoon I took Hugh out for a little walk on to the front lawn to feel the sun and spring air and look at the spring flowers coming through.

Hugh did not leave the house again after that.

Knowing that he could no longer digest solid food and remembering that he had a passion for oysters, Mike Daunt arranged for a supply, and put the word round among Hugh's friends. Peter Behan had a dozen from Loch Fyne sent to Cragg twice a week, and Hugh devoured them. At Daunt's suggestion Sandy Leventon, Editor of *Trout and Salmon*, sent a parcel of three dozen.

When Malcolm Greenhalgh, Mike Daunt and another friend, David Evans, turned up at the cottage the Tuesday after Thomas' visit, they found Kathleen out and the fridge stuffed with oysters and champagne. They trudged upstairs to find Hugh in bed and barely conscious. Gradually he revived and started to take an interest in his guests.

When he came round he told us that we must help ourselves, and said he would join us. We offered to help him, but he insisted on getting down by himself. We laid the table in the kitchen. He managed to get down the stairs in the end, but it must have taken him fifteen minutes.

Finally, in he tottered. "There's no brown bread and butter!" he said, so we found some and buttered the bread. "No sideplates!" he said, so we dug those out and put them round. "Now, I want to hear the slurping of oysters and the clinking of glasses," said Hugh. We did as we were told. Hugh sat down with us and drank some champagne and ate about sixteen oysters. Then we could see he was going to pass out, so we helped him into his chair in the sitting-room and put a glass of whisky and water in his hand.

That was the last food Hugh was able to take. Two days later, Bill went in to see him.

Usually he would tell me to fill a glass of whisky and have a drink with him. I pulled him up on to his pillows and held a glass to his lips, which he sipped.

By now he was on a morphine driver. He took my hand and said, "Not long now William, look after Kath for me." Then he closed his eyes and went into his final coma. I saw him the next day, the Friday, and the morning after, but by then he was unconscious.

That Saturday night was a savage one; a deep depression had brought a storm in from the Atlantic. A March westerly raged in the cottage chimneys, and driving rain battered the windows. It was a real old wildfowler's night.

If Hugh could hear it, he was long past giving any sign. There was nothing more to be done for him, other than to keep him comfortable. Kathleen and Marjorie kept watch, chatting about old times in the kitchen and taking it in turns to check on him every so often.

At a quarter to midnight, Marjorie went upstairs, checked Hugh's pulse and saw that he had gone. It was 30th March, the day before the anniversary of his wife Doris' death and a year and a day after that of their son Christopher.

Towards the end Falkus, still the dramatist even *in extremis*, had kept quoting Keats' *The Nightingale*: 'Now more than ever seems it rich to die, to cease upon the midnight with no pain.' He achieved that to within fifteen minutes.

Mike Daunt sensed Hugh's passing.

I was having dinner with some friends at home in Berkshire - I knew that the end must be very near. A few minutes after midnight I felt him go through the room. I turned to my neighbour, an old friend who knows me well, and who knew how much I loved him, and said to her: "He's gone," and looked at my watch to check the time. The next morning Bill rang me early to tell me that he had died.

Dr Gallagher was called, and certified death; the causes were given as bronchiopneumonia, carcinomatosis and rectal carcinoma.

The funeral was fixed for the following Thursday, 4th April, at Distington Hall Crematorium, near Workington. Falkus had left instructions that he wanted it kept as low-key as possible, with just his family and inner circle in attendance. He had also insisted that it must be free of any taint of religion, which for the mourners, particularly Bill Arnold and Fred Buller, made it an unsatisfactory and rather awkward affair. Bill did his best to fill the gap with a brief homily, and Malcolm Greenhalgh read from Hugh's much-recycled story *The Sea Trout*. Alongside the Arnolds and Armstrongs there were just the three Woodall brothers and their wives, the two Freds with theirs, Malcolm and Yvonne Greenhalgh, Peter Behan, Anthony Desbruslais, Tim Thomas, Hugh's daughter-in-law Gila and Kathleen's two older brothers, Benny junior and Les.

Tim escorted Kath in; she was 'very brave and dignified'. But as the curtains closed on the coffin, her composure crumbled and she rushed forward to shout an anguished farewell to Hugh.

Despite the partial reconciliation with her father, Mary Falkus was not at the cremation, nor did she attend the wake. She had written to Bill to explain why.

'I'm afraid Hugh's life is not one I wish to celebrate with champagne' she told him. 'It is more than sad that I am not able to feel proud of my own father and that I feel no sense of loss. His behaviour towards his first wife and family is, and always will be, a mystery to me. You may imagine the deep pain the *Times* obituary caused me and others of my family.' (It had made no mention of Doris, or of Mary and her twin brother.)

The burial and wake were fixed for noon on Sunday, 14th April, ten days after the funeral. It was Hugh's idea that his ashes should be buried next to his old dog's grave at Meadow Dub, in the spot where the couple had shared midnight picnics and love on the haysack in those long-ago summers when the Esk had run silver with sea trout and Hugh's heart had leapt with the joy of pursuing them. It was at Meadow Dub too, nearly forty years before, that Hugh had stalked, hooked and landed his fifteen-pound monster. 'It would have been no good burying him in a churchyard, next to other people - imagine the ructions he'd have caused' Kathleen told *Salmon, Trout and Sea Trout* a year or two later.

Falkus had stipulated in writing that his departure should be celebrated with the help of a wagonload of authentic champagne on ice - he left £1000 for the purpose - and that the guests must stay until the last bottle had been drained. Bill laid on a ten-foot farm trailer for the job. A local fisherman, Andy Graham, supplied the ice and John Mason, another friend, arranged the champagne - eight cases of it. Some of the guests added their own bottles to the pile. 'I never saw so many bottles of bubbly, or so much ice' says Fred J. Taylor.

Well over a hundred of Hugh's family and friends assembled. In addition to most of those who had attended the funeral and the entire Armstrong family, they included Arthur and Grace Oglesby, David Burnett, Hugh's niece Daphne Smyth and her partner Richard. It was too late for Frank Plum - he had died two years before, in his late seventies - but his partner, Mary Smallbone, was there. So was Bill Bruxby, despite his excision from Hugh's greatest work. Members of Hugh's wider angling network included Ken and David Reid from Scotland. From the valley came the Woodall clan in strength, Sheila Barron who had once been very close to Hugh, Eileen Tonge of the Pennington Arms and her son Ian, Roger Putnam, whose guest house had put up many of Hugh's pupils, and Hugh's boating companions Paul Pedersen and Frank Chamberlain. Kathleen, tearful but composed, busied herself as usual making sure everyone felt welcome.

It was a cold, dull spring day, and the interment was a damp affair. The guests stood about the grass in waxproofs and cagoules, some sharing umbrellas against the drizzle, as Bill gave his homily and Mike Daunt, at Bill's suggestion, read the somewhat unseasonal opening paragraphs of Hugh's introduction to *Sea Trout Fishing*: 'It was a dark mid-August night with a heavy tumble of cloud and a hint of rain, the little river at summer low . . .'

On a summer's morning twenty-one years before, filming a scene for *Self Portrait of a Happy Man*, Falkus had leaned on his stick by the old sycamore tree at Meadow Dub and described how by this little corner of the Esk he had released Dog from the pain of terminal cancer; a walk down to the river with dog and gun, a piece of chocolate, and as old Dog put his head down for the titbit and wagged his tail for the last time, the 12-bore had

Final farewell.

done its work. 'I expect you think I'm very sentimental, and perhaps I am' Falkus had told the camera. 'But I can pass this spot without regret. I gave that dog as good a life as I could, and when the time came, as quick a death. I only hope that one day, if necessary, someone will do as much for me.'

An impractical wish, but on his death Bill and Kathleen came as close to meeting it as they could. Before the ceremony Bill had carved 'HUGH FALKUS 30/3/96' on a large, rectangular sandstone slab and dug a hole on the top of the bank beside Dog's grave, among the early shoots of bluebell and wild garlic. Now Kath, in her blue hooded coat and green Hunters, knelt down to place the casket containing Hugh's ashes in the hole and Bill's son Peter, helped by David Evans, lifted the stone into position over them. Kath leaned on Sheila Barron, and Sheila leaned on Kath. Marie Arnold hugged both of them. Kath shouted "Goodbye, Falk!" and the stone dropped into place.

And then as the ceremony concluded, a remarkable thing; a little group of greylag geese appeared, flying up the river from the estuary. They circled Hugh's grave once, honking softly to one another, then flew back downriver through the drizzle the way they had come.

The party retired to the fishing hut at Knott End to finish off the champagne. There was also, naturally, plenty of whisky. Daphne remembers Kath drinking rather too much of it. Some time around nine in the evening, a mellow nucleus of Hugh's confederates drove in convoy up to the Bower House at Eskdale Green, where Mike Daunt had booked a back room for them. Here they stayed until the small hours. When the bar closed, Daunt unilaterally reopened it. Bill Arnold remembers that the party did not truly end until Daunt and Malcolm Greenhalgh left, at teatime the following day.

In the riverside glade where Hugh's ashes lay, Marie Arnold planted daffodils and fire-orange montbretia among the bluebells and wood anemones. The valley was beginning to put on its green cloak, ready for another season. Below the bank, beside Hugh's stone, the Esk ran bright and clear. The year's first sea trout would soon be on their way.

XVII

After Hugh

Drake was Falk's dog. He was in an awful state for a long while after Hugh died.
Sometimes I think he blames me for his master going.

KATHLEEN FALKUS, INTERVIEW WITH *Salmon, Trout and Sea Trout*

FALKUS' WILL was short and simple. The money came to just over £140,000. Of this he left £2000 to Sheila Barron (no one is quite sure why), and £1000 'to drink to the memory of my old friends'. His beloved William Armstrong 12-bore went to Bill Arnold. Everything else went to Kathleen.

The obituaries were generous and eloquent (most of them were of course written by his allies). Mike Daunt in *Trout and Salmon* dubbed him 'the greatest writer and communicator on salmon and sea-trout fishing that Britain has seen this century'. In the *Weekend Telegraph*, David Profumo recalled his 'physically powerful presence, with a burning blue gaze and quite remarkable charisma' and talked of the 'angry demon' in Falkus' nature. Brian Clarke in *The Times* called him 'a restless, iconoclastic figure who had the stature and looks of a *Boy's Own Paper* hero, and lived a life to match'.

A subdued peace descended on Cragg. With Hugh gone Kathleen finally lost all incentive to cook, and the kitchen which had fuelled so much conviviality over the years became cold and silent. Her few proper meals were taken at the Arnolds', where she dined two or three times a week (though she would pick at her food and leave most of it), or sometimes at the home of Les Stout and his partner Lesley in Eskdale Green - Les had just retired to the valley after a gillieing career on the Tay.

She had Drake and Leo, their two labradors, of course, and would take

311

them on long and rambling walks. On fine days she would spend hours sitting up on the slopes of Latterbarrow Crag or down by the river. Often she would walk up to Knott End by way of Hugh's grave at Meadow Dub, where she would pick a piece of nature's bric-a-brac for him and leave it lying on his stone; a wild daffodil, a sprig of purple loosestrife, a pebble, a spray of gorse.

Without the masterful Hugh, there was a lack of domestic decision-making. Bill Arnold remembers Kath agonising over whether to keep the heating on in his study, to ward off damp, or leave it off, to save on heating bills. She discussed with Fred Buller a strategy for the sale of his remaining books, but the plan was never carried out.

She lived life from day to day, with little forward planning. The annuity Bill had set up for Hugh had died with him, so Bill arranged a pensioner bond for her to make sure she could manage comfortably.

There were some small attempts at merry widowhood. The year after Hugh died, Kath went on a short cruise in the Mediterranean with Mary Smallbone. She acquired a credit card (Hugh had always scorned such things) and started ordering clothes and shoes indiscriminately from catalogues. But she gave her old dress size, so most of the clothes, when they arrived, were far too big for her.

She was not left alone. Hugh's friends had been Kath's friends too, and they had no intention of abandoning her. Fred Buller continued to drive up every few weeks as he had always done, though to see Kathleen, not to fish; Fred had not wet a line in the Esk for years. David Burnett was a regular visitor, and Malcolm Greenhalgh and Tim Thomas came up when they could. Marjorie and Geoff would drive down from Workington. With everyone, the talk would come back to Hugh and times past.

Anthony Desbruslais would arrive to fish on summer weekends, and the invitation was returned; Kathleen, who had a maternal fondness for Anthony, spent her first two Christmases after Hugh died with his family at their home in Nottinghamshire. The dogs went with her.

Kathleen refused to make a will, so eventually Anthony sorted one out for her. There is an apple orchard alongside the cottage which Kathleen loved, and Bill Arnold, concerned that the cottage would be worth much less without it, arranged for her to put £1500 of her capital into buying it from her brother Benny.

In 1997, thanks to the efforts of Malcolm Greenhalgh and David Burnett, the 'till book' finally arrived. *The Salmon & Sea Trout Fisher's Handbook* was well received and sold steadily, the print run of 3500 copies selling out in 2004.

As time went on, Anthony Desbruslais could not help noticing how con-fused Kathleen was becoming. 'If you tried to get her to discuss any particular subject she would wander off the point all the time. She would ask the same questions again and again, which was very trying. The alcohol was not doing her any good at all.'

In July 1997 a new event celebrating the sea trout took place on the river Annan. The National Sea Trout Festival included a week-long angling competition. Hugh might not have thought much of that idea, but one hopes he would have approved the presentation by Kathleen of the Hugh Falkus Memorial Award for wildlife art, a glass bowl with engravings designed by Kath herself.

Roland Carson, an angler from nearby Bootle who had met Kathleen by chance not long before Falkus died when he went up to the cottage to get his copy of *Sea Trout Fishing* autographed, had spoken to her at the funeral and received an invitation to visit Cragg and fish the river. As a result he spent several evenings with her at the cottage. He remembers her as a 'lovely, kind woman' who could be vague and eccentric, but generally seemed happy, active and well.

Roland saw her for the last time in the spring of 2002, when he found her in good spirits. 'She loved the music of Abba, and my last memory is of her dancing around the sitting-room to one of their albums' he says. 'I thought she had years ahead of her.'

But when she was alone, Kathleen would increasingly sink into self-neglect. The drinking got worse. Under its influence she would frequently go to pieces.

The dogs' regime had become progressively slacker. They began to spend more time in the house than out of it. After a while Kath gave up putting them in the kennel at night altogether, which made the house, to visiting human noses, less than pleasant.

She got into the habit of sleeping on the sofa in the sitting-room, and one morning in June 2002 Bill Arnold arrived to find her lying there semi-conscious. It was obvious that there was no alternative to full-time care, whether she liked it or not. Rodney Gallagher, her GP, was called, but she refused to see him. It was only when Bill called her sister Marjorie to inter-vene that she relented. Gallagher returned, examined her, and immediately arranged a bed at Whitehaven Hospital.

Kath died a few days later, on 26th June, of pneumonia and liver failure. She was four months short of her seventieth birthday.

The funeral, like Hugh's, was held at Distington Hall Crematorium.

The valley folk again turned out in force. A few days later, in the presence of the entire Armstrong family and a few close friends, Kath's ashes were buried beside Hugh's at Meadow Dub.

Bill gave a short reading. He had carved a stone for her to match the one he had done for Hugh; it read simply 'KATHLEEN 26.6.02'.

Bill found a temporary sanctuary for the two labradors, Leo and Drake, together with Kathleen's ancient cat, Sooty, in a local pets' home. The cat survived the uprooting by no more than a few days. Anthony Desbruslais adopted the dogs and took them home to Nottinghamshire, where Leo died shortly afterwards after suffering a prolonged and violent fit. Drake was now twelve years old and barely able to walk. Nevertheless he wandered away from the Desbruslais home one day and managed to disappear without a trace; to this day no one knows what happened to him.

At first Bill Arnold continued to fish the Derwent on Mondays with Anthony - Sir Frank Barlow took over Falkus' rod - but to Bill and Marie, Eskdale had become a very empty place. In 2003 they sold Knott End and moved south to Arnside, on the estuary of the Kent in north-west Lancashire. Bill has only once returned to Cragg, and found it difficult to go beyond the kitchen.

Marie Arnold died in April 2006 after a short illness. Bill now has his own place on the farm where their daughter and son-in-law live, high in the Lancashire hills above the valley of the Lune. In his seventy-eighth year, he still goes fishing and shooting as often as possible. He is the Secretary of the Lune and Wyre Fisheries Association and continues to take a keen interest in river management.

Cragg Cottage and its contents, including Hugh's remaining books, pictures and papers, were left to Kathleen's niece Jane. She and her husband have repaired and updated the cottage to allow it to be rented as a holiday home, though Hugh's study has been preserved much as it was when he last used it.

The money Kathleen left went to her handicapped niece Marie, daughter of her youngest brother Bruce (Marie also inherited Falkus' royalties, which continue to pay for her care). She left her little stretch of the fishing to Anthony Desbruslais, who still goes up to fish there with friends. They have competition these days; the right bank of that part of the Esk has been let to the Prince Albert Angling Society, the largest angling club in Europe.

The Esk itself flows on, as swift and sparkling as it ever was, though there is widespread agreement among those who remember the good old days

that the runs are not what they were, and probably never will be again. All the same, it still manages to produce a few hundred sea trout and salmon in a good year.

So far Hugh's valley, superficially at least, has remained as little troubled by the twenty-first century as it was by the twentieth. From the cottage garden at Cragg you can still admire the view that entranced him when he first came to this spot more than half a century ago; the bog-and-pasture patchwork, the ambling stone walls, the blue fells, the rooks and the ravens. Only the distant scars of mechanised forestry work under Muncaster Fell and a neat stack of black-plastic-bound silage bales in the middle distance remind you that the world outside the valley has moved on.

Out beyond the estuary, the sands of Ravenglass where Hugh shot those pioneering films with Niko Tinbergen are wild and beautiful still, though they are not as they were forty years ago - this was always a transient land-scape. Vegetation has locked down the free-flowing dunes, and the black-headed gulls are long gone.

Niko died at his home in Oxford in 1988, aged eighty-one. Arthur Oglesby died at the age of seventy-six on 2nd December, 2000; Jack Hemingway died on the same day.

Fred J. Taylor's wife Carrie died in 2005, after sixty-one years of marriage to one of the most highly-regarded men in angling. At eighty-nine Fred is not as active as he was, but he still goes fishing on the Test when he can, with occasional outings after pike or tench.

Down in Berkshire, the irrepressible Mike Daunt continues to run the Hugh Falkus School of Speycasting, where his pupils have included Eric Clapton, Ronnie Corbett, Jeremy Paxman and Chris Tarrant. Daunt has found new fame as the 'Bounder' in a BBC2 country documentary, *The Bart and the Bounder*, which has now become a book.

At eighty, Fred Buller is as busy with various writing projects as ever. In 2001, the book Fred had laboured on with Hugh's help for more than thirty years finally saw the light of day. *Dame Juliana, The Angling Treatyse and its Mysteries* was published by the Flyfisher's Classic Library in an edition of three hundred and fifty copies, stylishly bound in leather with a silk marker ribbon and slipcase. It was well received. John Betts in *The American Fly Fisher* called it 'one of the most thoughtful angling books published in the last hundred or more years'.

As to the books for which Hugh is chiefly remembered, *Sea Trout Fishing* has now remained in print for an astonishing forty-five years, with *Salmon Fishing* passing the thirty-three-year mark alongside it. These days, Falkus fans and angling book enthusiasts will pay three-figure sums for first editions of *The Stolen Years*, the single edition of *Speycasting* and even *The Salmon & Sea Trout Fisher's Handbook*.

The latest, and presumably the last, new work from Falkus is an audio CD, published in 2004 by the Flyfisher's Classic Library. *Hugh Falkus - Salmon and Sea Trout Fishing* is sixty minutes of Falkus talking about fishing, including 'scenes' on the river, compiled from material recorded by Keith Allan at the end of the 1970s. 'The voice of the Master comes over beautifully, clear and precise, a lesson to those who babble and gabble rather than seek to communicate sensibly and clearly' said *Trout and Salmon*. 'I suggest you don't, as is recommended, listen to it on the car radio, lest your driving suffers . . . it deserves one's full concentration.'

After almost four decades, *Signals for Survival*, the film that made Falkus' name as a wildlife broadcaster, has not been forgotten. This year the UK-based charity Wildscreen, with BBC backing, launched Wild Film History, the world's first centralised collection of films and information documenting the history and heritage of wildlife film-making. Only the most influential and innovative films have been selected as the foundation for the collection, and *Signals* is among them.

Even in death, Hugh Falkus has not given up fishing. He remains Honorary Vice President of Bowland Game Fishing Association, the only club he would allow his name to be associated with. Each year the members dedicate an evening to him. There is a Hugh Falkus Memorial Lecture, with generous acknowledgement of the contribution he made to the sport.

Hugh would appreciate that.

Bibliography

Angling

Angler's Bedside Book, The, edited by Maurice Wiggin (1965, B. T. Batsford).

Angler's Companion: A Popular and Practical Handbook to the Art of Angling, The, Thomas Tod Stoddart (1847).

Arthur Ransome on Fishing, Jeremy Swift (1994, Jonathan Cape).

Book on Angling, A, Francis Francis (1867).

Book of the All-Round Angler, The, John Bickerdyke (1888).

Border River Angling, William Lawrie (1939, Oliver & Boyd).

Book of the Sea Trout, The, Hamish Stuart (1917, Martin Secker).

Catching the Wily Sea Trout, A. R. Harris Cass (1946, Herbert Jenkins).

Fishing for Sea Trout, H. P. Henzell (1949, Black).

Fishing for Trout and Salmon, Terence Horsley (1944, H. F. & G. Witherby).

Life of the Sea Trout, The, G. Herbert Nall (1930, Seeley Service).

Modern Salmon and Sea Trout Fishing, Kenneth Dawson (1938, Country Life).

North Country Angler, or the Art of Angling as Practised in the Northern Counties of England, The, (1786, anon).

Passionate Angler, The, Maurice Wiggin (1949, Sylvan Press).

Practical Angler, The, subtitled '*The Art of Trout-Fishing, More Particularly Applied to Clear Water*', W. C. Stewart (1857).

River Fishing for Sea Trout, F. W. Holiday (1960, Herbert Jenkins).

Salmon and Sea Trout Fishing, W. E. Davies, (1957, Elliott Right Way Books).

Salmon and Sea Trout in Wild Places, Sidney Spencer (1968, H. F. & G. Witherby).

Salmon and Women: The Feminine Angle, Wilma Paterson and Prof. Peter Behan, with foreword by H. F. (1990, H. F. & G. Witherby).

Sea Trout and Occasional Salmon, Jeffrey Bluett (1948, Cassell).

Sea Trout - A Study in Natural History, The, by Henry Lamond (1916, Sherratt & Hughes).

Sea Trout Fishing, R. C. Bridgett (1929, Herbert Jenkins).

Successful Sea Trout Angling, Moc Morgan and Graeme Harris (1989, Blandford Press).

Troubled Waters, Maurice Wiggin (1960, Hutchinson).

General

Endangered Species - The Bart and The Bounder's Countryside Year, Michael Daunt and Sir Richard Heygate (2007, John Murray).

Cottage Idyll, A, Maurice Wiggin (1969, Thomas Nelson).

Countryman's Cooking, W. M. W. Fowler (1965, Arlington Books; 2006, Excellent Press).

Escape from Germany 1939-45, Aidan Crawley (2001, Stationery Office).

Harpoon at a Venture, Gavin Maxwell (1952 Rupert Hart-Davis, 1980 Penguin).

Moonless Night, B. A. 'Jimmy' James (2001, Leo Cooper).

Niko's Nature, Hans Kruuk (2002, Oxford University Press).

Not All Glory, Victor F Gambon (1996, Arms & Armour Press).

Not Only Golf, Pat Ward-Thomas (1981, Hodder & Stoughton).

Riddle of the Sands, The, Erskine Childers (1903).

Silent Twins, The, Marjorie Wallace (1986 Chatto & Windus, 1987 Penguin).

Society's Queen: Edith, Marchioness of Londonderry by Anne de Courcy (2004, Weidenfeld). (Originally published in 1992 by Sinclair-Stevenson as *Circe: The Life of Edith, Marchioness of Londonderry*).

Southern Fells, The, A. Wainwright (1960, Marshall).

Stalag Luft III, the Full Story, Charles Rollings (1992, Hyperion Books).

Winged Life, The, Richard Rumbold and Lady Margaret Stewart (1953, Weidenfeld & Nicholson).

Nature Detective (1978) (published in the USA as *Wildtrack - Reminiscences of a Nature Detective*).

Salmon & Sea Trout Fisher's Handbook, with Malcolm Greenhalgh (1997, Excellent Press).

Salmon Fishing, A Practical Guide (1984, H. F. & G. Witherby).

Sea Trout, The (1987, H. F. & G. Witherby; 1995, Flyfisher's Classic Library).

Sea Trout Fishing (1962, 1975 et al, H. F. & G. Witherby).

Signals for Survival (with Niko Tinbergen) (1970, Clarendon Press).

Speycasting (1994, Excellent Press).

Some of it Was Fun (2003, Medlar Press).

Stolen Years, The (1965 Museum Press, 1979 H. F. & G. Witherby).

Successful Angling (1977, Stanley Paul) with Fred Buller, Fred J. Taylor and Richard Walker.

Books by Hugh Falkus

Dame Juliana - The Angling Treatyse and its Mysteries, with Fred Buller (2001, Flyfisher's Classic Library).

Freshwater Fishing, (with Fred Buller) (1975, Macdonald, 1988 Stanley Paul, 1994 Grange Books).

From Sydney Cove to Duntroon (with Joan Kerr) (1982, Gollancz).

Master of Cape Horn (1982, Gollancz).

Footnotes

1. There were only seven Zeppelin raids on the whole of the London area in 1917, all in the early months - by this stage of the war Germany had lost faith in the Zeppelins because of poor results and high cost. Instead they were turning to Gotha bombers. No raid is recorded for 15th May, but on 25th May, when Hugh was barely a week old, there was a mass bombing raid on South East England. Only two of the twenty-three Gothas found their targets, but they succeeded in doing more damage than any of the Zeppelin raids that had gone before, killing ninety-five people and wounding one hundred and ninety-two.

2. www.terrynorm.ic24.net/gospel%20hall.htm

3. According to *Stalag Luft III, The Full Story*, by Charles Rollings, Falkus also spent a short time at Lübeck, north-east of Hamburg - he was transferred there from Stalag Luft I in August 1941.

4. *Not All Glory*, Victor F. Gambon, Arms and Armour Press, 1996.

5. *A Cottage Idyll* (Thomas Nelson, 1969).

6. Weather details by courtesy of the Met Office National Meteorological Archive.

7. Lee's widow Pippa was told that the actual cause of death was exposure.

8. *Society's Queen: Edith, Marchioness of Londonderry* (Weidenfeld) (earlier published by Sinclair Stevenson as *Circe: The Life of Edith, Marchioness of Londonderry*).

9. *The Winged Life* by Richard Rumbold and Lady Margaret Stewart, Weidenfeld & Nicholson 1953.

10. The largest sea trout recorded from the Esk is a fish of 21lb taken by a poacher in a net in 1984. The poacher, who was indiscreet enough to photograph his prize, got away on that occasion but was caught and prosecuted for a later offence.

11. *Niko's Nature*, Oxford University Press, 2002.

12. Letter, Bodleian Library, quoted in *Niko's Nature*.

13. The full story is told in *The Silent Twins*, by Marjorie Wallace, Penguin 1987.

14. Buller's company, Chubbs Ltd, was, and still is, a book wholesaler to the gun and fishing tackle trade.

15. In 1995 the Flyfisher's Classic Library published a new edition, limited to two hundred and fifty copies, each furnished with an example of the Medicine Fly tied for the occasion by Annie Douglas.

Index